C For Dummies®

2nd Edition

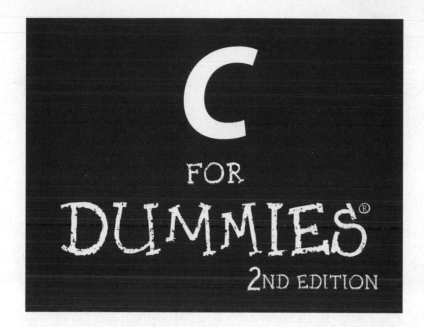

C FOR DUMMIES®

2ND EDITION

by Dan Gookin

WILEY
John Wiley & Sons, Inc.

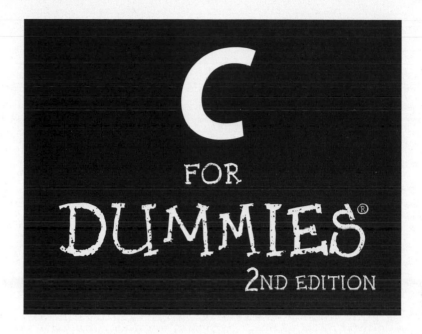

C For Dummies®, 2nd Edition

Published by
John Wiley & Sons, Inc.
111 River Street
Hoboken, NJ 07030-5774

Published by John Wiley & Sons, Inc., Hoboken, New Jersey

Published simultaneously in Canada

For general information on our other products and services, please contact our Customer Care Department within the U.S. at 877-762-2974, outside the U.S. at 317-572-3993, or fax 317-572-4002.

For technical support, please visit `www.wiley.com/techsupport`.

Wiley publishes in a variety of print and electronic formats and by print-on-demand. Some material included with standard print versions of this book may not be included in e-books or in print-on-demand. If this book refers to media such as a CD or DVD that is not included in the version you purchased, you may download this material at `http://booksupport.wiley.com`. For more information about Wiley products, visit `www.wiley.com`.

Library of Congress Control Number: 2004101965

ISBN 978-0-764-57068-1 (pbk); ISBN 978-0-470-19699-1 (ebk); ISBN 978-0-764-57392-7 (ebk)

Manufactured in the United States of America

10 9 8 7 6 5

2B/RZ/QU/QY/IN

WILEY

About the Author

Dan Gookin has been writing about technology for 20 years. He has contributed articles to numerous high-tech magazines and written more than 90 books about personal computing technology, many of them accurate.

He combines his love of writing with his interest in technology to create books that are informative and entertaining, but not boring. Having sold more than 14 million titles translated into more than 30 languages, Dan can attest that his method of crafting computer tomes does seem to work.

Perhaps Dan's most famous title is the original *DOS For Dummies,* published in 1991. It became the world's fastest-selling computer book, at one time moving more copies per week than the *New York Times* number-one best seller (although, because it's a reference book, it could not be listed on the *NYT* best seller list). That book spawned the entire line of *For Dummies* books, which remains a publishing phenomenon to this day.

Dan's most recent titles include *PCs For Dummies,* 9th Edition; *Buying a Computer For Dummies,* 2004 Edition; *Troubleshooting Your PC For Dummies; Dan Gookin's Naked Windows XP;* and *Dan Gookin's Naked Office.* He also publishes a free weekly computer newsletter, "Weekly Wambooli Salad," full of tips, how-tos, and computer news. He also maintains the vast and helpful Web page `www.wambooli.com`.

Dan holds a degree in communications and visual arts from the University of California, San Diego. He lives in the Pacific Northwest, where he enjoys spending time with his four boys in the gentle woods of Idaho.

Publisher's Acknowledgments

We're proud of this book; please send us your comments through our online registration form located at http://dummies.custhelp.com.

Some of the people who helped bring this book to market include the following:

Acquisitions, Editorial, and Vertical Websites

Project Editor: Rebecca Whitney

Acquisitions Editor: Gregory Croy

Technical Editors: Greg Guntle, Kip Warner (http://TheVertigo.com)

Editorial Manager: Carol Sheehan

Vertical Websites Supervisor: Richard Graves

Editorial Assistant: Amanda M. Foxworth

Cartoons: Rich Tennant (www.the5thwave.com)

Composition Services

Project Coordinator: Maridee Ennis

Layout and Graphics: Amanda Carter, Andrea Dahl, Lauren Goddard, Denny Hager, Michael Kruzil, Lynsey Osborn

Proofreaders: Laura Albert, Andy Hollandbeck, Aptara

Indexer: Johnna VanHoose

Publishing and Editorial for Technology Dummies

Richard Swadley, Vice President and Executive Group Publisher

Andy Cummings, Vice President and Publisher

Mary C. Corder, Editorial Director

Publishing for Consumer Dummies

Kathleen Nebenhaus, Vice President and Executive Publisher

Composition Services

Debbie Stailey, Director of Composition Services

Contents at a Glance

Introduction 1

Part I: Introduction to C Programming 7

Chapter 1: Up from the Primordial C 9
Chapter 2: C of Sorrow, C of Woe..19
Chapter 3: C Straight..29
Chapter 4: C What I/O 39
Chapter 5: To C or Not to C..55
Chapter 6: C More I/O with `gets()` and `puts()` 65

Part II: Run and Scream from Variables and Math 73

Chapter 7: A + B = C..75
Chapter 8: Charting Unknown Cs with Variables 93
Chapter 9: How to C Numbers 107
Chapter 10: Cook That C Variable Charred, Please..121

Part III: Giving Your Programs the Ability to Run Amok 131

Chapter 11: C More Math and the Sacred Order of Precedence 133
Chapter 12: C the Mighty `if` Command..147
Chapter 13: What If `C==C`? 165
Chapter 14: Iffy C Logic..175
Chapter 15: C You Again 185
Chapter 16: C the Loop, C the Loop++..201
Chapter 17: C You in a While Loop 215
Chapter 18: Do C While You Sleep..225
Chapter 19: Switch Case, or, From 'C' to Shining 'c'..239

Part IV: C Level 251

Chapter 20: Writing That First Function..253
Chapter 21: Contending with Variables in Functions..265
Chapter 22: Functions That Actually Funct 275
Chapter 23: The Stuff That Comes First 293

Chapter 24: The `printf()` Chapter 305
Chapter 25: Math Madness! 313
Chapter 26: The Old Random-Number Function 325

Part V: Part of Tens 337

Chapter 27: Ten More Things You Need to Know about the C Language 339
Chapter 28: Ten Tips for the Budding Programmer 347
Chapter 29: Ten Ways to Solve Your Own Programming Problems 353

Appendix A: The Stuff You Need to Know before You Read All the Other Stuff in This Book 359

Appendix B: ASCII Table 371

Index 377

Table of Contents

Introduction 1

"What Will Understanding C Do for Me?" 1
About This Here Dummies Approach 2
How to Work the Examples in This Book 2
Foolish Assumptions 3
Icons Used in This Book 3
What's New with This Edition? 4
Final Thots 4

Part I: Introduction to C Programming 7

Chapter 1: Up from the Primordial C 9

An Extremely Short and Cheap History of the C Language 9
The C Development Cycle 11
From Text File to Program 11
  The source code (text file) 12
  Creating the GOODBYE.C source code file 13
  The compiler and the linker 14
  Compiling GOODBYE.C 15
  Running the final result 16
Save It! Compile and Link It! Run It! 16

Chapter 2: C of Sorrow, C of Woe 19

The Required Woes of Editing and Recompiling 19
  Reediting your source code file 20
  Recompiling (or the C equivalent of the "do-over") 21
Dealing with the Heartbreak of Errors 22
  Yikes! An error! But, before you shoot yourself. 22
  The autopsy 23
  Repairing the malodorous program 24
  Now try this error! 26

Chapter 3: C Straight 29

The Big Picture 29
C Language Pieces' Parts 30
The C Language Itself — the Keywords 32
Other C Language Components 34
Pop Quiz! 35
The Helpful RULES Program 36
  The importance of being `\n` 36
  Breaking up lines\ is easy to do 37

Chapter 4: C What I/O 39

Introduce Yourself to Mr. Computer 39
  Compiling WHORU.C 40
  The reward 41
More on `printf()` 41
  Printing funky text 42
  Escape from `printf()`! 44
  The f means "formatted" 46
  A bit of justification 47
`scanf` Is Pronounced "Scan-Eff" 49
  Putting `scanf` together 49
  The miracle of `scanf()` 51
  Experimentation time! 52

Chapter 5: To C or Not to C 55

Adding Comments 55
  A big, hairy program with comments 56
  Why are comments necessary? 58
Comment Styles of the Nerdy and Not-Quite-Yet-Nerdy 58
  Bizarr-o comments 59
  C++ comments 60
Using Comments to Disable 61
The Perils of "Nested" Comments 62

Chapter 6: C More I/O with `gets()` and `puts()` 65

The More I Want, the More I `gets()` 65
  Another completely rude program example 66
  And now, the bad news about `gets()` 67
The Virtues of `puts()` 67
  Another silly command-prompt program 68
  `puts()` and `gets()` in action 68
  More insults 69
  `puts()` can print variables 70

Part II: Run and Scream from Variables and Math 73

Chapter 7: A + B = C 75

The Ever-Changing Variable 75
  Strings change 76
  Running the KITTY 77
Welcome to the Cold World of Numeric Variables 77
  Hello, integer 78
  Using an integer variable in the Methuselah program 79

Assigning values to numeric variables 80
Entering numeric values from the keyboard 81
The `atoi()` function 81
So how old is this Methuselah guy, anyway? 83
You and Mr. Wrinkles 85
A Wee Bit o' Math 86
Basic mathematical symbols 86
How much longer do you have to live to break the Methuselah record? 88
Bonus modification on the final Methuselah program! 90
The direct result 91

Chapter 8: Charting Unknown Cs with Variables 93

Cussing, Discussing, and Declaring Variables 93
"Why must I declare a variable?" 94
Variable names verboten and not 95
Presetting variable values 96
The old random-sampler variable program 98
Maybe you want to chance two pints? 99
Multiple declarations 100
Constants and Variables 101
Dreaming up and defining constants 101
The handy shortcut 102
The `#define` directive 104
Real, live constant variables 106

Chapter 9: How to C Numbers 107

There Are Numbers, and Then There Are Numbers 107
Numbers in C 108
Why use integers? Why not just make every number floating-point? 110
Integer types (short, long, wide, fat, and so on) 110
Signed or unsigned, or "Would you like a minus sign with that, Sir?" 111
How to Make a Number Float 113
"Hey, Carl, let's write a floating-point number program!" 114
The E notation stuff 116
Bigger than the Float, It's a Double! 118
Formatting Your Zeroes and Decimal Places 119

Chapter 10: Cook That C Variable Charred, Please 121

The Other Kind of Variable Type, the `char` 121
Single-character variables 122
`Char` in action 123
Stuffing characters into character variables 124

Reading and Writing Single Characters 125
The `getchar()` function 126
The `putchar()` function 127
Character Variables As Values 128

Part III: Giving Your Programs the Ability to Run Amok 131

Chapter 11: C More Math and the Sacred Order of Precedence ...133

An All-Too-Brief Review of the Basic C Mathematical Operators 133
The old "how tall are you" program 135
Unethical alterations to the old "how tall are you" program 136
The Delicate Art of Incrementation (Or, "Just Add One to It") 137
Unhappily incrementing your weight 138
Bonus program! (One that may even have a purpose in life) 140
The Sacred Order of Precedence 141
A problem from the pages of the dentistry final exam 141
What's up, Sally? 142
The confounding magic-pellets problem 144
Using parentheses to mess up the order of precedence 145

Chapter 12: C the Mighty `if` Command 147

If Only. 147
The computer-genie program example 148
The `if` keyword, up close and impersonal 150
A question of formatting the `if` statement 154
The final solution to the income-tax problem 155
If It Isn't True, What Else? 157
Covering all the possibilities with `else` 158
The `if` format with `else` 159
The strange case of `else-if` and even more decisions 160
Bonus program! The really, really smart genie 163

Chapter 13: What If `C==C`? 165

The World of `if` without Values 165
Which is greater: S or T, $ or –? 166
The problem with `getchar()` 168
Fixing GREATER.C to easily read standard input 170
"Can I get `getchar()` to read only one character?" 171
Meanwhile, back to the GREATER problem 171
Another, bolder example 173
Using the `if` Keyword to Compare Two Strings 174

Chapter 14: Iffy C Logic 175

Exposing Flaws in logic 175
If, And, Or, But 177
    A solution (but not the best one) 177
    A better solution, using logic 178
    The `if` command's logical friends 180
    A logical `AND` program for you 183

Chapter 15: C You Again 185

For Going Loopy 185
    Repetitive redundancy, I don't mind 187
    For doing things over and over, use the `for` keyword 188
    Tearing through OUCH.C a step at a time 190
    Having fun whilst counting to 100 192
I'm Bustin' Outta Here! 193
    At last — the handy ASCII program 193
    Beware of infinite loops! 195
    Breaking out of a loop 197
    The `break` keyword 198

Chapter 16: C the Loop, C the Loop++ 201

The Art of Incrementation 201
    Cryptic C operator symbols, Volume I: The `inc` operator (++) 202
    Another look at the LARDO.C program 203
The Mysterious Practice of Decrementation 204
    O, to count backward 205
    How counting backward fits into the `for` loop 206
    Cryptic C operator symbols, Volume II: The `dec` operator ( ) 207
    A final improvement to OLLYOLLY.C 208
More Incrementation Madness 209
    Leaping loops! 210
    Counting to 1,000 by fives 211
    Cryptic C operator symbols, Volume III:
        The madness continues 211
    The answers 213

Chapter 17: C You in a While Loop 215

The Lowdown on `while` Loops 215
    Whiling away the hours 216
    The `while` keyword (a formal introduction) 218
    Deciding between a `while` loop and a `for` loop 219
    Replacing those unsightly `for(;;)` loops
        with elegant `while` loops 220
    C from the inside out 222
Not to Beat a Dead Horse or Anything. 223

Chapter 18: Do C While You Sleep 225

The Down-Low on Upside-Down do-while Loops 225
The devil made me do-while it! 226
do-while details 227
A flaw in the COUNTDWN.C program 228
The always kosher number-checking do-while loop 229
Nested Loops and Other Bird-Brained Concepts 231
Adding a tense, dramatic delay to the COUNTDWN.C program 231
The nitty GRID.C of nested loops 234
Break the Brave and Continue the Fool 235
Please continue. 236
The continue keyword 237

Chapter 19: Switch Case, or, From 'C' to Shining 'c' 239

The Sneaky switch-case Loops 239
The switch-case Solution to the LOBBY Program 241
The Old switch-case Trick 243
The Special Relationship between while and switch-case 248

Part IV: C Level 251

Chapter 20: Writing That First Function 253

Meet Mr. Function 253
A silly example you don't have to type 254
A potentially redundant program in need of a function 255
The noble jerk() function 256
How the jerk() function works in BIGJERK2.C 257
Prototyping Your Functions 258
Prototypical prototyping problems 259
A sneaky way to avoid prototyping problems 260
The Tao of Functions 262
The function format 262
How to name your functions 263

Chapter 21: Contending with Variables in Functions 265

Bombs Away with the BOMBER Program! 265
Will the dual variable BOMBER.C program bomb? 267
Adding some important tension 267
How We Can All Share and Love with Global Variables 269
Making a global variable 270
An example of a global variable in a real, live program 271

Chapter 22: Functions That Actually Funct 275

Marching a Value Off to a Function.....275
How to send a value to a function.....276
An example (and it's about time!).....277
Avoiding variable confusion (must reading).....279
Sending More than One Value to a Function.....280
Functions That Return Stuff.....282
Something for your troubles.....282
Finally, the computer tells you how smart it thinks you are.....284
Return to sender with the `return` keyword.....285
Now you can understand the `main()` function.....287
Give that human a bonus!.....288
No Need to Bother with This C Language Trivia If You're in a Hurry.....289

Chapter 23: The Stuff That Comes First 293

Please Don't Leave Me Out!.....294
Say! Aren't you the `#include` construction?.....294
What's up with STDIO.H?.....297
Writing your own dot-H file.....298
A final warning about header files.....300
What the `#defines` Are Up To.....302
Avoiding the Topic of Macros.....303

Chapter 24: The `printf()` Chapter 305

A Quick Review of `printf()`.....305
The Old Displaying-Text-with-`printf()` Routine.....306
The `printf()` Escape Sequences.....306
The `printf()` escape-sequence testing program deluxe.....307
Putting PRINTFUN to the test.....308
The Complex `printf()` Format.....310
The `printf()` Conversion Characters.....311

Chapter 25: Math Madness! 313

More on Math.....313
Taking your math problems to a higher power.....314
Putting `pow()` into use.....315
Rooting out the root.....317
Strange Math? You Got It!.....319
Something Really Odd to End Your Day.....320
The perils of using `a++`.....320
Oh, and the same thing applies to a `--`.....322
Reflections on the strange `++a` phenomenon.....322

Chapter 26: The Old Random-Number Function 325

On Being Random.....325
Using the `rand()` function.....326
Planting a random-number seed.....328
Randoming up the RANDOM program.....329
Streamlining the randomizer.....331
The Diabolical Dr. Modulus.....333
Rolling the Dice with the Final RANDOM Program.....335

Part V: Part of Tens.....337

Chapter 27: Ten More Things You Need to Know about the C Language.....339

Arrays.....339
Strings.....340
Structures.....341
Pointers.....343
Linked Lists.....343
Binary Operators.....344
Interacting with the Command Line.....345
Disk Access.....345
Interacting with the Operating System.....345
Building Big Programs.....346

Chapter 28: Ten Tips for the Budding Programmer.....347

Use the Command-Line History.....347
Keep Your Editor Open in Another Window.....348
Use a Context-Colored Text Editor.....348
Know the Line-Number Commands in Your Editor.....349
Keep a Command Prompt Window Open If You're Using the IDE.....350
Know a Few Handy Command-Prompt Commands.....350
Carefully Name Your Variables.....351
Know Your Post- and Pre-Incrementing and Decrementing Riddles.....351
Breaking Out of a Loop.....352

Chapter 29: Ten Ways to Solve Your Own Programming Problems.....353

Work on One Thing at a Time.....354
Break Up Your Code.....354
Simplify.....355
Talk through the Program.....355
Set Breakpoints.....356

Monitor Your Variables 356
Document Your Work 356
Use Debugging Tools 357
Use a C Optimizer 357
Read More Books! 358

Appendix A: The Stuff You Need to Know before You Read All the Other Stuff in This Book 359

Setting Things Up 359
The C language compiler 360
The place to put your stuff 361
Making Programs 363
Finding your `learn` directory or folder 363
Running an editor 364
Compiling and linking 365

Appendix B: ASCII Table 371

Index 377

Introduction

Welcome to *C For Dummies,* 2nd Edition — your last, desperate, and final attempt to understand the C programming language.

Although I can't promise that you'll become a C guru after wading through this text, I can guarantee that you will

- Know how to recognize a C program and, when one is grouped with an IRS Form 1040, the morning stock report, baseball statistics, and anything written in Braille, you'll be able to pick out which one is the C program.
- Be able to write C programs that no other publisher would let an author print in its C books.
- Appreciate the following code, but be unable to use it at cocktail parties to impress your friends:

```
while(dead_horse)
     beat();
```

- Find out how to speak in C Talk, which is the ability to look at character groupings, such as `printf`, `putchar`, and `clock`, and pronounce them as "print-f," "put-kar," and "see-lock."
- Have fun.

I can't really guarantee that last point. However, this book was written minus the sword of mathematics hanging over anyone's head. Let's leave stern programming up to those who fuss over Avogadro's number and Fibonacci sequences and who debate the merits of how to indent their C program source code. Serious work is for the nerds. Fun happens when you read *C For Dummies,* 2nd Edition.

"What Will Understanding C Do for Me?"

Look at your computer screen. Imagine something happening there. Anything. As long as you know how to program a computer, what you imagine will take place. Okay, maybe not as fast as you like — but it can be done.

Programming is the ultimate way to get even with a computer. *You* are in charge. *You* tell the beast what to do. And it will obey you, even when you tell it to do something stupid. Computers are fast and obedient, not smart.

Anything your computer does, any devices it talks with or controls, can be manipulated by using a programming language and writing programs that pull the right levers. The C programming language has been crowned the best and most common way to program any personal computer. C may not be the easiest programming language to figure out, but it's not the most difficult, either. It's tremendously popular and well supported, which makes it a good choice.

About This Here Dummies Approach

Most programming books start out by assuming that you don't know anything. The author may remember that for, oh, maybe two or three chapters. Then, after that initial pressure is off, there he goes! Chapter 4 is written not to teach you how to program, but, rather, to impress the author's programming buddies back at college. So your learning journey ends with a whimper. You will *not* find that problem in this book.

The best way to learn something is one piece at a time. With programming, I prefer to show you things by using small programs, tiny models, and quick-to-type examples. That way, you're not overwhelmed with an initial program that's three pages long, and you don't get lost after a few chapters. That's because the pace stays the same throughout the book. I insist on it!

This book also gets you started right away. When researching other books, I noticed that often the first program you have to type is not only several dozen lines long, but also nearly 50 pages into the book on average! In this book, you get started right away with a program example on Page 13. *That* quick!

How to Work the Examples in This Book

Part of the fun of finding out how to program by reading a book is that you type the programs yourself. That's the way I figured out how to program a computer. I sat down with Dr. David Lien's *Learning TRS-80 BASIC* (Compusoft) and, 36 solid hours later, I finished. Then I slept. Then I did it again because I completely forgot everything, but remembered enjoying doing it the first time.

Your first task is to read Appendix A. It tells you how to set up a C language compiler on your computer and get things all ready to work.

Next, you need to know how to type stuff. This stuff looks like this:

```
Here I go, typing some stuff. La, la, la.
```

Mostly, you type complete programs, consisting of several lines like the one before this paragraph. Type them all, and press Enter at the end of each line. Because this book is only so wide, however, occasionally you see a line split in two. It looks like this:

```
This is an example of a very long line that was painfully
         split in two by this book's cruel typesetters.
```

When you see that, *don't* type two lines. If you just keep typing, everything fits on one line on your screen. If you forget this advice, your programs mess up, so I toss in several reminders throughout this book whenever such a thing happens.

Foolish Assumptions

This book makes the following assumptions about you, your computer, your compiler, and — most important — your state of mind:

- You have a computer, or at least you have access to one. It can be just about any computer; this book is *not* specific to Windows.
- You're pretty good with the computer. You understand things. You may even fix your own problems or help others with their problems.
- You know how to look things up on the Web, download stuff, and find things you need.
- You have a passing familiarity with your operating system's command prompt or terminal window. This is important, and it's explained in Appendix A.
- You're willing to find out how to program — perhaps even desperate to do so!

Icons Used in This Book

Technical information you can merrily skip over.

Something you should remember to do.

Something you should remember not to do.

A healthy suggestion worthy of note.

What's New with This Edition?

This book isn't really the second edition of any previous book, but it does borrow material from the old *C For Dummies* books, Volumes I and II. This book represents a compilation of basic material from both books. And, by reading this book, you'll have a broad, basic knowledge of the C language.

Unlike the older books, this one is organized on a chapter-by-chapter level, not by lessons. Each chapter is self-contained and, where necessary, cross references to other chapters are included.

Gone are the quizzes and tests. This book has no homework, per se.

Alas, this book is only so big, and only so much ground could be covered, given this book's gentle pace. Because of that, those interested in pursuing the C language further should check out the companion book, *C All-in-One Desk Reference For Dummies* (Wiley). That book is for more experienced programmers, which is what you will become after reading this book.

Final Thots

Understanding how to use C is an ongoing process. Only a dweeb would say "I know everything about programming in C." There are new things to be learned every day and different approaches to the same problems. Nothing is perfect, but many things are close.

My thoughts on the matter are this: Sure, people who took 20 years of C programming and paid too much per semester at A Major University will have some C snobbishness in them. Whatever. Ask yourself this question: Does my program run? Okay. Does it do what I want? Better. Does it meet their artificial standards? Who cares? I'll be happy if your sloppy C program works. But keep this in mind: The more you learn, the better you get. You'll discover new tricks and adapt your programming style to them.

This book has a companion Web page, replete with bonus material and all sorts of fun information:

```
http://www.c-for-dummies.com
```

I hope that you enjoy the journey you're about to begin. Crack your knuckles, power up that compiler, and prepare yourself for a few solid hours of eyeball frazzle. You're going C programming!

Part I
Introduction to C Programming

"We're here to clean the code."

In this part . . .

You have never programmed anything in your life. The VCR? Forget it! On your microwave oven, you use the Popcorn and Add a Minute buttons. You know that you can punch numbers into your cell phone and hit the Send button, yet you dare not touch any of the other buttons, for fear of entering that dark realm, that dank and musty dungeon of *programming*. If that's you, get ready to turn your life around.

Contrary to what you may believe, it's *nothing* to program a computer. Anyone can do it. Programmers may carry themselves with an air of mysticism and treat their skills like priests performing sacred religious rites. Poppycock. Programming is painless. It's easy. It's fun.

It's now *your* turn to tell the computer exactly what to do with itself. In just a few pages, you will be programming your PC. It's time to get even! Time to twist its arm and wait until it bellows "Uncle! *UNCLE!*" Get ready to take charge.

Chapter 1

Up from the Primordial C

In This Chapter

- Hysterical C history
- How C programs are created
- Building the source code
- Compiling and linking
- Running the result

As the most useful device you have ever used, a computer can become anything — as long as you have the ability to program it. That's what makes computers unique in the pantheon of modern devices. And although most computer users shy away from programming — confusing it with mathematics or electrical engineering — the fact is that programming a computer is really a rather simple and straightforward thing. It's easy.

This chapter introduces you to the basics of programming. Although it has some yabber-yabber and background information, the meat of the chapter involves creating, compiling, and running your first program. Feel the power! Finally, it's *you* who can tell the computer what to do with itself!

TIP

Because you probably didn't read this book's Introduction (for shame), know that you should preview Appendix A before starting here.

An Extremely Short and Cheap History of the C Language

First, there was the B programming language. Then there was the C programming language.

Stuff you don't need to know about language levels

Programming languages have different levels, depending on how much they resemble human languages. Programming languages that use common words and are relatively easy for most folks to read and study are called *high-level* languages. The opposite of those are *low-level* languages, which are not easy to read or study.

High-level languages include the popular BASIC programming language as well as other languages that just aren't that popular any more. BASIC reads almost like English, and all its commands and instructions are English words — or at least English words missing a few vowels or severely disobeying the laws of spelling.

The lowest of the low-level programming languages is machine language. That language is the actual primitive grunts and groans of the microprocessor itself. Machine language consists of numbers and codes that the microprocessor understands and executes. Therefore, no one really writes programs in machine language; rather, they use assembly language, which is one step above the low-level machine language because the grunts and groans are spelled out rather than entered as raw numbers.

Why would anyone use a low-level language when high-level languages exist? Speed! Programs written in low-level languages run as fast as the computer can run them, often many times faster than their high-level counterparts. Plus, the size of the program is smaller. A program written in Visual Basic may be 34K in size, but the same program written in assembly language may be 896 bytes long. On the other hand, the time it takes to develop an assembly language program is much longer than it would take to write the same program in a higher-level language. It's a trade-off.

The C programming language is considered a mid-level language. It has parts that are low-level grunting and squawking, and also many high-level parts that read like any sentence in a Michael Crichton novel, but with more character development. In C, you get the best of the high-level programming languages and the speed of development they offer, and you also get the compact program size and speed of a low-level language. That's why C is so bitchen.

No, I'm not being flip. C was developed at AT&T Bell Labs in the early 1970s. At the time, Bell Labs had a programming language named B — B for Bell. The next language they created was C — one up on B.

- C is the offspring of both the B programming language and a language named BCPL, which stood for Basic Combined Programming Language. But you have to admit that the B story is cute enough by itself.
- You would think that the next, better version of C would be called the D language. But, no; it's named C++, for reasons that become apparent in Chapter 16.
- C is considered a *mid-level language*. See the nearby sidebar, "Stuff you don't need to know about language levels," for the boring details.

- The guy who created the C programming language at Bell Labs is Dennis Ritchie. I mention him in case you're ever walking on the street and you happen to bump into Mr. Ritchie. In that case, you can say "Hey, aren't you Dennis Ritchie, the guy who invented C?" And he'll say "Why — why, yes I am." And you can say "Cool."

The C Development Cycle

Here is how you create a C program in seven steps — in what's known as the *development cycle:*

1. Come up with an idea for a program.
2. Use an editor to write the source code.
3. Compile the source code and link the program by using the C compiler.
4. Weep bitterly over errors (optional).
5. Run the program and test it.
6. Pull out hair over bugs (optional).
7. Start over (required).

No need to memorize this list. It's like the instructions on a shampoo bottle, though you don't have to be naked and wet to program a computer. Eventually, just like shampooing, you start following these steps without thinking about it. No need to memorize anything.

- The C development cycle is not an exercise device. In fact, programming does more to make your butt fit more snugly into your chair than anything.
- Step 1 is the hardest. The rest fall naturally into place.
- Step 3 consists of two steps: compiling and linking. For most of this book, however, they are done together, in one step. Only later — if you're still interested — do I go into the specific differences of a compiler and a linker.

From Text File to Program

When you create a program, you become a programmer. Your friends or relatives may refer to you as a "computer wizard" or "guru," but trust me when I say that *programmer* is a far better title.

As a programmer, you job is not "programming." No, the act of writing a program is *coding*. So what you do when you sit down to write that program is *code* the program. Get used to that term! It's very trendy.

The job of the programmer is to write some code! Code to do what? And what type of code do you use? Secret code? Morse Code? Zip code?

The purpose of a computer program is to make the computer do something.

The object of programming is to "make it happen." The C language is only a tool for communicating with the PC. As the programmer, it's your job to translate the intentions of the computer user into something the computer understands and then give users what they want. And if you can't give them what they want, at least make it close enough so that they don't constantly complain or — worse — want their money back.

The tool you have chosen to make it happen is the C programming language. That's the code you use to communicate with the PC. The following sections describe how the process works. After all, you can just pick up the mouse and say "Hello, computer!"

- Programming is what TV network executives do. Computer programmers *code*.
- You use a programming language to communicate with the computer, telling it exactly what to do.

The source code (text file)

Because the computer can't understand speech and, well, whacking the computer — no matter how emotionally validating that is for you — does little to the PC, your best line of communications is to write the computer a note — a file on disk.

To create a PC epistle, you use a program called a text editor. This program is a primitive version of a word processor minus all the fancy formatting and printing controls. The text editor lets you type text — that's about all.

Using your text editor, you create what's called a *source code file*. The only special thing about this file is that it contains instructions that tell the computer what to do. And although it would be nice to write instructions like "Make a funny noise," the truth is that you must write instructions in a tongue the computer understands. In this case, the instructions are written in the C language.

- The source code file is a text file on disk. The file contains instructions for the computer that are written in the C programming language.
- You use a text editor to create the source code file. See Appendix A for more information on text editors.

Creating the GOODBYE.C source code file

Use your text editor to create the following source code. Carefully type each line exactly as written; *everything* you see below is important and necessary. Don't leave anything out:

```
#include <stdio.h>

int main()
{
    printf("Goodbye, cruel world!\n");
    return(0);
}
```

As you review what you have typed, note how much of it is familiar to you. You recognize some words (`include`, `main`, `"Goodbye, cruel world!"`, and `return`), and some words look strange to you (`stdio.h`, `printf`, and that `\n` thing).

When you have finished writing the instructions, save them in a file on disk. Name the file GOODBYE.C. Use the commands in your text editor to save this file, and then return to the command prompt to compile your instructions into a program.

- See Appendix A for information on using a text editor to write C language programs as well as for instructions on where you should save the source code file on disk.
- In Windows Notepad, you must ensure that the file ends in `.C` and not in `.TXT`. Find a book about Windows for instructions on showing the filename extensions, which makes saving a text file to disk with a .C extension easier.
- Note that the text is mostly in lowercase. It must be; programming languages are more than case sensitive — they're case-*fussy*. Don't worry when English grammar or punctuation rules go wacky; C is a *computer* language, not English.
- Also note how the program makes use of various parentheses: the angle brackets, `<` and `>`; the curly braces, `{` and `}`; and the regular parentheses, `(` and `)`.

Extra help in typing the GOODBYE.C source code

The first line looks like this:

```
#include <stdio.h>
```

Type a pound sign (press Shift+#) and then **include** and a space. Type a left angle bracket (it's above the comma key) and then **stdio**, a period, **h**, and a right angle bracket. Everything must be in lowercase — no capitals! Press Enter to end this line and start the second line.

Press the Enter key alone on the second line to make it blank. Blank lines are common in programming code; they add space that separates pieces of the code and makes it more readable. And, trust me, anything that makes programming code more readable is okay by me!

Type the word **int**, a space, **main**, and then two parentheses hugging nothing:

```
int main()
```

There is no space between `main` and the parentheses and no space inside the parentheses. Press Enter to start the fourth line.

Type a left curly brace:

```
{
```

This character is on a line by itself, right at the start of the line. Press Enter to start the fifth line.

```
printf("Goodbye, cruel
    world!\n");
```

If your editor was smart enough to automatically indent this line, great. If not, press the Tab key to indent. Then type **printf**, the word *print* with a little *f* at the end. (It's pronounced "print-eff.") Type a left parenthesis. Type a double quote. Type **Goodbye, cruel world**, followed by an exclamation point. Then type a backslash, a little **n**, double quotes, a right parenthesis, and, finally, a semicolon. Press Enter to start the sixth line.

```
return(0);
```

If the editor doesn't automatically indent the sixth line, press the Tab key to start the line with an indent. Then type **return**, a paren, **0** (zero), a paren, and a semicolon. Press Enter.

On the seventh line, type the right curly brace:

```
}
```

Some editors automatically unindent this brace for you. If not, use your editor to back up the brace so that it's in the first column. Press the Enter key to end this line.

Leave the eighth line blank.

The compiler and the linker

After the source code is created and saved to disk, it must be translated into a language the computer can understand. This job is tackled by the compiler.

The *compiler* is a special program that reads the instructions stored in the source code file, examines each instruction, and then translates the information into the machine code understood only by the computer's microprocessor.

If all goes well and the compiler is duly pleased with your source code, the compiler creates an object code file. It's a middle step, one that isn't necessary for smaller programs but that becomes vital for larger programs.

Finally, the compiler links the object code file, which creates a real, live computer program.

If either the compiler or the linker doesn't understand something, an error message is displayed. At that point, you can gnash your teeth and sit and stew. Then go back and edit the source code file again, fixing whatever error the compiler found. (It isn't as tough as it sounds.) Then you attempt to compile the program again — you recompile and relink.

TECHNICAL STUFF

- The compiler translates the information in the source code file into instructions the computer can understand. The linker then converts that information into a runnable program.
- The GCC compiler recommended and used in this book combines the compiling and linking steps. An object file *is* created by GCC, but it is automatically deleted when the final program file is created.
- Object code files end in OBJ or sometimes just O. The first part of the object file name is the same as the source code filename.
- Feel free to cheerfully forget all this object code nonsense for now.
- Text editor⇨Compiler.
- Source code⇨Program.

Compiling GOODBYE.C

The gritty details for compiling a program are in Appendix A. Assuming that you have thumbed through it already, use your powerful human memory to recall the proper command to compile and link the GOODBYE.C source code. Here's a hint:

```
gcc goodbye.c -o goodbye
```

Type that command at your command prompt and see what happens.

Well?

Nothing happens! If you have done everything properly, the GCC compiler merely creates the final program file for you. The only time you see a message is if you goof up and an error occurs in the program.

If you do get an error, you most likely either made a typo or forgot some tiny tidbit of a character: a missing " or ; or \ or) or (or — you get the idea. *Very carefully* review the source code earlier in this chapter and compare it with what you have written. Use the editor to fix your mistake, save the code to disk, and then try again.

Note that GCC reports errors by line number, or it may even specifically list the foul word it found. In any event, note that Chapter 2 covers error-hunting in your C programs.

Running the final result

If you used the proper compiling command, the name of the program to run is identical to the first part of your source code. So why not run that program!

In Windows, the command to type is

```
goodbye
```

In the Unix-like operating systems, you must specify the program's path or location before the program name. Type this command:

```
./goodbye
```

Press the Enter key and the program runs, displaying this marvelous text on your screen:

```
Goodbye, cruel world!
```

Welcome to C language programming!

(See Appendix A for more information on running programs.)

Save It! Compile and Link It! Run It!

Four steps are required in order to build any program in C. They are save, compile, link, and run. Most C programming language packages automatically perform the linking step, though whether or not it's done manually, it's still in there.

Save! Saving means to save your source code. You create that source code in a text editor and save it as a text file with the C (single letter C) extension.

Compile and link! Compiling is the process of transforming the instructions in the text file into instructions the computer's microprocessor can understand. The linking step is where the instructions are finally transformed into a program file. (Again, your compiler may do this step automatically.)

Run! Finally, you run the program you have created. Yes, it's a legitimate program, like any other on your hard drive.

You have completed all these steps in this chapter, culminating in the creation of the GOODBYE program. That's how C programs are built. At this stage, the hardest part is knowing what to put in the source file, which gets easier as you progress through this book. (But by then, getting your program to run correctly and without errors is the hardest part!)

You find the instructions to save, compile, and run often in this book. That's because these steps are more or less mechanical. What's more important is understanding how the language works. That's what you start to find out about in the next chapter.

Chapter 2

C of Sorrow, C of Woe

In This Chapter

- Reediting and recompiling
- Fixing an error
- Understanding the error message
- Dealing with heinous linker errors

Don't let the success of a first-time compile spoil an otherwise normal day of programming.The fact is, most of your programming time is spent dealing with errors, from typos to flaws in logic. Those errors have to be fixed. It happens so often that one guru I know commented that the process should be called *debugging* and not *programming*.

This chapter gets you used to the idea of errors and how to deal with them. As you may note, it's the *second* chapter of this book. That must mean that dealing with errors is a larger part of the programming picture than you may have otherwise imagined.

The Required Woes of Editing and Recompiling

As a human, you may commit the vocal sin of pronouncing the *t* in *often* or adding an *r* after the *a* in *Washington*. Big deal! But just once, type `pirntf` rather than `printf` and your entire programming world becomes unglued. Or, worse, forget a curly brace. One missing curly brace can lead to a screen full of embarrassing error messages.

Before you cower in shame, fear not, gentle programmer newbie person. Errors happen. You deal with them. Like this:

1. **Reedit your source code, saving the fixed-up file to disk.**
2. **Recompile the source code.**
3. **Run the result.**

Errors can still happen. Heck, you may *never* get to Step 3! But these steps show you how to deal with them.

- It happens.
- I might remind you to look at the C language development cycle from Chapter 1. Note Steps 4 and 6. Nod your head wisely in agreement.

Reediting your source code file

Source code is not carved in stone — or silicon, for that matter. It can be changed. Sometimes, the changes are necessary, in the case of errors and boo-boos. At other times, you may just want to modify your program, adding a feature or changing a message or prompt — what the hard-core C geeks call *tweaking* or *twiddling*. To do that, you have to reedit your source code file.

For example, the GOODBYE program from Chapter 1 displays a message on the screen:

```
Goodbye, cruel world!
```

This program can easily be modified to show any message you like. To do so, use your editor and change the source code file, replacing the original message with your newer, pithier message. Follow these steps:

1. **Use your text editor to reedit the GOODBYE.C source code.**
2. **Edit Line 5, which looks like this:**

   ```
   printf("Goodbye, cruel world!\n");
   ```

3. **Replace the text** `Goodbye, cruel world!` **with** `Farewell, you ugly toad!`

   ```
   printf("Farewell, you ugly toad!\n");
   ```

   Change only the text between the double quotes. That's the information that is displayed on the screen. Everything else — don't touch!

4. **Double-check your work.**
5. **Save the file to disk.**

   It's okay to overwrite the original; your modified file becomes the new GOODBYE.C source code file.

Now you're ready to recompile your source code, as covered in the next section.

- "Reedit your source code file" means to use your text editor to modify the source code, the text file that contains the C language instructions.
- You reedit the source code file to repair an error caught by the compiler or linker or to modify the program. This situation happens a lot.
- If you're using the command prompt to run your editor, don't forget that you can use the up-arrow key to recall previous commands (in certain command-prompt environments). In this case, press the up-arrow key a few times until the original command to edit the GOODBYE.C source code file reappears at the prompt.

Recompiling (or the C equivalent of the "do-over")

Recompiling means to make the program one more time — to rework the steps you went through to create the program originally. This process usually happens after you modify or change the source code, such as you do in the preceding section. Because the source code is different, you have to feed it to the compiler again to generate the new, better (and, hopefully, bug-free) program.

To recompile the new GOODBYE.C source code, use your compiler as outlined in Appendix A. For most everyone, that's

```
gcc goodbye.c -o goodbye
```

Press the Enter key and pray that no error messages appear, and then you're done. The new program has been created.

Run the program! Type the proper command — either **goodbye** or **./goodbye** — at the prompt to see the new, stunning output.

Who knew that it would be so darn easy to display such crap on the computer's screen?

- After you reedit your source code file, you have to recompile to re-create the program file. That is how you fix an error or modify the program.
- If you're programming in an IDE (Integrated Development Environment) such as Dev-C++ or Microsoft Visual C++, you may need to use a Rebuild or Rebuild All command to create a new program after modifying your source code.
- If you see any errors after recompiling, you must re-reedit your source code and then re-recompile again. (You only "reedit" and "recompile"; no sense in getting re-happy.)

Dealing with the Heartbreak of Errors

Errors happen. Even the best of programmers get errors, from the innocent code-writing cog at Microsoft to the sneering, snooty Linux programmer whose only contact with humanity is the pizza guy — they all get errors. Every day.

Errors are nothing to be embarrassed about. Consider them learning tools or gentle reminders. That's because the compiler tells you, with uncanny accuracy, just what the error is and where it is. Contrast this with your most nightmarish math class: The wicked pedant would write only "WRONG!" next to your calculations, no matter how innocent a mistake you made. Yes, computers can be forgiving — and this can even teach you something.

Yikes! An error! But, before you shoot yourself. . . .

Here is a new program, ERROR.C. Note the optimism in its name. It's a flawed C program, one that contains an error (albeit an on-purpose error):

```
#include <stdio.h>

int main()
{
 printf("This program will err.\n")
 return(0);
}
```

Type the source code exactly as it appears here. Do not use the GOODBYE.C source code as a base; start over here with a clean editor window.

When you're done entering the source code, save it to disk as ERROR.C. Compile it, and then. . . .

Unfortunately, when you compile this program, it produces an error. The next section provides the autopsy.

- Pay careful attention as you type! Each little oddball character and nutty parenthesis is important to the C language!
- Here's a hint on the common GCC command to compile this source code:

```
gcc error.c -o error
```

That's the last compiling hint you get in this book!

The autopsy

The ERROR.C program erred! What a shock.

Don't be alarmed — it was expected. (In fact, you may have seen this type of error before.) Here is a sample of what the cruel message may look like:

```
error.c: In function `main':
error.c:6: parse error before "return"
```

How rude! It's not that reassuring hand on your shoulder and the kind, avuncular voice explaining that you boo-booed. Still, what the error message lacks in personality, it makes up for in information.

On the up side, though the error message is cryptic, it's informative. Whatever your compiler, you should be able to single out the following bits of information:

- The source code file that contained the error, `error.c`
- The line that contains the error, Line 6 (though it may not be — you can't really trust computers too much)
- The type of error, a `parse error` or `syntax error` or something similar
- The location of the error (before the word `return`)

It still may not be clear exactly what's wrong, but you're given many clues. Most important, you're given a line number: *The error is in Line 6.*

Okay, it's really in Line 5, but the C programming language is flexible, and the compiler doesn't discover that "something's missing" until Line 6. (You can cut the compiler some slack here.)

The error type is also important. A *parse,* or *syntax,* error means that an item of C language punctuation is missing, and, therefore, two things that aren't supposed to run together have run together. In this case, a missing semicolon character at the end of Line 5 is to blame.

The solution? You have to reedit the source code file and fix what's wrong. In this case, you would reedit ERROR.C and add the semicolon to the end of Line 5. Even if you looked at Line 6 (per the output's insistence), you would see nothing wrong there. If so, your eyes would wander back and — because you're aware of the Missing Semicolon Syndrome — you would see the problem and mend it.

- Errors are not the end of the world! Everyone gets them.
- *Syntax* refers to the way a language is put together. Some compilers use that term rather than *parse,* which means "the order in which things are put together." Eh.
- Some versions of GCC put double quotes around "`return`" rather than the tick marks shown in the preceding example. Beyond that, GCC is remarkably consistent with its error messages.
- Missing semicolons are one of the most popular types of errors in the C language. You find out in the next chapter more about semicolons and the role they play.
- The error message's *line number* refers to a line in the source-code text file. That's why nearly all text editors use line numbers, which you can see at the top or bottom of the screen or editing window.
- The line number may or may not be accurate. In the case of a missing semicolon, the next line may be the "error line." This statement holds true with other types of errors in C. Oh, well — at least it's close and not a generic honk of the speaker and "ERRORS GALORE, YOU FOOL" plastered onscreen.
- A good habit is to fix the first error listed and then recompile. Often, the first error is the only real one, but the compiler lists others that follow because it becomes confused.
- Of course, you may be thinking "Okay, smarty-pants computer, you know what's wrong — fix it!" But computers don't just jump to conclusions like that. That is the evil of the statement "Do what I mean": Computers can't read minds, so you must be precise. They are champs, however, at pointing out what's wrong (and almost snobbishly so).

Repairing the malodorous program

To make the world right again, you have to fix the program. This process requires editing the source code file, making the needed correction, saving the source code file back to disk, and then recompiling.

No need to fill your head with this

C programming has two degrees of errors: warnings and errors. Some compilers call the errors *critical* errors. (Sounds like a mistake Roger Ebert would make.) Other times, they're *fatal* errors, like opening a creepy closet in one of those *Scream* movies.

The warning error means "Ooo, this doesn't look tasty, but I'll serve it to you anyway." Chances are, your program runs, but it may not do what you intend. Or, it may just be that the compiler is being touchy. With most C compilers, you can switch off some of the more persnickety warning error messages, which tend to get in the way at this early stage of your C education.

The critical error means "Dear Lordy, you tried to do something so criminal that I cannot morally complete this program." Okay, maybe it's not that severe. But the compiler cannot complete its task because it just doesn't understand your instructions.

You can fix the ERROR.C program by adding a semicolon. Edit Line 5 and add a semicolon to the end of the line. Also correct the sentence displayed on the screen so that it reads as follows:

```
printf("This program will no longer err.\n");
```

Other than changing Line 5, everything else in the program remains untouched.

Save ERROR.C back to disk. Recompile the program and then run it:

```
This program will no longer err.
```

Indeed, it does not!

- I can't always tell you where to fix your programs. ERROR.C is the only program listed in this book that contains an on-purpose error. When you get an error message, you should check it to see where the error is in your source code. Then cross-check your source code with what's listed in this book. That way, you find what's wrong. But when you venture out on your own and experiment, you have only the error message to go by when you're hunting down your own errors.
- Pull two *R*s out of ERRORS and you have Eros, the Greek god of love. The Roman god of love was Cupid. Replace the *C* in Cupid with *St* and you have Stupid. Stupid errors — how lovely!

Now try this error!

Don't dispense with the ERROR.C file just yet. Don't close the window, and don't zap the project. (If you did, use your editor to load the ERROR.C file and prepare to reedit.)

Change Line 6 in the ERROR.C source code file to read this way:

```
retrun(0);
```

In case you don't see it, the word `return` has been mangled to read `retrun`; the second *r* and the *u* are transposed. Otherwise, the zero in the parentheses and the semicolon are unchanged.

The way C works is that it just assumes that `retrun` is something you're serious about and not a typo. The compiler couldn't care less. But the *linker* goes nuts over it. That's because it's the linker that glues program files together. It catches the error when it doesn't find the word `retrun` in any of its libraries. And, like any frazzled librarian, the linker spews forth an error message.

Save the modified ERROR.C file to disk. Then recompile. Brace yourself for an error message along the lines of

```
temporary_filename.o: In function 'main':
temporary_filename.o: undefined reference to 'retrun'
```

Or, the message may look like this:

```
temporary_filename.o(blah blah):error.c: undefined reference
         to 'retrun'
```

It's harder to tell where the error took place here; unlike compiler errors, linker errors tend to be vague. In this case, the linker is explaining that the error is in reference to the word `retrun`. So, rather than use a line-number reference, you can always just search for the bogus text.

To fix the error, reedit the source code and change `retrun` back to `return`. Save. Recompile. The linker should be pleased.

- As I mention elsewhere in this book, the GCC compiler both compiles and links.
- If the linker is run as a separate program, it obviously produces its own error messages.
- A temporary file is created by the compiler, an *object code* file that ends in .O — which you can see in the error message output. This object code file is deleted by GCC.

- The linker's job is to pull together different pieces of a program. If it spots something it doesn't recognize, such as `retrun`, it assumes, "Hey, maybe it's something from another part of the program." So the error slides by. But, when the linker tries to look for the unrecognized word, it hoists its error flags high in the full breeze.

All about errors!

A common programming axiom is that you don't write computer programs as much as you remove errors from them. Errors are everywhere, and removing them is why it can take years to write good software.

Compiler errors: The most common error, initially discovered by the compiler as it tries to churn the text you write into instructions the computer can understand. These errors are the friendly ones, generally self-explanatory with line numbers and all the trimmings. The errors are caught before the program is built.

Linker errors: Primarily involve misspelled commands. In advanced C programming, when you're working with several source files, or modules, to create a larger program, linker errors may involve missing modules. Also, if your linker requires some "library" file and it can't be found, another type of error message is displayed. Pieces of the program are built, but errors prevent it from them being glued together.

Run-time errors: Generated by the program when it runs. They aren't bugs; instead, they're things that look totally acceptable to the compiler and linker but just don't do quite what you intended. (This happens often in C.) The most common run-time error is a *null pointer assignment.* You aggravate over this one later. The program is built, but usually gets shut down by the operating system when it's run.

Bugs: The final type of error you encounter. The compiler diligently creates the program you wrote, but whether that program does what you intended is up to the test. If it doesn't, you must work on the source code some more. Bugs include everything from things that work slowly to ones that work unintentionally or not at all. These are the hardest things to figure out and are usually your highest source of frustration. The program is built and runs, but it doesn't behave the way you think it would.

Chapter 3

C Straight

In This Chapter

- Looking at the C language
- Dissecting source code
- Obeying the RULES
- Using `\n`
- Splitting up lines with `\`

Any new language looks weird to you. Your native tongue has a certain cadence or word pattern. And the letters all fit together in a certain way. Foreign languages, they have weird characters: ç, ü, and ø and letter combinations that look strange in English — Gwynedd, Zgierz, Qom, and Idaho.

Strange new things require getting used to. You need a road map to know what's what. There's really no point in blindly typing in a C program unless you have a faint idea of what's going on. That's what this chapter shows. After reading through two chapters and compiling two different C programs and dealing with the heartbreak of errors, this chapter finally and formally introduces you to the C language.

The Big Picture

Figure 3-1 outlines the GOODBYE.C program's source code, which I use as an example in Chapter 1.

Each program must have a starting point. When you run a program, the operating system (OS) sends it off on its way — like launching a ship. As its last dockmaster duty, the OS hurls the microprocessor headlong into the program. The microprocessor then takes the program's helm at a specific starting point.

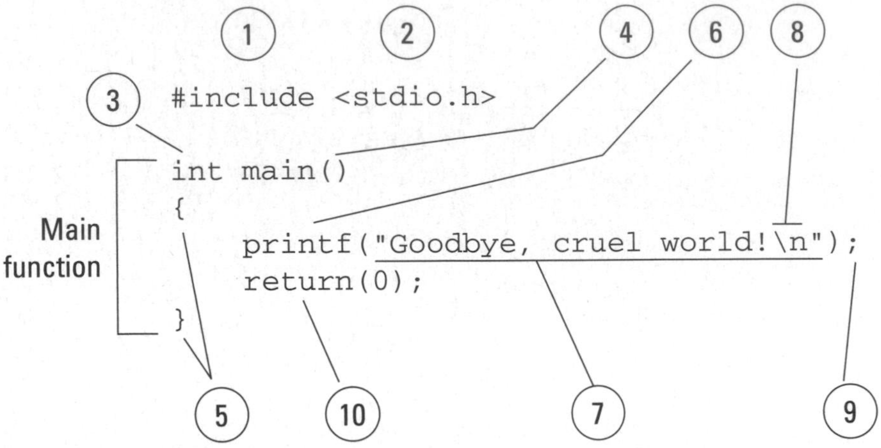

Figure 3-1: GOODBYE.C and its pieces' parts.

In all C programs, the starting point is the `main()` function. Every C program has one; GOODBYE.C, ERROR.C, and all the other C programs you ever create. The `main()` function is the engine that makes the program work. The `main()` function is also the skeleton upon which the rest of the program is built.

- `main()` is the name given to the first (or primary) function in every C program. C programs can have other functions, but `main()` is the first one.
- In C, functions are followed by parentheses. The parentheses can be empty, or they can contain information — it all depends on the individual function.
- When I write about C language functions in this book, I include the parentheses, as in `main()`.
- A *function* is a machine — it's a set of instructions that does something. C programs can have many functions in them, though the `main()` function is the first function in a C program. It's required.

Function. Get used to that word.

C Language Pieces' Parts

Here are some interesting pieces of the C program shown in Figure 3-1:

1. `#include` is known as a *preprocessor directive,* which sounds impressive, and it may not be the correct term, but you're not required to memorize it anyhow. What it does is tell the compiler to "include" text from another file, stuffing it right into your source code. Doing this avoids lots of little, annoying errors that would otherwise occur.

2. `<stdio.h>` is a filename hugged by angle brackets (which is the C language's attempt to force you to use all sorts of brackets and whatnot). The whole statement `#include <stdio.h>` tells the compiler to take text from the file STDIO.H and stick it into your source code before the source code is compiled. The STDIO.H file itself contains information about the STanDard Input/Output functions required by most C programs. The *H* means "header." You read more about header files in Chapter 23.

3. `int main` does two things. First, the `int` identifies the function `main` as an integer function, meaning that `main()` must return an integer value when it's done. Second, that line names the function `main`, which also identifies the first and primary function inside the program.

   You find out more about functions returning values in Chapter 22.

4. Two empty parentheses follow the function name. Sometimes, items may be in these parentheses, which I cover in Chapter 22.

5. All functions in C have their contents encased by curly braces. So, the function name comes first (`main` in Item 3), and then its contents — or the machine that performs the function's job — is hugged by the curly braces.

6. `printf` is the name of a C language function, so I should write it as `printf()`. It's job is to display information on the screen. (Because printers predated computer monitors, the commands that display information on the screen are called *print* commands. The added *f* means "formatted," which you find out more about in the next few chapters.)

7. Like all C language functions, `printf()` has a set of parentheses. In the parentheses, you find text, or a "string" of characters. Everything between the double quote characters (") is part of `printf`'s text string.

8. An interesting part of the text string is `\n`. That's the backslash character and a little *n*. What it represents is the character produced by pressing the Enter key, called a *newline* in C. You read more about this and other weird backslash-character combinations in Chapter 7.

9. The `printf` line, or statement, ends with a semicolon. The semicolon is C language punctuation — like a period in English. The semicolon tells the C compiler where one statement ends and another begins. Note that all statements require semicolons in C, even if only one statement is in a program or function.

10. The second statement in GOODBYE.C is the `return` command. This command sends the value 0 (zero) back to the operating system when the `main()` function is done. Returning a value is required as part of the `main()` function. You read why in Chapter 22. Note that even though this command is the last one in the program, this statement ends in a semicolon.

- Text in a program is referred to as a *string.* For example, "la-de-da" is a string of text. The string is enclosed by double quotes.
- A C language function starts with the function type, such as `int`, and then the function name and parentheses, as in `main()`. Then come a set of curly braces, `{` and `}`. Everything between the `{` and `}` is part of the function.
- The C language is composed of keywords that appear in statements. The statements end in semicolons, just as sentences in English end in periods. (Don't frazzle your wires over memorizing this right yet.)

The C Language Itself — the Keywords

The C language is really rather brief. C has only 32 *keywords.* If only French were that easy! Table 3-1 shows the keywords that make up the C language.

Table 3-1 C Language Keywords

auto	double	int	struct
break	else	long	switch
case	enum	register	typedef
char	extern	return	union
const	float	short	unsigned
continue	for	signed	void
default	goto	sizeof	volatile
do	if	static	while

Not bad, eh? But these aren't all the words you use when writing programs in C. Other words or instructions are called *functions.* These include jewels like `printf()` and several dozen other common functions that assist the basic C language keywords in creating programs.

Beyond keywords, programming languages (like human languages) also involve grammar, or properly sticking together the words so that understandable ideas are conveyed. This concept is completely beyond the grasp of the modern legal community.

Even more keyword madness!

Keywords are worth noting because their use is restricted or reserved. For example, you cannot think up your own function and name it `short`. That's because `short` is a keyword, reserved only for its specific purpose in the core C language. That's one way the keywords are special.

In addition to the 32 keywords shown in Table 3-1 are these two depreciated C language keywords:

fortran

entry

C once had these keywords, but no longer. Still, I would avoid using them in your programs. (That's what "depreciated" means.)

Also, the C++ language has a hoard of reserved words. If you plan to study C++, include these words in your do-not-use, reserved C language vocabulary:

asm	false	private	throw
bool	friend	protected	true
catch	inline	public	try
class	mutable	reinterpret_cast	typeid
const_cast	namespace	static_cast	using
delete	new	template	virtual
dynamic_cast	operator	this	

It's better to know these words now and not use them than to use one (such as `new` or `friend`) and run into trouble later when you eventually find out how to use C++.

In addition to grammar, languages require rules, exceptions, jots and tittles, and all sorts of fun and havoc. Programming languages are similar to spoken language in that they have various parts and lots of rules.

- The keywords can also be referred to as *reserved words.*
- Note that all keywords are lowercase. This sentence is always true for C: Keywords, as well as the names of functions, are lowercase. C is case sensitive, so there is a difference between `return`, `Return`, and `RETURN`.
- You are never required to memorize the 32 keywords.
- In fact, of the 32 keywords, you may end up using only half on a regular basis.
- Some keywords are real words! Others are abbreviations or combinations of two or more words. Still others are cryptograms of the programmers' girlfriends' names.
- Each of the keywords has its own set of problems. You don't just use the keyword `else`, for example; you must use it *in context.*

- Functions such as printf() require a set of parentheses and lots of stuff inside the parentheses. (Don't fret over this statement right now; just nod your head and smile in agreement, "Yes, printf() does require lots of stuff.")
- By the way, the fact that printf() is a C function and not a keyword is why the #include <stdio.h> thing is required at the beginning of a program. The STDIO.H file contains instructions telling the compiler what exactly printf() is and does. If you edit out the #include <stdio.h> line, the compiler produces a funky "I don't know what to do with this printf() thing" type of error.

Other C Language Components

The C language has many other parts, making it look rather bizarre to the new programmer. Right now, all that's standing between ignorance and knowledge is *time,* so don't dwell on what you don't know. Instead, keep these few points rolling around in your mind, like so many knowledge nuggets:

- The C language uses words — keywords, functions, and so forth — as its most basic elements.
- Included with the words are symbols. Sometimes these symbols are called *operators,* and at other times they're called something else. For example, the plus sign (+) is used in C to add things.
- The words have options and rules about how they're used. These rules are all referenced in the C reference material that came with your compiler. You don't have to memorize all of them, though a few of them become second nature to you as you study and use C.
- Parentheses are used to group some of the important items required by C words.

  The words are put together to create *statements,* which are similar to sentences in English. The statements all end with a semicolon.
- Braces are used to group parts of a program. Some words use braces to group their belongings, and all the separate functions you create within a program are grouped by braces. In Figure 3-1 and in all your C programs in the first two chapters, for example, the braces have been used to contain the belongings of the main() function.
- All this stuff put together (and more stuff I dare not discuss at this point) makes up the syntax of the C language. *Syntax* is how languages are put together.

Pop Quiz!

1. The core function in every C language program is called

    A. `numero_uno()`.

    B. `main()`.

    C. `primus()`.

    D. `core()`.

2. C language keywords are

    A. The "words" of the C language.

    B. Held together with string and earwax.

    C. Uttered only in candlelit reverence by the C Language Gurus.

    D. As numerous as the stars and nearly as distant.

3. In addition to keywords are

    A. Functions, such as `printf()`.

    B. Operators, such as +, -, and other weird things.

    C. Curly braces or brackets, angle brackets — all sorts of brackets. Man, do we have a bracket problem!

    D. Probably all of the above.

4. Functions require parentheses because

    A. They talk in whispers.

    B. The parentheses keep the function warm.

    C. The parentheses hold various things required by or belonging to the function.

    D. What's a function?

5. A telltale sign of any C program is its curly braces. Using what you know of C, draw in the braces where they should appear in the following program:

```
int main()
___
    printf("Goodbye, cruel world!\n");
           return(0);
___
```

Answers on page 516.

The Helpful RULES Program

I just can't let you go without a program in this chapter. To help you understand the most easily offended C rules, I have summarized them in the following program. It displays several lines of text that remind you of the basic rules of C that you know about:

```
#include <stdio.h>

int main()
{
 printf("Braces come in pairs!");
 printf("Comments come in pairs!");
 printf("All statements end with a semicolon!");
 printf("Spaces are optional!");
 printf("Must have a main function!");
 printf("C is done mostly in lowercase.\
   It's a case-sensitive language.");
 return(0);
}
```

Type the preceding source code into your editor. Save the code to disk as RULES.C. Compile and run.

The resulting program is named RULES, and you can run it whenever you need a reminder about some basic C do's and don'ts.

- This program is really no different from those shown in previous chapters. It merely has more `printf()` functions.
- The final `printf()` function (in Line 10) may seem a little odd. That's because it's split between two lines. This weird contraption is covered later in this chapter.

The importance of being `\n`

Did you notice something odd about the output of the RULES program? Yes, it resembles an ugly clot of text:

```
Braces come in pairs!Comments come in pairs!All statements
          end with a semicolon!Spaces are optional!Must have
          a main function!C is done mostly in lowercase.
          It's a case-sensitive language.
```

The source code looks okay, but what's missing from the output is the character you get when you press the Enter key, or what's called the *newline* character. You have seen it before. It's that weird `\n` thing:

```
\n
```

This line is C-speak for "Gimme a new line of text." The `n` stands for *new* in *new line* (though they write it as one word: newline).

The program you just created, RULES.C, needs the `\n` character at the end of each line to ensure that each line is displayed on a line by itself on the screen. This addition makes the output of the RULES program easy to read.

Edit the RULES.C source code file again. Before the last double-quote in each `printf()` string, add the `\n` newline character.

If you're good with search and replace, search for the `")` (quote-paren) and replace it with `\n")`.

Save the file to disk and recompile it. The output should now be more pleasing:

```
Braces come in pairs!
Comments come in pairs!
All statements end with a semicolon!
Spaces are optional!
Must have a main function!
C is done mostly in lowercase. It's a case-sensitive
          language.
```

- In C, the `\n` character is used in a text string as though the Enter key were pressed.
- It's always `\n` with a little *n*. C is mostly lowercase.
- The `\n` is called *newline,* though calling it "slash-n" or "backslash-n" is acceptable as long as you don't say it aloud.
- Table 24-1, in Chapter 24, lists other characters of a similar nature to `\n`.

Breaking up lines\ is easy to do

Another anomaly of the RULES program is that rogue \ character found at the end of the tenth line. When used to end a line, the sole \ tells the compiler that the rest of the line is merely continued on the line that follows. So, these two lines:

```
printf("C is done mostly in lowercase\
          It's a case-sensitive language.\n");
```

are both seen as one single line when it comes time to compile; all the compiler sees is this:

```
printf("C is done mostly in lowercase It's a case-sensitive
          language.\n");
```

You may find such a trick necessary for extra-long lines as your programs grow more complex. The \ simply lets you split up a long line between several lines in your source code. That can be handy.

Depending on how your editor and compiler behave, the result of splitting a line with a string of text in it may not be what you want. For example, the output on your screen may look like this:

```
Braces come in pairs!
Comments come in pairs!
All statements end with a semicolon!
Spaces are optional!
Must have a main function!
C is done mostly in lowercase.                 It's a case-
           sensitive language.
```

That happens because the split line includes a few tabs to indent things — which looks pretty in your source code, but looks like blech when the program runs. The solution is merely to edit the source code so that the extra tabs are removed from the string of text.

To wit, change Lines 10 and 11 in the source code from this:

```
        printf("C is done mostly in lowercase.\
                  It's a case-sensitive language.");
```

to this:

```
        printf("C is done mostly in lowercase. \
It's a case-sensitive language.");
```

Note the extra space after the period in the first line (before the backslash), which keeps the two lines of text from running into each other. Save that mess. Compile and run. The output shall be most pleasing to the eye.

- Do note that some programs elsewhere in this book may use the \ to split long lines.
- Don't worry about using the \ to split any lines. It's a trick you see others use occasionally, but in my travels I prefer using a sideways-scrolling editor to splitting up long lines.
- Although split lines are treated as a single line, any errors that happen on either line are given their proper line number in the source code file. So, if a semicolon were missing at the end of Line 11 in the RULES.C example, the compiler would flag it on that line, not on the line before it.

Chapter 4

C What I/O

In This Chapter

- Reading the keyboard
- Understanding `printf()`
- Creating formatted output
- Understanding `scanf()`

Computers are all about input and output — the old I/O of days gone by, what the pioneers once sang about. The wimminfolk would want to dance real slow. Maybe cry. It was a sentimental thing, y'all — something that fancy, dooded-up city slickers read about in dime magazines.

A-hem!

Input and output: You type something in and get a response, ask a question and get an answer, put in two dollars in coins and get your soda pop — things along those lines. This goes along with what I present in Chapter 3: It is your job as a programmer to write a program that does something. At this point in the learning process, triviality is okay. Soon, however, you begin to write programs that really do something.

Introduce Yourself to Mr. Computer

To meet the needs of input and output — the old I/O — you can try the following program, WHORU.C — which is "who are you" minus a few letters. Please don't go calling this program "horror-you" (which could be spelled another way, but this is a family book).

The purpose of this program is to type your name at the keyboard and then have the computer display your name on the screen, along with a nice, friendly greeting:

```
#include <stdio.h>

int main()
{
    char me[20];

    printf("What is your name?");
    scanf("%s",me);
    printf("Darn glad to meet you, %s!\n",me);

    return(0);
}
```

Type the preceding source code into your editor. Double-check everything. Don't bother with any details just yet. Type and hum, if it pleases you.

Save the file to disk. Name it WHORU.C.

Don't compile this program just yet. That happens in the next section.

- The `char me[20];` thing is a *variable declaration*. It provides storage for the information you enter (the *I* in I/O). You find out more about variables in Chapter 8.
- The new function here is `scanf()`, which is used to read input from the keyboard and store it in the computer's memory.
- Left paren is the `(` character. Right paren is the `)` character. *Paren* is short for parenthesis or a type of steak sauce. (It's also not a "real" word and is frowned on by English teachers of the high-and-tight bun.)

Compiling WHORU.C

Compile the WHORU.C source code. If you see syntax or other errors, double-check your source code with what is listed in this book. Ensure that you entered everything properly. Be on the lookout for jots and tittles — parentheses, double quotes, backslashes, percent signs, sneeze splotches, or other unusual things on your monitor's screen.

If you need to fix any errors, do so now. Otherwise, keep reading in the next section.

- Refer to Chapter 2 for more information on fixing errors and recompiling.
- A common beginner error: Unmatched double quotes! Make sure that you always use a set of "s (double quotes). If you miss one, you get an error. Also make sure that the parentheses and curly braces are included in pairs; left one first, right one second.

The reward

Enough waiting! Run the WHORU program now. Type **whoru** or **./whoru** at the command prompt and press the Enter key. The output looks like this:

```
What is your name?
```

The program is now waiting for you to type your name. Go ahead: Type your name! Press Enter.

If you typed **Buster**, the next line is displayed:

```
Darn glad to meet you, Buster!
```

- If the output looks different or the program doesn't work right or generates an error, review your source code again. Reedit to fix any errors and then recompile.
- I/O is input/output, what computers do best.
- I/O, I/O, it's off to code I go. . . .
- This program is an example that takes input and generates output. It doesn't do anything with the input other than display it, but it does qualify for I/O.

The WHORU.C source code mixes two powerful C language functions to get input and provide output: `printf()` and `scanf()`. The rest of this chapter tells more about these common and useful functions in detail.

More on `printf()`

The `printf()` function is used in the C programming language to display information on the screen. It's the all-purpose "Hey, I want to tell the user something" display-text command. It's the universal electric crayon for the C language's scribbling muscles.

The format for using the basic printf function is

```
printf("text");
```

printf is always written in lowercase. It's a must. It's followed by parentheses, which contain a quoted string of text, *text* (see the example). It's printf()'s job to display that text on the screen.

In the C language, printf()is a complete statement. A semicolon always follows the last parenthesis. (Okay, you may see an exception, but it's not worth fussing over at this point in the game.)

- Although *text* is enclosed in double quotes, they aren't part of the message that printf() puts up on the screen.
- You have to follow special rules about the text you can display, all of which are covered in Chapter 24.
- The format shown in the preceding example is simplified. A more advanced format for printf() appears later in this chapter.

Printing funky text

Ladies and gentlemen, I give you the following:

```
Ta da!  I am a text string.
```

It's a simple collection of text, numbers, letters, and other characters — but it's not a string of text. Nope. For those characters to be considered as a unit, they must be neatly enclosed in double quotes:

```
"Ta da!  I am a text string."
```

Now you have a string of text, but that's still nothing unless the computer can manipulate it. For manipulation, you need to wrap up the string in the bun-like parentheses:

```
("Ta da!  I am a text string.")
```

Furthermore, you need an engine — a *function* — to manipulate the string. Put printf on one side and a semicolon on the other:

```
printf("Ta da!  I am a text string.");
```

And, you have a hot dog of a C command to display the simple collection of text, numbers, letters, and other characters on the screen. Neat and tidy.

Consider this rabble:

```
He said, "Ta da! I am a text string."
```

Is this criminal or what? It's still a text string, but it contains the double-quote characters. Can you make that text a string by adding even more double quotes?

```
"He said, "Ta da! I am a text string.""
```

Now there are four double quotes in all. That means eight tick marks hovering over this string's head. How can it morally cope with that?

```
""Damocles" if I know."
```

The C compiler never punishes you for "testing" anything. There is no large room in a hollowed-out mountain in the Rockies where a little man sits in a chair looking at millions of video screens, one of which contains your PC's output, and, no, the little man doesn't snicker evilly whenever you get an error. Errors are safe! So why not experiment?

Please enter the following source code, DBLQUOTE.C. The resulting program is another "`printf()` displays something" example. But this time, what's displayed contains a double quote. Can you do that? This source code is your experiment for the day:

```
#include <stdio.h>

int main()
{
    printf("He said, "Ta da! I am a text string."");
    return(0);
}
```

Type the source code exactly as it appears, including the double quotes — four in all. (You notice right away that something is wrong if your editor color-codes quoted text. But work with me here.)

Save the source code file to disk as DBLQUOTE.C.

Compile and run the preceding program — if you can. Chances are that you encounter one of these errors instead:

```
dblequote.c: In function 'main':
dblequote.c:5: parse error before "Ta"
```

or

```
dblequote.c: In function 'main':
dblequote.c:6: syntax error before "Ta"
```

The `printf()` function requires a text string enclosed in double quotes. Your compiler knows that. After the second double quote in the string was encountered (before the word *Ta*), the compiler expected something else — something other than "Ta." Therefore, an error was generated. Figure 4-1 illustrates this in a cute way.

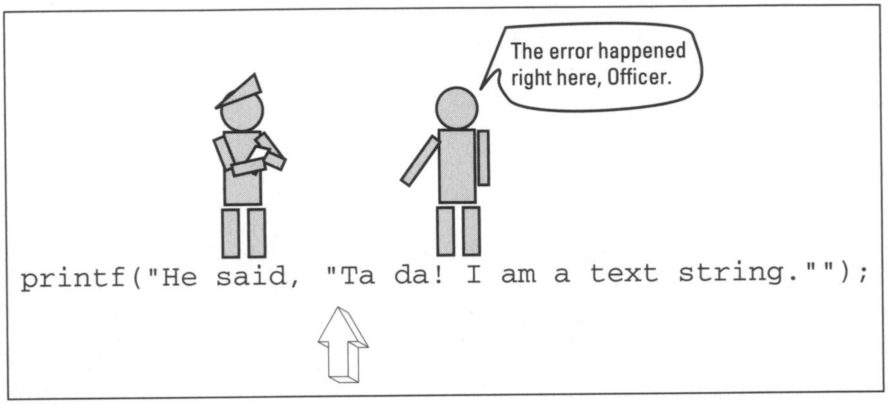

Figure 4-1: The C compiler detects something amiss in the `printf()` statement.

Obviously, there is a need to use the double-quote character in a string of text. The question is how to pass that character along to `printf()` without it ruining the rest of your day. The answer is to use an escape sequence.

In the olden days, programmers would have simply gone without certain characters. Rather than trip up a string with a double quote, they would have used two single quotes. Some ancient programmers who don't know about escape sequences still use these tricks.

Escape from `printf()`*!*

Escape sequences are designed to liven up an otherwise dull action picture with a few hard-cutting, loud-music moments of derring-do. In a programming language, *escape sequences* are used to sneak otherwise forbidden characters, or characters you cannot directly type at the keyboard, into text strings.

In the C language, escape sequences always begin with the backslash character (\). Locate this character on your keyboard now. It should be above the Enter key, though they often hide it elsewhere.

The backslash character signals the `printf()` function that an escape sequence is looming. When `printf()` sees the backslash, it thinks, "Omigosh, an escape sequence must be coming up," and it braces itself to accept an otherwise forbidden character.

To sneak in the double-quote character without getting `printf()` in a tizzy, you use the escape sequence `\"` (backslash, double quote). Behold, the new and improved Line 5:

```
printf("He said, \"Ta da! I am a text string.\"");
```

Notice the `\"` escape sequences in the text string. You see two of them, prefixing the two double quotes that appear in the string's midsection. The two outside double quotes, the ones that really are bookmarks to the entire string, remain intact. Looks weird, but it doesn't cause an error.

(If your text editor color-codes strings, you see how the escaped double quotes appear as special characters in the string, not as boundary markers, like the other double quotes.)

Edit your DBLQUOTE.C source code file. Make the escape-sequence modification to Line 5, as just shown. All you have to do is insert two backslash characters before the rogue double quotes: `\"`.

Save the changed source code file to disk, overwriting the original DBLQUOTE.C file with the newer version.

Compile and run. This time, it works and displays the following output:

```
He said, "Ta da! I am a text string."
```

- The `\"` escape sequence produces the double-quote character in the middle of a string.
- Another handy escape sequence you may have used in Chapter 1 is `\n`. That produces a "new line" in a string, just like pressing the Enter key. You cannot "type" the Enter key in a text string, so you must use the `\n` escape sequence.
- All escape sequences start with the backslash character.
- How do you stick a backslash character into a string? Use two of them: `\\` is the escape sequence that sticks a backslash character into a string.
- An escape sequence can appear anywhere in a text string: beginning, middle, or end and as many times as you want to use them. Essentially, the \ thing is a shorthand notation for sticking forbidden characters into any string.
- Other escape sequences are listed in Chapter 24 (in Table 24-1).

The f means "formatted"

The function is called `printf()` for a reason. The *f* stands for *formatted.* The advantage of the `printf` function over other, similar display-this-or-that functions in C is that the output can be formatted.

Earlier in this chapter, I introduce the format for the basic `printf` function as

```
printf("text");
```

But the real format — *shhh!* — is

```
printf("format_string"[,var[,...]]);
```

What appears in the double quotes is really a *formatting string.* It's still text that appears in `printf()`'s output, but secretly inserted into the text are various *conversion characters,* or special "placeholders," that tell the `printf()` function how to format its output and do other powerful stuff.

After the format string comes a comma (still inside the parentheses) and then one or more items called *arguments.* The argument shown in the preceding example is *var,* which is short for *var*iable. You can use `printf()` to display the content or value of one or more variables. You do this by using special conversion characters in `format_string`. Figure 4-2 illustrates this concept rather beautifully.

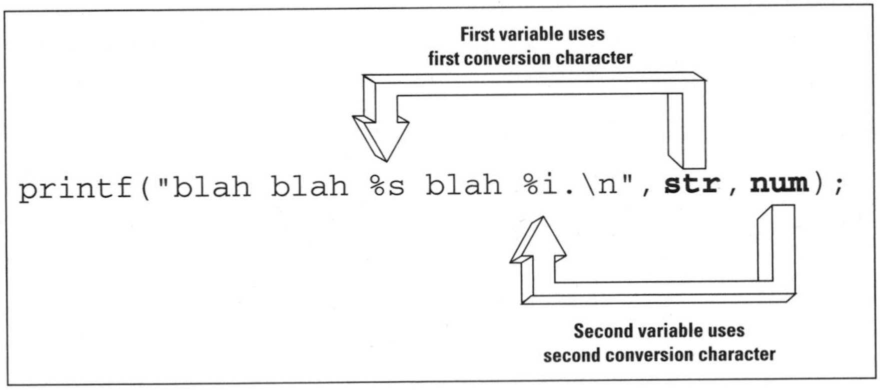

Figure 4-2: How `printf()` solves arguments.

The `[,...]` doohickey means that you can have any number of *var* items specified in a single `printf` function (before the final paren). Each *var* item, however, must have a corresponding placeholder (or conversion character) in `format_string`. They must match up, or else you get an error when the program is compiled.

A bit of justification

To demonstrate how `printf()` can format text, as well as use those handy *conversion characters* and *var* things I scared you with in the preceding section, how about a sample program?

For your consideration is the following source code, which I have named JUSTIFY.C. Marvel at it:

```
#include <stdio.h>

int main()
{
    printf("%15s","right\n");
    printf("%-15s","left\n");
    return(0);
}
```

What JUSTIFY.C does is to display two strings: `right` is right-justified, and `left` is left-justified. This makes more sense when you see the program's output rather than just look at the source code.

Enter this source code into your text editor.

In the first `printf` statement, the first string is `%15s` (percent sign, 15, little *s*). That's followed by a comma and then `right`, followed by the newline escape sequence, `\n` (backslash, little *n*).

The second `printf` statement is nearly the same thing, though with a minus sign before the 15 and the string `left` rather than `right`.

This program contains more C doodads than any other program introduced in the first three chapters in this book. Be careful with what you type! When you're certain that you have it right, save the file to disk as JUSTIFY.C.

Compile JUSTIFY.C. Fix any errors if you need to. Then run the program. Your output should look something like this:

```
          right
left
```

The word `right` is right-justified 15 spaces over; `left` is left-justified. This arrangement was dictated by the `%15s` formatting command in `printf()`. The `%15s` part of the formatting string didn't print at all. Instead, it *controlled* how the other string's contents appeared on the screen. That's the formatting power of `printf()` at work.

Maybe a little more help in understanding conversion characters

To drive home how `printf()` uses its formatting string and arguments, bring up the source code for the GOODBYE.C program into your text editor. Change Line 5 to read:

```
printf("%s","Goodbye, cruel
    world!\n");
```

`printf()` has been modified to contain a formatting string and an argument.

The formatting string is `%s`, which is the *string* (for *s*) placeholder.

The argument is a string of text: `"Goodbye, cruel world\!n"`.

Save the source code under a new filename, BYE.C. Compile and run. The output is the same as the original; you have merely used the `%s` in the `printf()` function to "format" the output.

Try this modification of Line 5:

```
printf("%s, %s
    %s\n","Goodbye","cruel",
    "world!");
```

Carefully edit Line 5 to look like what's shown in the preceding line. It has three string placeholders, `%s`, and three strings in double quotes (with commas between them). Save. Compile. Run. The output should be the same.

(If you get a compiling error, you probably have put a comma *inside* the double quotes, rather than between them.)

The JUSTIFY.C program shows you only a hint of what the `printf()` function can do. `printf()` can also format numbers in a remarkable number of ways, which is a little overwhelming to present right now in this chapter.

- In the `printf()` function, the first item in quotes is a formatting string, though it can also contain text to be displayed right on the screen.
- The percent character holds special meaning to `printf()`. It identifies a *conversion character* — what I call a "placeholder" — that tells `printf` how to format its output.
- The conversion character `s` means string: `%s`.
- Any numbers between the `%` and the `s` are used to set the *width* of the text string displayed. So, `%15s` means to display a string of text using 15 characters. A minus sign before the `15` means to left-justify the string's output.
- Doesn't "left-justify" sound like a word processing term? Yup! It's formatting!
- `printf()` doesn't truncate or shorten strings longer than the width specified in the `%s` placeholder.

- All this conversion-character stuff can get complex. Rest assured that seldom does anyone memorize it. Often, advanced programmers have to consult their C language references and run some tests to see which formatting command does what. Most of the time, you aren't bothered with this stuff, so don't panic.

`scanf` *Is Pronounced "Scan-Eff"*

Output without input is like Desi without Lucy, yang without yin, Caesar salad without the garlic. It means that the seven dwarves would be singing "Oh, Oh, Oh" rather than "I/O, I/O." Besides — and this may be the most horrid aspect of all — without input, the computer just sits there and talks *at* you. That's just awful.

C has numerous tools for making the computer listen to you. A number of commands read input from the keyboard, from commands that scan for individual characters to the vaunted `scanf()` function, which is used to snatch a string of text from the keyboard and save it in the cuddly, warm paws of a string variable.

- `scanf()` is a function like `printf()`. Its purpose is to read text from the keyboard.
- Like the *f* in `printf()`, the *f* in `scanf()` means *formatted*. You can use `scanf()` to read a specifically formatted bit of text from the keyboard. In this chapter, however, you just use `scanf()` to read a line of text, nothing fancy.

Putting `scanf` *together*

To make `scanf()` work, you need two things. First, you need a storage place to hold the text you enter. Second, you need the `scanf` function itself.

The storage place is called a *string variable*. *String* means a string of characters — text. *Variable* means that the string isn't set — it can be whatever the user types. A string variable is a storage place for text in your programs. (Variables are discussed at length in Chapter 8.)

The second thing you need is `scanf()` itself. Its format is somewhat similar to the advanced, cryptic format for `printf()`, so there's no point in wasting any of your brain cells covering that here.

An example of using `scanf()` reads in someone's first name. First, you create a storage place for the first name:

```
char firstname[20];
```

This C language statement sets aside storage for a string of text — like creating a safe for a huge sum of money that you wish to have some day. And, just like the safe, the variable is "empty" when you create it; it doesn't contain anything until you put something there.

Here's how the preceding statement breaks down:

`char` is a C language keyword that tells the compiler to create a character variable, something that holds text (as opposed to numbers).

`firstname` is the name of the storage location. When the source code refers to the variable, it uses this name, `firstname`.

`[20]` defines the size of the string as being able to hold as many as 20 characters. All told, you have set aside space to hold 20 characters and named that space — that *variable* — `firstname`.

The semicolon ends the C language statement.

The next step is to use the `scanf()` function to read in text from the keyboard and store it in the variable that is created. Something like the following line would work:

```
scanf("%s",firstname);
```

Here's how this statement works:

`scanf()` is the function to read information from the keyboard.

`%s` is the string placeholder; `scanf()` is looking for plain old text input from the keyboard. Pressing the Enter key ends input.

The text input is stored in the string variable named `firstname`.

The semicolon ends the C language statement.

Between the variable and `scanf()`, text is read from the keyboard and stored in the computer's memory for later use. The next section coughs up an example.

- If you're writing a C program that requires input, you must create a place to store it. For text input, that place is a string variable, which you create by using the `char` keyword.
- Variables are officially introduced in Chapter 8 in this book. For now, consider the string variable that `scanf()` uses as merely a storage chamber for text you type.
- The formatting codes used by `scanf()` are identical to those used by `printf()`. In real life, you use them mostly with `printf()` because there are better ways to read the keyboard than to use `scanf()`. Refer to Table 24-2 in Chapter 24 for a list of the formatting percent-sign placeholder codes.
- Forgetting to stick the `&` in front of `scanf()`'s variable is a common mistake. Not doing so leads to some wonderful *null pointer assignment* errors that you may relish in the years to come. As a weird quirk, however, the ampersand is optional when you're dealing with string variables. Go figure.

The miracle of `scanf()`

Consider the following pointless program, COLOR.C, which uses two string variables, `name` and `color`. It asks for your name and then your favorite color. The final `printf()` statement then displays what you enter.

```
#include <stdio.h>

int main()
{
    char name[20];
    char color[20];

    printf("What is your name?");
    scanf("%s",name);
    printf("What is your favorite color?");
    scanf("%s",color);
    printf("%s's favorite color is %s\n",name,color);
    return(0);
}
```

Enter this source code into your editor. Save this file to disk as COLOR.C. Compile.

If you get any errors, double-check your source code and reedit the file. A common mistake: forgetting that there are two commas in the final `printf()` statement.

Run the program! The output looks something like this:

```
What is your name?dan
What is your favorite color?brown
dan's favorite color is brown
```

In Windows XP, you have to run the command by using the following line:

```
.\color
```

The reason is that COLOR is a valid console command in Windows XP, used to change the foreground and background color of the console window.

Experimentation time!

Which is more important: the order of the `%s` doodads or the order of the variables — the arguments — in a `printf` statement? Give up? I'm not going to tell you the answer. You have to figure it out for yourself.

Make the following modification to Line 12 in the COLOR.C program:

```
printf("%s's favorite color is %s\n",color,name);
```

The order of the variables here is reversed: `color` comes first and then `name`. Save this change to disk and recompile. The program still runs, but the output is different because you changed the variable order. You may see something like this:

```
brown's favorite color is Dan.
```

See? Computers *are* stupid! The point here is that you must remember the order of the variables when you have more than one listed in a `printf()` function. The `%s` thingies? They're just fill-in-the-blanks.

How about making this change:

```
printf("%s's favorite color is %s\n",name,name);
```

This modification uses the `name` variable twice — perfectly allowable. All `printf()` needs are two string variables to match the two `%s` signs in its formatting string. Save this change and recompile. Run the program and examine the output:

```
Dan's favorite color is Dan
```

Okay, Lois — have you been drinking again? Make that mistake on an IRS form and you may spend years playing golf with former stockbrokers and congressmen. (Better learn to order your variables now.)

Finally, make the following modification:

```
printf("%s's favorite color is %s\n",name,"blue");
```

Rather than the `color` variable, a *string constant* is used. A *string constant* is simply a string enclosed in quotes. It doesn't change, unlike a variable, which can hold anything. (It isn't variable!)

Save the change to disk and recompile your efforts. The program still works, though no matter which color you enter, the computer always insists that it's "blue."

- The string constant `"blue"` works because `printf()`'s `%s` placeholder looks for a string of text. It doesn't matter whether the string is a variable or a "real" text string sitting there in double quotes. (Of course, the advantage to writing a program is that you can use variables to store input; using the constant is a little silly because the computer already knows what it's going to print. I mean, ladies and gentlemen, where is the I/O?)
- The `%s` placeholder in a `printf()` function looks for a corresponding string variable and plugs it in to the text that is displayed.
- You need one string variable in the `printf()` function for each `%s` that appears in `printf()`'s formatting string. If the variable is missing, a syntax boo-boo is generated by the compiler.
- In addition to string variables, you can use string constants, often called *literal* strings. That's kind of dumb, though, because there's no point in wasting time with `%s` if you already know what you're going to display. (I have to demonstrate it here, however, or else I have to go to C Teacher's Prison in Connecticut.)
- TIP: Make sure that you get the order of your variables correct. This advice is especially important when you use both numeric and string variables in `printf`.
- The percent sign (%) is a holy character. *Om!* If you want a percent sign (%) to appear in `printf`'s output, use two of them: `%%`.

Chapter 5

To C or Not to C

In This Chapter

- Inserting notes for yourself
- Using fancy commenting techniques
- Borrowing C++ comments
- Disabling code with comments
- Avoiding nested comments

An important part of programming is remembering what the heck it is you're doing. I'm not talking about the programming itself — that's easy to remember, and you can buy books and references galore in case you don't. Instead, the thing you have to remember is what you are attempting to make a program do at a specific spot. You do that by inserting a *comment* in your source code.

Comments aren't really necessary for the small programs you're doing in this book. Comments don't begin to become necessary until you write larger programs — on the scope of Excel or Photoshop — where you can easily lose your train of thought. To remind yourself of what you're doing, you should stick a comment in the source code, explaining your approach. That way, when you look at the source code again, your eyes don't glaze over and the drool doesn't pour, because the comments remind you of what's going on.

Adding Comments

Comments in a C program have a starting point and an ending point. Everything between those two points is ignored by the compiler, meaning that you can stick any text in there — anything — and it doesn't affect how the program runs.

```
/* This is how a comment looks in the C language */
```

This line is a fine example of a comment. What follows is another example of a comment, but the type that gives this book its reputation:

```
/*
Hello compiler!  Hey, error on this: pirntf!
Ha! Ha! You can't see me!  Pbbtbtbt!
Nya! Nya! Nya!
*/
```

- The beginning of the comment is marked by the slash and the asterisk: `/*`.
- The end of the comment is marked by the asterisk and the slash: `*/`.
- Yup, they're different.
- The comment is not a C language statement. You do not need a semicolon after the `*/`.

A big, hairy program with comments

The following source code is MADLIB1.C. It uses the `printf()` and `scanf()` functions described in Chapter 4 to create a short yet interesting story:

```
/*
MADLIB1.C Source Code
Written by (your name here)
*/

#include <stdio.h>

int main()
{
    char adjective[20];
    char food[20];
    char chore[20];
    char furniture[20];

/* Get the words to use in the madlib */

    printf("Enter an adjective:");          /* prompt */
    scanf("%s",&adjective);                  /* input */
    printf("Enter a food:");
    scanf("%s",&food);
    printf("Enter a household chore (past tense):");
    scanf("%s",&chore);
    printf("Enter an item of furniture:");
    scanf("%s",&furniture);

/* Display the output */
```

```
    printf("\n\nDon't touch that %s %s!\n",adjective,food);
    printf("I just %s the %s!\n",chore,furniture);

    return(0);
}
```

Type the source code exactly as written. The only thing new should be the comments. Each one begins with /* and ends with */. Make sure that you get those right: A slash-asterisk begins the comment, and an asterisk-slash ends it. (If you're using a color-coded editor, you see the comments all coded in the same color.)

Save the file to disk and name it MADLIB1.C.

Compile. Run.

Here is a sample of the program's output:

```
Enter an adjective:hairy
Enter a food:waffle
Enter a household chore (past tense):vacuumed
Enter an item of furniture:couch

Don't touch that hairy waffle!
I just vacuumed the couch!
```

Oh, ha-ha! Ouch! My sides!

- This program is long and looks complex, but it doesn't use any new tricks. Everything here, you have seen already: `char` to create string variables, `printf()` to display text and string variables, and `scanf()` to read the keyboard. Yawn.
- MADLIB1.C uses these four string variables: `adjective`, `food`, `chore`, and `furniture`. All four are created by the `char` keyword, and 20 characters of storage are set aside for each one. Each of the string variables is filled by `scanf()` with your keyboard input.
- Each of the final `printf()` functions contains two `%s` placeholders. Two string variables in each function supply the text for the `%s` placeholders.
- The second-to-last `printf()` function begins with two newline characters, `\n \n`. These characters separate the input section, where you enter the bits of text, from the program's output. Yes, newlines can appear anywhere in a string, not just at the end.
- MADLIB1.C has five comments. Make sure that you can find each one. Notice that they're not all the same, yet each one begins with `/*` and ends with `*/`.

Why are comments necessary?

Comments aren't necessary for the C compiler. It ignores them. Instead, comments are for you, the programmer. They offer bits of advice, suggestions for what you're trying to do, or hints on how the program works. You can put anything in the comments, though the more useful the information, the better it helps you later on.

TIP

Most C programs begin with a few lines of comments. All my C programs start with information such as the following:

```
/* COOKIES.C
Dan Gookin, 1/20/05 @ 2:45 a.m.
Scan Internet cookie files for expired
dates and delete.
*/
```

These lines tell me what the program is about and when I started working on it.

In the source code itself, you can use comments as notes to yourself, such as

```
/* Find out why this doesn't work */
```

or this:

```
save=itemv;    /* Save old value here */
```

or even reminders to yourself in the future:

```
/*
Someday you will write the code here that makes
the computer remember what it did last time this
program ran.
*/
```

The point is that comments are notes *for yourself.* If you were studying C programming in school, you would write the comments to satiate the fixations of your professor. If you work on a large programming project, the comments placate your team leader. For programs you write, the comments are for you.

Comment Styles of the Nerdy and Not-Quite-Yet-Nerdy

The MADLIB1.C program contains five comments and uses three different commenting styles. Though you can comment your programs in many more ways, these are the most common:

```
/*
MADLIB1.C Source Code
Written by Mike Rowsoft
*/
```

Ever popular is the multiline approach, as just shown. The first line starts the comment with the `/*` all by itself. Lines following it are all comments, remarks, or such and are ignored by the compiler. The final line ends the comment with `*/` all by itself. Remember that final`* /`; otherwise, the C compiler thinks that your whole program is just one big, long comment (possible, but not recommended).

```
/* Get the words to use in the madlib */
```

This line is a single-line comment, not to be confused with a C language statement. The comment begins with `/*` and ends with `*/` all on the same line. It's 100 percent okey-dokey, and, because it's not a statement, you don't need a semicolon.

Finally, you can add the "end of line" comment:

```
    printf("Enter an adjective:");        /* prompt */
```

After the preceding `printf` statement plus a few taps of the Tab key, the `/*` starts a comment, and `*/` ends it on the same line.

Bizarr-o comments

During my travels, I have seen many attempts to make comments in C programs look interesting. Here's an example:

```
/*****************************************
**  Commander Zero's Excellent Program  **
*****************************************/
```

This comment works. It contains lots of asterisks, but they're all still stuck between `/*` and `*/`, making it a viable comment.

I have used this before in my programs:

```
/*
 * This is a long-winded introduction to an
 * obscure program written by someone at a
 * university who's really big on himself and
 * thinks no mere mortal can learn C -- and who
 * has written three "C" books to prove it.
 */
```

The idea in this example is to create a "wall of asterisks" between the /* and */, making the comment stick out on the page.

Another example I often use is this:

```
/********************************************/
```

That line of asterisks doesn't say anything, yet it helps to break up different sections in a program. For example, I may put a line of asterisks between different functions so that I can easily find them.

The bottom line: No matter what you put between them, a comment must start with /* and end with */.

C++ comments

Because today's C compilers also create C++ code, you can take advantage of the comment style used by C++ in your plain old C programs. I mention it simply because the C++ comment style can be useful, and it's permitted if you want to borrow it.

In C++, comments can start with a double slash, //. That indicates that the rest of the text on the line is a comment. The end of the line marks the end of the comment:

```
//This is another style of comment,
//one used in C++
```

This commenting style has the advantage that you don't have to both begin and end a comment, making it ideal for placing comments at the end of a C language statement, as shown in this example:

```
    printf("Enter an adjective:");              // prompt
    scanf("%s",&adjective);                     // input
```

These modifications to the MADLIB1.C program still keep the comments intact. This method is preferred because it's quick; however, /* and */ have the advantage of being able to rope in a larger portion of text without typing // all over the place.

Using Comments to Disable

Comments are ignored by the compiler. No matter what lies between the /* and the */, it's skipped over. Even vital, lifesaving information, mass sums of cash, or the key to eternal youth — all these are ignored if they're nestled in a C language comment.

Modify the MADLIB1.C source code, changing the last part of the program to read:

```
/* Display the output */

/*
    printf("\n\nDon't touch that %s %s!\n",adjective,food);
    printf("I just %s the %s!\n",chore,furniture);
*/
```

To make the modification, follow these cinchy steps:

1. Insert a line with /* on it before the first printf() function in this example.
2. Insert a line with */ on it after the second printf() function.

With the last two printf() statements disabled, save the file to disk and recompile it. It runs as before, but the resulting "mad lib" isn't displayed. The reason is that the final two printf() functions are "commented out."

- You can use comments to disable certain parts of your program. If something isn't working correctly, for example, you can "comment it out." You may also want to include a note to yourself, explaining why that section is commented out.
- Sometimes you may notice that something which should be working isn't working. The reason is that you may have *accidentally* commented it out. Always check your /* and */ comment bookends to make sure that they match up the way you want them to.
- By using an editor with color-coded text, you can easily spot missing */ characters to end a comment. If you notice that a greater chunk of your source code is colored as a comment, a misplaced */ is probably to blame.

The Perils of "Nested" Comments

The most major of the faux pas you can commit with comments is to "nest" them, or to include one set of comments inside another. To wit, I present the following C program fragment:

```
if(all_else_fails)
    {
        display_error(erno);          /* erno is already set */
        walk_away();
    }
else
    get_mad();
```

Don't worry about understanding this example; it all comes clear to you later in this book. However, notice that the `display_error` function has a comment after it: `erno is already set`. But suppose that, in your advanced understanding of C that is yet to come, you want to change the gist of this part of the program so that only the `get_mad()` function is executed. You comment out everything except that line to get it to work:

```
/*
if(all_else_fails)
    {
    display_error(erno);      /* erno is already set */
    walk_away();
    }
else
*/
    get_mad();
```

Here, the C compiler sees only the `get_mad` function, right?

Wrong! The comment begins on the first line with the `/*`. But it ends on the line with the `display_error()` function. Because that line ends with `*/` — the comment bookend — that's the end of the "comment." The C compiler then starts again with the `walk_away` function and generates a parse error on the rogue curly brace floating in space. The second comment bookend (just above the `get_mad()` function) also produces an error. Two errors! How heinous.

This example shows a *nested comment,* or a comment within a comment. It just doesn't work. Figure 5-1 illustrates how the C compiler interprets the nested comment.

To avoid the nested-comment trap, you have to be careful when you're disabling portions of your C program. The solution in this case is to uncomment the `erno is already set` comment. Or, you can comment out each line individually, in which case that line would look like this:

```
/*  display_error(erno);    /* erno is already set */
```

This method works because the comment still ends with */. The extra /* inside the comment is safely ignored.

- Yeah, nested comments are nasty, but nothing you need to worry about at this point in the game.
- Note that the C++ style of comments, //, doesn't have a nesting problem.

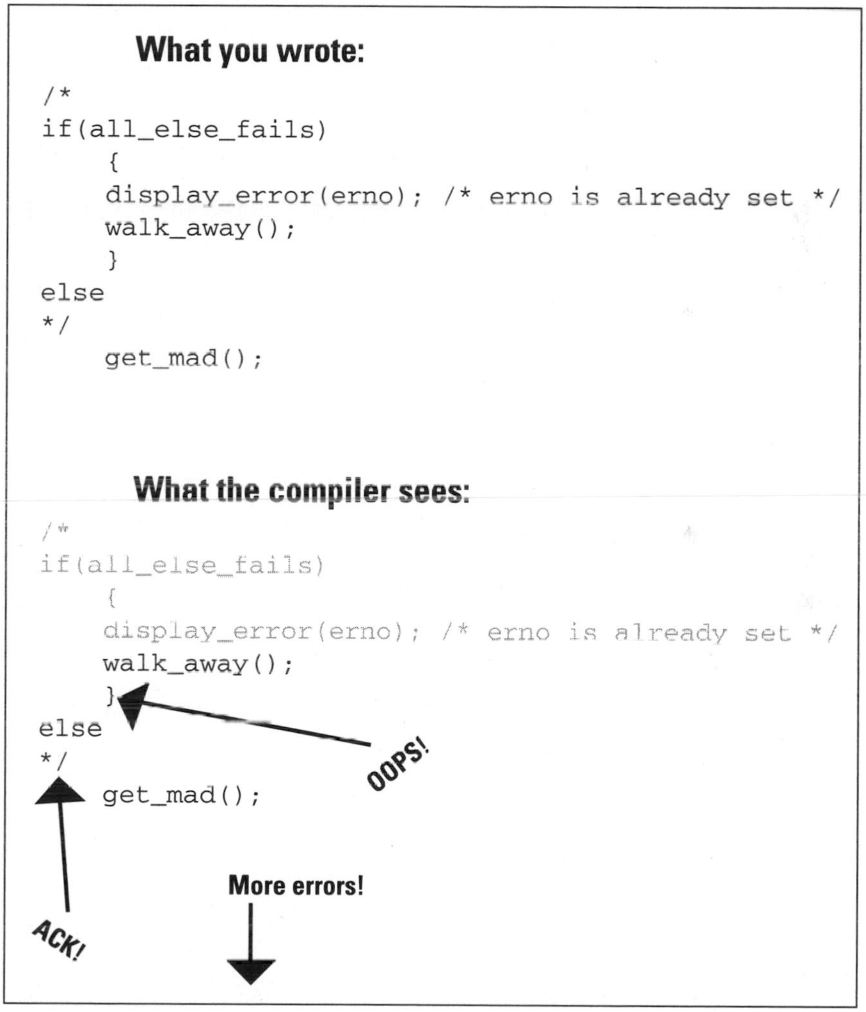
What you wrote:
/*
if(all_else_fails)
{
display_error(erno); /* erno is already set */
walk_away();
}
else
*/
get_mad();
What the compiler sees:
/*
if(all_else_fails)
{
display_error(erno); /* erno is already set */
walk_away();
}
else
*/
get_mad();
OOPS!
ACK!
More errors!

Figure 5-1: The perils of a nested comment.

Chapter 6

C More I/O with gets() and puts()

In This Chapter

- Reading strings of text with gets()
- Avoiding some gets() problems
- Using puts() to display text
- Displaying variables with puts()
- Knowing whether to use puts() or printf()

The printf() and scanf() functions aren't the only way you can display information or read text from the keyboard — that old I/O. No, the C language is full of I/O tricks, and when you find out how limited and lame printf() and scanf() are, you will probably create your own functions that read the keyboard and display information just the way you like. Until then, you're stuck with what C offers.

This chapter introduces the simple gets() and puts() functions. gets() reads a string of text from the keyboard, and puts() displays a string of text on the screen.

The More I Want, the More I gets()

Compared to scanf(), the gets() function is nice and simple. Both do the same thing: They read characters from the keyboard and save them in a variable. gets() reads in only text, however. scanf() can read in numeric values and strings and in a number of combinations. That makes it valuable, but for reading in text, clunky.

Like scanf() reading in text, gets() requires a char variable to store what's entered. It reads everything typed at the keyboard until the Enter key is pressed. Here's the format:

```
gets(var);
```

gets(), like all functions, is followed by a set of parentheses. Because gets() is a complete statement, it always ends in a semicolon. Inside the parentheses is *var,* the name of the string variable text in which it is stored.

Another completely rude program example

The following is the INSULT1.C program. This program is almost identical to the WHORU.C program, introduced in Chapter 4, except that gets() is used rather than scanf().

```
#include <stdio.h>

int main()
{
    char jerk[20];

    printf("Name some jerk you know:");
    gets(jerk);
    printf("Yeah, I think %s is a jerk, too.\n",jerk);
    return(0);
}
```

Enter this source code into your editor. Save the file to disk and name it INSULT1.C.

Compile the program. Reedit the text if you find any errors. Remember your semicolons and watch how the double quotes are used in the printf() functions.

Run the resulting program. The output looks something like this:

```
Name some jerk you know:Bill
Yeah, I think Bill is a jerk, too.
```

- gets() reads a variable just like scanf() does. Yet no matter what reads it, the printf() statement can display it.
- gets(var) is the same as scanf("%s",var).
- If you get a warning error when compiling, see the next section.

- You can pronounce `gets()` as "get-string" in your head. "Get a string of text from the keyboard." However, it probably stands for "Get stdin," which means "Get from standard input." "Get string" works for me, though.

And now, the bad news about gets()

The latest news from the C language grapevine is *not* to use the `gets()` function, at least not in any serious, secure programs you plan on writing. That's because `gets()` is not considered a safe, secure function to use.

The reason for this warning — which may even appear when you compile a program using `gets()` — is that you can type more characters at the keyboard than were designed to fit inside the `char` variable associated with `gets()`. This flaw, known as a *keyboard overflow,* is used by many of the bad guys out there to write worms and viruses and otherwise exploit well-meaning programs.

For the duration of this book, don't worry about using `gets()`. It's okay here as a quick way to get input while finding out how to use C. But for "real" programs that you write, I recommend concocting your own keyboard-reading functions.

The Virtues of puts()

In a way, the `puts()` function is a simplified version of the `printf()` function. `puts()` displays a string of text, but without all `printf()`'s formatting magic. `puts()` is just a boneheaded "Yup, I display this on the screen" command. Here's the format:

```
puts(text);
```

`puts()` is followed by a left paren, and then comes the *text* you want to display. That can either be a string variable name or a string of text in double quotes. That's followed by a right paren. The `puts()` function is a complete C language statement, so it always ends with a semicolon.

The `puts()` function's output always ends with a newline character, `\n`. It's like `puts()` "presses Enter" after displaying the text. You cannot avoid this side effect, though sometimes it does come in handy.

Another silly command-prompt program

To see how `puts()` works, create the following program, STOP.C. Yeah, this program is really silly, but you're just starting out, so bear with me:

```
#include <stdio.h>

int main()
{
    puts("Unable to stop: Bad mood error.");
    return(0);
}
```

Save this source code to disk as STOP.C. Compile it, link it, run it.

This program produces the following output when you type **stop** or **./stop** at the command prompt:

```
Unable to stop: Bad mood error.
```

Ha, ha.

- `puts()` is not pronounced "putz."
- Like `printf()`, `puts()` slaps a string of text up on the screen. The text is hugged by double quotes and is nestled between two parentheses.
- Like `printf()`, `puts()` understands escape sequences. For example, you can use `\"` if you want to display a string with a double quote in it.
- You don't have to put a `\n` at the end of a `puts()` text string. `puts()` always displays the newline character at the end of its output.
- If you want `puts()` not to display the newline character, you must use `printf()` instead.

`puts()` *and* `gets()` *in action*

The following program is a subtle modification to INSULT1.C. This time, the first `printf()` is replaced with a `puts()` statement:

```
#include <stdio.h>

int main()
{
    char jerk[20];
```

```
    puts("Name some jerk you know:");
    gets(jerk);
    printf("Yeah, I think %s is a jerk, too.",jerk);
    return(0);
}
```

Load the source code for INSULT1.C into your editor. Change Line 7 so that it reads as just shown; the `printf` is changed to `puts`.

Use your editor's Save As command to give this modified source code a new name on disk: INSULT2.C. Save. Compile. Run.

```
Name some jerk you know:
Rebecca
Yeah, I think Rebecca is a jerk, too.
```

Note that the first string displayed (by `puts()`) has that newline appear afterward. That's why input takes place on the next line. But considering how many command-line or text-based programs do that, it's really no big deal. Otherwise, the program runs the same as INSULT1. But you're not done yet; continue reading with the next section.

More insults

The following source code is another modification to the INSULT series of programs. This time, you replace the final `printf()` with a `puts()` statement. Here's how it looks:

```
#include <stdio.h>

int main()
{
    char jerk[20];

    puts("Name some jerk you know:");
    gets(jerk);
    puts("Yeah, I think %s is a jerk, too.",jerk);
    return(0);
}
```

Load the source code for INSULT2.C into your editor. Make the changes just noted, basically replacing the `printf` in Line 9 with puts. Otherwise, the rest of the code is the same.

Save the new source code to disk as INSULT3.C. Compile and run.

Whoops! Error! Error!

```
Insult3.c:9: too many arguments to function 'puts'
```

The compiler is smart enough to notice that more than one item appears to be specified for the puts() function; it sees a string, and then a variable is specified. According to what the compiler knows, you need only one or the other, not both. Oops.

- puts() is just not a simpler printf().
- If you got the program to run — and some compilers may — the output looks like this:

  ```
  Name some jerk you know:
  Bruce
  Yeah, I think that %s is a jerk, too.
  ```

  Ack! Who is this %s person who is such a jerk? Who knows! Remember that puts() isn't printf(), and it does not process variables the same way. To puts(), the %s in a string is just %s — characters — nothing special.

puts() *can print variables*

puts() can display a string variable, but only on a line by itself. Why a line by itself? Because no matter what, puts() always tacks on that pesky newline character. You cannot blend a variable into another string of text by using the puts() function.

Consider the following source code, the last in the INSULT line of programs:

```
#include <stdio.h>

int main()
{
    char jerk[20];

    puts("Name some jerk you know:");
    gets(jerk);
    puts("Yeah, I think");
    puts(jerk);
    puts("is a jerk, too.");
    return(0);
}
```

Feel free to make the preceding modifications to your INSULT3.C program in your editor. Save the changes to disk as INSULT4.C. Compile. Run.

```
Name some jerk you know:
David
Yeah, I think
David
is a jerk, too.
```

The output looks funky, like one of those "you may be the first person on your block" sweepstakes junk mailers. But the program works the way it was intended.

- TIP: Rather than replace `printf()` with `puts()`, you have to rethink your program's strategy. For one, `puts()` automatically sticks a newline on the end of a string it displays. No more strings ending in `\n`! Second, `puts()` can display only one string variable at a time, all by itself, on its own line. And, last, the next bit of code shows the program the way it should be written by using only `puts()` and `gets()`.
- REMEMBER: You must first "declare" a string variable in your program by using the `char` keyword. Then you must stick something in the variable, which you can do by using the `scanf()` or `gets` function. Only then does displaying the variable's contents by using `puts()` make any sense.
- WARNING! Do not use `puts()` with a nonstring variable. The output is weird. (See Chapter 8 for the lowdown on variables.)

When to use puts()
When to use printf()

- Use `puts()` to display a single line of text — nothing fancy.
- Use `puts()` to display the contents of a string variable on a line by itself.
- Use `printf()` to display the contents of a variable nestled in the middle of another string.
- Use `printf()` to display the contents of more than one variable at a time.
- Use `printf()` when you don't want the newline (Enter) character to be displayed after every line, such as when you're prompting for input.
- Use `printf()` when fancy formatted output is required.

Part II
Run and Scream from Variables and Math

The 5th Wave   By Rich Tennant

©RICHTENNANT
Oh come on-
how fatal
can it be?
FATAL
ERROR

In this part . . .

Programming a computer involves more than just splattering text on a screen. In fact, when you ask most folks, they assume that programming is some branch of mathematics or engineering. After all, computers have their roots in the calculators and adding machines of years gone by. And, early computers were heavily involved with math, from computing missile trajectories to landing men on the moon.

I have to admit: Programming a computer does involve math. That's the subject of the next several chapters, along with an official introduction to the concept of a variable (also a math thing). Before you go running and screaming from the room, however, consider that it's the computer that does the math. Unlike those sweaty days in the back of eighth-grade math class, with beady-eyed Mr. Perdomo glowering at you like a fat hawk eyeing a mouse, you merely have to jot down the problem. The computer solves it for you.

Relax! Sit back and enjoy reading about how you can slavishly make the computer do your math puzzles. And, if it gets the answer wrong, feel free to berate it until the computer feels like it's only about yay high.

Chapter 7

A + B = C

In This Chapter

- Changing a variable's value
- Introducing the `int`
- Converting text with the `atoi()` function
- Using +, -, *, and /
- Struggling with basic math

It's time to confirm your worst fears. Yes, computers have something to do with math. But it's more of a passing fancy than the infatuation you're now dreading. Unless you're some hard-core type of engineer (the engi*nerd*), mathematics plays only a casual role in your programs. You add, subtract, divide, multiply, and maybe do a few other things. Nothing gets beyond the skills of anyone who can handle a calculator. It's really fourth-grade stuff, but because we work with variables— which is more like eighth-grade algebra stuff — this material may require a little squeezing of the brain juices. In this chapter, I try to make it as enjoyable as possible for you.

The Ever-Changing Variable

A variable is a storage place. The C compiler creates the storage place and sets aside room for you to store strings of text or values — depending on the type of storage place you create. You do this by using a smattering of C language keywords that you soon become intimate with.

What's in the storage place? Could be anything. That's why it's called a variable. Its contents may depend on what's typed at the keyboard, the result of some mathematical operation, a campaign promise, or a psychic prediction. The contents can change too — just like the psychic prediction or campaign promise.

It's by juggling these variables that work gets done in most programs. When you play PacMan, for example, his position on the screen is kept in a variable because, after all, he moves (his position changes). The number of points PacMan racks up are stored in a variable. And, when you win the game, you enter your name, and that too is stored in a variable. The value of these items — PacMan's location, your points, your name — are changing or can change, which is why they're stored in variables.

- *Variables* are information-storage places in a program. They can contain numbers, strings of text, and other items too complex to get into right now.
- The contents of a variable? It depends. Variables are defined as being able to store strings of text or numbers. Their contents depend on what happens when the program runs, what the user types, or the computer's mood, for example. Variables can change.
- Where are variables stored? In your computer's memory. This information isn't important right now; the computer makes room for them as long as you follow proper variable-creating procedures in your C programs.

Strings change

The following program is brought to you by the keyword `char` and by the `printf()` and `gets()` functions. In this program, a string variable, `kitty`, is created, and it's used twice as the user decides what to name her cat. The changing contents of `kitty` show you the gist of what a variable is:

```
#include <stdio.h>

int main()
{
      char kitty[20];

      printf("What would you like to name your cat?");
      gets(kitty);
      printf("%s is a nice name. What else do you have in
            mind?",kitty);
      gets(kitty);
      printf("%s is nice, too.\n",kitty);
      return(0);
}
```

Enter the source code for KITTY.C into your text editor. Save the file to disk as KITTY.C.

Compile KITTY.C. If you get any errors, reedit your source code. Check for missing semicolons, misplaced commas, and so on. Then recompile.

Running the program is covered in the next section.

- The `char` keyword is used to create the variable and set aside storage for it.
- Only by assigning text to the variable can its contents be read.
- It's the `gets()` function that reads text from the keyboard and sticks it into the string variable.

Running the KITTY

After compiling the source code for KITTY.C in the preceding section, run the final program. The output looks something like this:

```
What would you like to name your cat?Rufus
Rufus is a nice name. What else do you have in mind?Fuzzball
Fuzzball is nice, too.
```

The `kitty` variable is assigned one value by using the first `gets()` function. Then, it's assigned a new value by the second `gets()` function. Though the same variable is used, its value changes. That is the idea behind variables.

- A single variable can be used many times in a program. It can be used over and over with the same value, or used over and over to store different values.
- It's the contents of the string variable that are displayed — not the variable name. In the KITTY.C program, the variable is named `kitty`. That's for your reference as a programmer. What's stored in the variable is what's important.

Welcome to the Cold World of Numeric Variables

Just as strings of text are stored in string variables, numbers are stored in numeric variables. This allows you to work with values in your program and to do the ever-dreaded math.

To create a numeric variable and set aside storage space for a number, a special C language keyword is used. Unlike `char`, which creates all types of strings, different keywords are used to create variables for storing different types of numbers. It all depends on how big or how weird the number is.

Hello, integer

To keep things sane for now, I show you only one of the numeric variable types. It's the simplest form of a number, the *integer.* Just say "IN-tuh-jur." Integer.

Here's how the typical C compiler defines an integer type of number:

- An integer is a whole number — no fractions, decimal parts, or funny stuff.
- An integer can have a value that ranges from 0 to 32,767.
- Negative numbers, from –32,768 up to 0 are also allowed.

Any other values — larger or smaller, fractions, or values with a decimal point, such as 1.5 — are *not* integers. (The C language can deal with such numbers, but I don't introduce those types of variables now.)

To use an integer variable in a program, you have to set aside space for it. You do this with the `int` keyword at the beginning of the program. Here's the format:

```
int var;
```

The keyword `int` is followed by a space (or a press of the Tab key) and then the name of the variable, *var.* It's a complete statement in the C language, and it ends with a semicolon.

- Some compilers may define the range for an `int` to be much larger than –32,768 through 32,767. To be certain, check with your compiler's documentation or help system.
- On older, 16-bit computers, an integer ranges in value from –32,768 through 32,767.
- On most modern computers, integer values range from –2,147,483,647 through 2,147,483,647.
- More information about naming a variable — and other C language trivia about variables — is offered in Chapter 8. For now, forgive me for the unofficial introduction.

- Yes! You're very observant. This type of `int` is the same one used to declare the `main()` function in every program you have written in this book — if you have been reading the chapters in order. Without getting too far ahead, you should now recognize that `main()` is known as an "integer function." It also ties into the `0` value in the `return` statement, but I tell you more about that in a few chapters.
- Computer geeks worldwide want you to know that an integer ranges from –32,768 up to 0 and then up to 32,767 only on personal computers. If, perchance, you ever program on a large, antique computer — doomed to ever-dwindling possibilities of employment, like those losers who program them — you may discover that the range for integers on those computers is somewhat different. Yeah, this information is completely optional; no need cluttering your head with it. But they would whine if I didn't put it in here.

Using an integer variable in the Methuselah program

If you need only small, whole-number values in a C program, you should use integer variables. As an example, the following program uses the variable `age` to keep track of someone's age. Other examples of using integer variables are to store the number of times something happens (as long as it doesn't happen more than 32,000-odd times), planets in the solar system (still 9), corrupt congressmen (always less than 524), and number of people who have seen Lenin in person (getting smaller every day). Think "whole numbers, not big."

The following program displays the age of the Biblical patriarch Methuselah, an ancestor of Noah, who supposedly lived to be 969 years old — well beyond geezerhood. The program is METHUS1.C, from Methus, which was his nickname:

```
#include <stdio.h>

int main()
{
      int age;

      age=969;
      printf("Methuselah was %d years old.\n",age);
      return(0);
}
```

Enter the text from METHUS1.C into your editor. Save the file to disk as METHUS1.C.

Compile the program. If you get any errors, reedit the source code and make sure that everything matches the preceding listing. Recompile.

Run the program and you see the following:

```
Methuselah was 969 years old.
```

The variable `age` was assigned the value 969. Then, the `printf()` statement was used, along with the `%d` placeholder, to display that value in a string.

- The fifth line creates the `age` variable, used to store an integer value.
- The seventh line assigns the value 969 to the `age` variable by using the equal sign (=). The variable `age` comes first, and then the equal sign, and then the value (969) to be placed in the `age` variable.
- In the eighth line, the `printf` function is used to display the value of the `age` variable. In `printf()`'s formatting string, the `%d` conversion character is used as a placeholder for an integer value. `%d` works for integers, just as `%s` is a placeholder for a string.

Assigning values to numeric variables

One thing worth noting in the METHUS1 program is that numeric variables are assigned values by using the equal sign (=). The variable goes on the left, and then the equal sign, and then the "thing" that produces the value on the right. That's the way it is, was, and shall be in the C language:

```
var=value;
```

var is the name of the numeric variable. `value` is the value assigned to that variable. Read it as "The value of the variable *var* is equal to the value `value`." (I know, too many *values* in that sentence. So shoot me.)

What could `value` be? It can be a number, a mathematical equation, a C language function that generates a value, or another variable, in which case *var* has that variable's same value. Anything that pops out a value — an integer value, in this case — is acceptable.

In METHUS1.C, the value for the variable `age` is assigned directly:

```
age=969;
```

Lo, the value 969 is safely stuffed into the `age` variable.

- The equal sign is used to assign a non-string value to a variable. The variable goes on the left side of the equal sign and gets its value from whatever's on the right side.
- String variables cannot be defined in this way, by using an equal sign. You cannot say

  ```
  kitty="Koshka";
  ```

  It just doesn't work! Strings can be read into variables from the keyboard by using the `scanf()`, `gets()`, or other C language keyboard-reading functions. String variables can also be preset, but you cannot use an equal sign with them, like you can with numeric variables!

Entering numeric values from the keyboard

Keep the METHUS1.C program warm in your editor's oven for a few seconds. What does it really do? Nothing. Because the value 969 is already in the program, there's no surprise. The real fun with numbers comes when they're entered from the keyboard. Who knows what wacky value the user may enter? (That's another reason for a variable.)

A small problem arises in reading a value from the keyboard: Only strings are read from the keyboard; the `scanf()` and `gets()` functions you're familiar with have been used to read string variables. And, there's most definitely a difference between the characters "969" and the number 969. One is a value, and the other is a string. (I leave it up to you to figure out which is which.) The object is to covertly transform the string "969" into a value — nay, an *integer* value — of 969. The secret command to do it is `atoi`, the A-to-I function.

The `atoi()` function

The `atoi()` (pronounced "A-to-I") function converts numbers at the beginning of a string into an integer value. The *A* comes from the acronym *ASCII,* which is a coding scheme that assigns secret code numbers to characters. So `atoi` means "convert an ASCII (text) string into an integer value." That's how you can read integers from the keyboard. Here's the format:

```
var=atoi(string);
```

var is the name of a numeric variable, an integer variable created by the `int` keyword. That's followed by an equal sign, which is how you assign a value to a variable.

On the difference between numbers and strings, if you dare to care

You have to know when a number in C is a value and when it's a string. A numeric value is what you find lurking in a numeric variable. This book calls those things *values,* and not *numbers.* A value is 5 apples, 3.141 (for example), the national debt, and the number of pounds you can lose on celebrity diets featured in this week's *Star.* Those are values.

Numbers are what appear in strings of text. When you type 255, for example, you're entering a string. Those are the characters 2, 5, and 5, as found on your keyboard. The string "255" is not a value. I call it a number. By using the `atoi()` function in the C language, you can translate it into a value, suitable for storage in a numeric variable.

There are numbers and there are values. Which is which? It depends on how you're going to use it. Obviously, if someone is entering a phone number, house number, or zip code, it's probably a string. (My zip code is 94402, but that doesn't mean that it's the 94-thousandth-something post office in the United States.) If someone enters a dollar amount, percentage, size, or measurement — anything you work with mathematically — it's probably a value.

The `atoi()` function follows the equal sign. Then comes the *string* to convert, hugged by `atoi()`'s parentheses. The string can be a string variable or a string "constant" enclosed in double quotes. Most often, the *string* to convert is the name of a string variable, one created by the `char` keyword and read from the keyboard by using `gets()` or `scanf()` or some other keyboard-reading function.

The line ends in a semicolon because it's a complete C language statement.

The `atoi` function also requires a second number-sign thingy at the beginning of your source code:

```
#include <stdlib.h>
```

This line is usually placed below the traditional #include <stdio.h> thing — both of them look the same, in fact, but it's `stdlib.h` in the angle pinchers that's required here. The line does not end with a semicolon.

- `atoi` is not pronounced "a toy." It's "A-to-I," like what you see on the spine of Volume One of a 3-volume encyclopedia.
- Numbers are values; strings are composed of characters.
- If the *string* that `atoi()` converts does not begin with a number, or if the number is too large or too weird to be an integer, `atoi` spits back the value 0 (zero).

- The purpose of `#include <stdlib.h>` is to tell the compiler about the `atoi()` function. Without that line, you may see some warning or "no prototype" errors, which typically ruin your programming day.
- STDLIB.H is the standard library header file, don't you know.
- Other C language functions are available for converting strings into non-integer numbers. That's how you translate input from the keyboard into a numeric value: You must squeeze a string by using a special function (`atoi`) and extract a number.

So how old is this Methuselah guy, anyway?

The following program is METHUS2.C, a gradual, creeping improvement over METHUS1.C. In this version of the program, you read a string that the user types at the keyboard. That string — and it is a string, by the way — is then magically converted into a numeric value by the `atoi()` function. Then, that value is displayed by using the `printf()` function. A miracle is happening here, something that the ancients would be truly dazzled by, probably to the point of offering you food and tossing fragrant posies your way.

```
#include <stdio.h>
#include <stdlib.h>

int main()
{
    int age;
    char years[13];

    printf("How old was Methuselah?");
    gets(years);
    age=atoi(years);
    printf("Methuselah was %d years old.\n",age);
    return(0);
}
```

Hunt and peck the METHUS2.C source code into your editor. You can edit the original METHUS1.C source code, but be careful to save it to disk under the new name, METHUS2.C.

Compile the program. Repair any errors you may have encountered.

Run the program. The output you see may look something like this:

```
How old was Methuselah?26
Methuselah was 26 years old.
```

No, you don't have to experiment with METHUS2.C, but I encourage you to try this

Thank goodness this book isn't *Surgery For Dummies.* Unlike that sober tome, this book allows you to freely fiddle, poke, pull, experiment, and have fun. Trying that with a cadaver is okay, but in Chapter 14 of *Surgery For Dummies,* "Finding That Pesky Appendix on Your Nephew," it's frowned on.

Run the METHUS2.C program again, and when the program asks you for Methuselah's age, type the following value:

```
10000000000
```

That's ten billion — a one with 10 zeroes and no commas. Press Enter and the output tells you that the old guy was 1,410,065,408 years old — or some other value, not what you typed. The reason is that you entered a value greater than an integer can hold. The value returned is the remainder of what you entered divided by the maximum size of an integer in your compiler.

How about typing the following value:

```
-64
```

Yes, Mr. M. could never be negative 64 years old, but the program accepts it. The reason is that integer values include negative numbers.

Here's one you need to try:

```
4.5
```

Is the oldest human really four-and-a-half? Probably at one time. Still, the program insists that he was only four. That's because the point-5 part is a fraction. Integers don't include fractions, so all the `atoi()` function reads is the `4`.

Finally, the big experiment. Type the following as Methus's age:

```
old
```

Yes, he was old. But when you enter **old** into the program, it claims that he was only zero. The reason is that the `atoi()` function didn't see a number in your response. Therefore, it generates a value of zero.

In this example, the user typed **26** for the age. That was entered as a string, transformed by `atoi()` into an integer value and, finally, displayed by `printf()`. That's how you can read in numbers from the keyboard and then fling them about in your program as numeric values. Other sections in this chapter, as well as in the rest of this book, continue to drive home this message.

- Okay, legend has it that the old man was 969 when he finally (and probably happily) entered into the hereafter. But by using this program, you can really twist history (though Methuselah probably had lots of contemporaries who lived as long as you and I do).
- If you forget the `#include <stdlib.h>` thing or you misspell it, a few errors may spew forth from your compiler. Normally, these errors are tame "warnings," and the program works just the same. Regardless, get

in the habit of including the `stdlib` thing when you use the `atoi()` function.

- The `age=atoi(years)` function is how the string `years` is translated into a numeric value. The `atoi()` function examines the string and spits up a number. That number is then placed in the `age` variable as a numeric value.

- Why not just print the string `years`? Well, you can. By replacing `age` with `years` and `%d` with `%s` in the final `printf()` function, the program displays the same message. To wit:

```
printf("Methuselah was %s years old.\n",years);
```

  The output is the same. However, only with a numeric variable can you perform mathematical operations. Strings and math? Give up now and keep your sanity!

You and Mr. Wrinkles

Time to modify the old Methuselah program again. This time, you create the METHUS3.C source code, as shown next. As with METHUS2.C, only subtle modifications are made to the original program. Nothing new, though you're building up to something later in this chapter.

```
#include <stdio.h>
#include <stdlib.h>

int main()
{
    int methus;
    int you;
    char years[8];

    printf("How old are you?");
    gets(years);
    you=atoi(years);

    printf("How old was Methuselah?");
    gets(years);
    methus=atoi(years);

    printf("You are %d years old.\n",you);
    printf("Methuselah was %d years old.\n",methus);
    return(0);
}
```

Double-check your source code carefully and save the file to disk as METHUS3.C.

Compile METHUS3.C. Fix any errors that sneak into the picture.

Run the program. You're asked two questions, and then two strings of text are displayed — something like the following:

```
How old are you?29
How old was Methuselah?969
You are 29 years old.
Methuselah was 969 years old.
```

Of course, this data is merely regurgitated. The true power of the computer is that math can be done on the values — and it's the computer that does the math, not you. Don't sweat it!

TIP

- You're not really 29.
- Yes, the `years` string variable is used twice. First, it reads in your age, and then the `atoi()` function converts it and saves the value in the `you` variable. Then, `years` is used again for input. This strategy works because the original value was saved in another variable — a cool trick.
- The METHUS3.C program has been divided into four sections. This is more of a visual organization than anything particular to the C programming language. The idea is to write the program in paragraphs — or thoughts — similar to the way most people try to write English.

A Wee Bit o' Math

Now is the time for all good programmers to do some math. No, wait! Please don't leave. It's cinchy stuff. The first *real* math explanation is several pages away.

When you do math in the C programming language, it helps to know two things: First, know which symbols — or, to be technical, *unique doodads* — are used to add, subtract, multiply, and divide numbers. Second, you have to know what to do with the results. Of course, you never have to do the math. That's what the computer is for.

Basic mathematical symbols

The basic mathematical symbols are probably familiar to you already if you have been around computers a while. Here they are:

- Addition symbol: +
- Subtraction symbol: –
- Multiplication symbol: *
- Division symbol: /

Incidentally, the official C language term for these dingbats is *operators.* These are mathematical (or arithmetic — I never know which to use) operators.

+ **Addition:** The addition operator is the plus sign, +. This sign is so basic that I can't really think of anything else you would use to add two numbers:

```
var=value1+value2;
```

Here, the result of adding `value1` to `value2` is calculated by the computer and stored in the numeric variable *var.*

– **Subtraction:** The subtraction operator is the minus sign, –:

```
var=value1-value2;
```

Here, the result of subtracting *value2* from *value1* is calculated and gently stuffed into the numeric variable *var.*

* **Multiplication:** Here's where we get weird. The multiplication operator is the asterisk — not the × character:

```
var=value1*value2;
```

In this line, the result of multiplying `value1` by `value2` is figured out by the computer, and the result is stored in the variable *var.*

/ **Division:** For division, the slash, /, is used; the primary reason is that the ÷ symbol is not on your keyboard:

```
var=value1/value2;
```

Here, the result of dividing `value1` by `value2` is calculated by the computer and stored in the variable `var`.

Note that in all cases, the mathematical operation is on the *right* side of the equal sign — something like this:

```
value1+value2=var;
```

TECHNICAL STUFF

Why the multiplication symbol is an asterisk (if you care to know)

In school, you probably learned that the X symbol means *multiply*. More properly, it's the × symbol, not the character X (or even little x). It's pronounced "times," as in "four times nine" for 4×9. In higher math, where it was harder for you to get an "easy A," the dot was also used for multiplication: 4•9 for "four times nine." I have even seen that expressed as 4(9) or (4)(9), though I fell right back asleep.

Why can't computers use the X? Primarily because they're stupid. The computer doesn't know when you mean X as in "ecks" and × as in "times." So, the asterisk (*) was accepted as a substitute. (The keyboard has no dot • character either.)

Using the * for multiplication takes some getting used to. The slash is kind of common — 3/$1 for "three for a dollar" or 33 cents each — so that's not a problem. But the * takes some chanting and bead counting.

It just doesn't work in the C language. The preceding line tells the C compiler to take the value of the `var` variable and put it into some numbers. Huh? And that's the kind of error you see when you try it: Huh? (It's called an `Lvalue` error, and it's shamefully popular.)

TIP

REMEMBER

- More mathematical symbols, or operators, are used in C programming. This chapter introduces only the four most common symbols.
- Having trouble remembering the math operators? Look at your keyboard's numeric keypad! The slash, asterisk, minus, and plus symbols are right there, cornering the number keys.
- Unlike in the real world, you have to keep in mind that the calculation is always done on the *right,* with the answer squirted out the equal sign to the left.
- You don't always have to work with two values in your mathematical functions. You can work with a variable and a value, two variables, functions — lots of things. C is flexible, but at this stage it's just important to remember that * means "multiply."

How much longer do you have to live to break the Methuselah record?

The following METHUS4.C source code uses a bit of math to figure out how many more years you have to live before you can hold the unofficial title of the oldest human ever to live (or at least tie with him).

Before you do this, I want you to think about it. What are the advantages of being the oldest person ever to live? What else do we know about Methuselah? He died before the flood. He was a good man, well received by The Man Upstairs. But, what else? I mean, like, did he eat weird or some thing? Did he avoid the grape? The Bible offers no hints.

```
#include <stdio.h>
#include <stdlib.h>

int main()
{
    int diff;
    int methus;
    int you;
    char years[8];

    printf("How old are you?");
    gets(years);
    you=atoi(years);

    methus=969;      /* Methuselah was 969 years old */

    diff=methus-you;

    printf("You are %d years younger than
           Methuselah.\n",diff);
    return(0);
}
```

The METHUS4.C program is eerily similar to METHUS3.C. It has only a few deviations, so you can edit the METHUS3.C source code and then save it to disk as METHUS4.C. Cross-check your work with the preceding source code listing, just to be sure.

Compile the program. Fix any errors that may crop up. Then run the final product. Your output may look something like the following:

```
How old are you?29
You are 940 years younger than Methuselah.
```

Try entering a different age to see how it compares with Methuselah's.

- It does math! It does math!
- This program uses four — four! — variables: `diff`, `methus`, and `you` are all integer variables. `years` is a string variable.
- What happens if you enter a negative age — or an age greater than 969?

- To figure out how much longer you have to live to match Methuselah's record, you subtract your age from his. Pay special attention to the order of events in the following statement:

  ```
  diff=methus-you;
  ```

  The math part always goes on the right side of the equal sign. Your age, stored in the `you` numeric variable, is subtracted from Methuselah's and stored in the `diff` numeric variable. The result then slides through the equal sign and into the `diff` numeric variable.

Bonus modification on the final Methuselah program!

Methuselah works hard until he's 65, and then he retires. Because he got his first job at 19, he has been contributing to Social Security. As soon as he hits 65, he starts drawing his money out. And out. And out. And out some more.

How about writing a program that can do what no bureaucrat in Washington can do: Figure out how much money Methuselah is drawing from the system? (We leave the "whether he earned it all" question up to future generations because, of course, if you ask Methuselah himself, he says that he did.)

```
#include <stdio.h>
#include <stdlib.h>

int main()
{
      int contributed;
      int received;

      contributed=65-19;
      received=969-65;

      printf("Methuselah contributed to Social Security for
           %d years.\n",contributed);
      printf("Methuselah collected from Social Security for
           %d years.\n",received);
      return(0);
}
```

Type into your editor the source code for METHUS5.C — which I promise is the last of the Methuselah suite of programs. Double-check your typing and all that stuff.

Your fine sense of logic wants you to type *i* before *e* in *received,* though the illogic of English dictates otherwise.

Save the file as METHUS5.C.

Compile it! Check for any errors or small pieces of meat the compiler may choke on. Dislodge them (reedit the source code) and compile again if you need to.

Run the program! Here's a sample of the output:

```
Methuselah contributed to Social Security for 46 years.
Methuselah collected from Social Security for 904 years.
```

- It seems fair to him.
- Line 10 calculates how long Methuselah has been receiving Social Security. If he died at 969 and began receiving checks at 65, the difference is the value you want. That's stored in the `received` variable.
- Notice how the smaller value is subtracted from the larger? C works from left to right with math: 65 minus 19; 969 minus 65. Still, the math part of the equation must be on the right. The variable that holds the result is on the left.
- When math is used in a program with numbers rather than variables, the numbers are called *constants*.
- You can find more information on the subject of constants in Chapter 8.

The direct result

Are variables necessary? Yes, when the value isn't known. In the last few Methuselah programs, the values were known, for the most part. Only when you enter your own age is there truly a need for a variable. Otherwise, *constant* values can be used.

For example, the following program is another version of METHUS5. You don't have to type this program, but look at the only two statements in the program. Gone are the variables and the statements that assigned them values, as well as the `#include <stdlib.h>` because `atoi()` isn't being used:

```
#include <stdio.h>

int main()
{
        printf("Methuselah contributed to Social Security for
             %d years.\n",65-19);
        printf("Methuselah collected from Social Security for
             %d years.\n",969-65);
        return(0);
}
```

The %d in the first printf() function looks for an integer value to "fill in the blank." The printf() function expects to find that value after the comma — and it does! The value is calculated by the C compiler as 65–19, which is 46. The printf() statement plugs the value 46 into the %d's placeholder. The same holds true for the second printf() function.

You can do the same thing without the math. You can figure out 65–19 and 969–65 in your head and then plug in the values directly:

```
printf("Methuselah contributed to Social Security for
     %d years.\n",46);
printf("Methuselah collected from Social Security for
     %d years.\n",904);
```

Again, the result is the same. The %d looks for an integer value, finds it, and plugs it in to the displayed string. It doesn't matter to printf() whether the value is a constant, a mathematical equation, or a variable. It must, however, be an integer value.

Chapter 8

Charting Unknown Cs with Variables

In This Chapter

- Declaring variables
- Naming variables
- Using `float` variables
- Declaring several variables at once
- Understanding constants
- Creating constants with `#define`
- Using the `const` keyword

Variables are what make your programs zoom. Programming just can't get done without them. You may have just dabbled with variables, but not been formally introduced. In this chapter, you're formally introduced!

Cussing, Discussing, and Declaring Variables

Along comes Valerie Variable. . . .

Valerie is a numeric variable. She loves to hold numbers — any number — it doesn't matter. Whenever she sees an equal sign, she takes to a value and holds it tight. But see another equal sign, and she takes on a new value. In that way, Valerie is a little flaky. You could say that Valerie's values vary, which is why she's a variable.

Victor is a string variable. He contains bits of text — everything from one character to several of them in a row. As long as it's a character, Victor doesn't mind. But which character? Victor doesn't care — because he's a variable, he can hold anything.

- Yes, I have a point here. C has two main types of variables: numeric variables, which hold only numbers or values, and string variables, which hold text, from one to several characters long.
- The C language has several different types of numeric variables, depending on the *size* and *precision* of the number. The details are in Chapter 9.
- Before you use a variable, it must be declared. This is — oh, just read the next section.

"Why must I declare a variable?"

You're required to announce your variables to the C compiler before you use them. You announce them by providing a list of variables near the top of the source code. That way, the compiler knows what the variables are called and what flavor of variables they are (what values they can contain). Officially, this process is known as *declaring* your variables.

For example:

```
int count;
char key;
char lastname[30];
```

Three variables are declared in this example: an integer variable, `count`; a character variable, `key`; and a character variable, `lastname`, which is a string that can be as many as 30 characters long.

Declaring variables at the beginning of the program tells the compiler several things. First, it says "These things are variables!" That way, when the compiler sees `lastname` in a program, it knows that it's a string variable.

Second, the declarations tell the compiler which type of variable is being used. The compiler knows that integer values fit into the `count` variable, for example.

Third, the compiler knows how much storage space to set aside for the variables. This can't be done "on the fly," as the program runs. The space must be set aside as the program is created by the compiler.

- Declare your variables near the beginning of your program, just after the line with the initial curly brace. Cluster them all up right there.
- Obviously, you don't know all the variables a program requires before you write it. (Though they teach otherwise at the universities, such mental overhead isn't required by you and me.) If you need a new variable, use your editor to declare it in the program. Rogue variables — those undeclared — generate syntax or linker errors (depending on how they're used).
- If you don't declare a variable, your program doesn't compile. A suitable complaint message is issued by the proper authorities.
- Most C programmers put a blank line between the variable declarations and the rest of the program.
- There's nothing wrong with commenting a variable to describe what it contains. For example:

```
int count; /* busy signals from tech support. */
```

- However, cleverly named variables can avoid this situation:

```
int busysignals;
```

  Or, even better:

```
int busy_signal_count;
```

Variable names verboten and not

What you can name your variables depends on your compiler. You have to follow a few rules, and you cannot use certain names for variables. When you break the rules, the compiler lets you know by flinging an error message your way. To avoid that, try to keep the following guidelines in the back of your head when you create new variables:

- The shortest variable name is a letter of the alphabet.
- Use variable names that mean something. Single-letter variables are just hunky-dory. But `index` is better than `i`, `count` is better than `c`, and `name` is better than `n`. Short, descriptive variable names are best.
- Variables are typically in lowercase. (All of C is lowercase, for the most part.) They can contain letters and numbers.
- Uppercase letters can be used in your variables, but most compilers tend to ignore the differences between upper- and lowercase letters. (You can tell the compiler to be case-sensitive by setting one of its options; refer to your compiler's online help system for the details.)

- You shouldn't begin a variable name with a number. It can contain numbers, but you begin it with a letter. Even if your compiler says that it's okay, other C compilers don't, so you should *not* begin a variable name with a number.
- C lords use the underline, or underscore, character in their variable names: `first_name` and `zip_code`, for example. This technique is fine, though it's not recommended to begin a variable name with an underline.

- Avoid naming your variables the same as C language keywords or functions. Don't name your integer variable `int`, for example, or your string variable `char`. This may not generate an error with your compiler, but it makes your source code confusing. (Refer to Table 3-1, in Chapter 3, for a list of the C language keywords.)
- Also avoid using the single letters *l* (lowercase *L*) and *o* (lowercase *O*) to name variables. Little *L* looks too much like a 1 (one), and *O* looks too much like a 0 (zero).
- Don't give similar names to your variables. For example, the compiler may assume that `forgiveme` and `forgivemenot` are the same variable. If so, an ugly situation can occur.
- Buried somewhere in the cryptic help files that came with your compiler are the official rules for naming variables. These rules are unique to each compiler, which is why I'm not mentioning them all here. After all, I'm not paid by the hour. And it's not part of my contract.

Presetting variable values

Suppose that this guy named Methuselah is 969 years old. I understand that this may be a new, bold concept to grasp, but work with me here.

If you were going to use Methuselah's age as a value in a program, you could create the variable `methus` and then shove the value `969` into it. That requires two steps. First comes the declaration:

```
int methus;
```

This line tells the compiler that `methus` is capable of holding an integer-size value in its mouth and all that. Then comes the assignment, when 969 is put into the variable `methus`:

```
methus=969;
```

In C, you can combine both steps into one. For example:

```
int methus=969;
```

This statement creates the integer variable `methus` and assigns it the value `969` — all at once. It's your first peek at C language shortcut. (C is full of shortcuts and alternatives — enough to make you kooky.)

You can do the same thing with string variables — but it's a little weird. Normally, string variables are created and given a size. For example:

```
char prompt[22];
```

Here, a character string variable, `prompt`, is created and given room for 22 characters. Then you use `gets()` or `scanf()` to stick text into that variable. (You don't use an equal sign!) When you create the variable and assign it a string, however, it's given this format:

```
char prompt[] = "So how fat are you, anyway?"
```

This command creates a string variable, `prompt`. That string variable already contains the text "So how fat are you, anyway?" Notice that you see no number in the brackets. The reason is that the compiler is smart enough to figure out how long the string is and use that value automatically. No guesswork — what joy!

- Numeric variables can be assigned a value when they're declared. Just follow the variable name with an equal sign and its value. Remember to end the line with a semicolon.
- You can even assign the variable a value concocted by using math. For example:

  ```
  int video=800*600;
  ```

  This statement creates the integer variable `video` and sets its value equal to 800 times 600, or 480,000. (Remember that * is used for multiplication in C.)
- Even though a variable may be assigned a value, that value can still change. If you create the integer variable `methus` and assign it the value `969`, there's nothing wrong with changing that value later in the program. After all, a variable is still a variable.

The old random-sampler variable program

To demonstrate how variables can be defined with specific values, the ICKYGU.C program was concocted. It works like those old Chinese all-you-can-eat places, where steaming trays of yummy glop lie waiting under grease-smeared panes of sneeze-protecting glass. Ah . . . reminds me of my college days and that bowel infection I had. Here's the source code:

```
#include <stdio.h>

int main()
{
        char menuitem[] = "Slimy Orange Stuff \"Icky Woka
             Gu\"";
        int pints=1;
        float price = 1.45;

        printf("Today special - %s\n",menuitem);
        printf("You want %d pint.\n",pints);
        printf("That be $%f, please.\n",price);
        return(0);
}
```

Type this source code into your editor. Double-check everything. Save the program as ICKYGU.C.

Compile the program. Repair any unexpected errors — as well as those you may have been expecting — and recompile if need be.

Run the final program. You see something like the following example displayed:

```
Today special - Slimy Orange Stuff "Icky Woka Gu"
You want 1 pint.
That be $1.450000, please.
```

Whoa! Is that lira or dollars? Of course, it's dollars — the dollar sign in `printf()`'s formatting string is a normal character, not anything special. But the `1.45` value was printed with four extra zeroes. Why? Because you didn't tell the compiler *not* to. That's just the way the `%f`, or floating-point conversion character, displays numbers.

To have the output make more dollars and sense, edit Line 11 and change the `%f` placeholder to read `%.2f`:

```
printf("That be $%.2f, please.\n",price);
```

Squeezing extra characters between the `%` and the `f` should be familiar to you; I show you how to it a few chapters back, to limit the formatting for the `%s` placeholder. Here, you're telling `printf()` to format the floating-point number to only two places after the decimal point.

Save the change to disk. Recompile and run. The output is more appealing:

```
Today special - Slimy Orange Stuff "Icky Woka Gu"
You want 1 pint.
That be $1.45, please.
```

- This program contains three types of variables: a string, `menuitem`; an integer value, `pints`; and a floating-point value, `price`.
- The price is a floating-point value because it contains a decimal part. It's another type of numeric variable. Unlike an integer, floating-point values can contain a decimal part.
- The "floating point" is that dot in the middle of the number — 1.45 — which is technically incorrect, but it's the way I remember it.
- Table 24-2 in Chapter 24 contains a list of the `printf()` function's placeholders. There, you find that `%f` is used to display a floating-point number, such as the one that appears in ICKYGU.C.
- The final `printf()` statement is used to display the value of the floating-point price variable:

  ```
  printf("That be $%.2f, please.\n",price);
  ```

  To do that, you use the `%f` (*f* for float) placeholder. However, `%f` requires some extra formatting power to display the value as a monetary amount. To meet this end, you insert a "dot-2" between the `%` and the little *f*. That formats the output to only two decimal places. Rather than use `%f`, the formatting string uses `%.2f`.

Maybe you want to chance two pints?

You can easily twist ICKYGU.C into doing some math for you. Suppose that you want to figure out how much two pints of the orange stuff is. First, you change the `pints` variable in the sixth line to read

```
int pints=2;
```

That fills the pints variable with 2. Then you have to stick some math into the final printf() function, which calculates how much two pints of the sticky stuff would be. Make these alterations:

```
printf("That be $%.2f, please.\n",pints*price);
```

The only true change is in the last part of the line. Before, you had only the price variable. Now, you have pints*price, which multiplies the value in price by the value in pints. Because price is a floating-point, or decimal, value, the result still is floating-point. That is the reason that the %f placeholder is still used in the formatting string.

Save these changes and recompile the program. You have to pay more, but — *mmmm* — your tummy will thank you.

Multiple declarations

C is full of abbreviations and shortcuts. That's one reason that no two C programs look alike: Programmers always take advantage of the different ways of doing things. One such trick is to declare several variables in one statement. I know — this used to be illegal in parts of the South, but it's now done aboveboard everywhere in the Union.

The following three int statements create three integer variables: methus, you, and diff:

```
int methus;
int you;
int diff;
```

The following single-line statement does the same thing:

```
int methus,you,diff;
```

Each of the variables is specified after the int keyword and a space. Each is followed by a comma, with the final variable followed by a semicolon to end the statement.

This shortcut is primarily a space-saving technique. It just takes up less screen space to declare all variables of one type on a single line than to have individual, itsy-bitsy int statements lining up at the beginning of a program.

TIP

You can declare variables of only the same type in a multiple declaration. For example:

```
int top,bottom,right,left;
float national_debt,pi;
```

The integer variables are declared on one line, and the floating-point (non-integer) variables on another.

Keep variables that are defined with a value on a line by themselves. To wit:

```
int first=1;
int the_rest;
```

Constants and Variables

In addition to the variable, the C language has something called a *constant*. It's used like a variable, though its value never changes.

Suppose that one day someone dupes you into writing a trigonometry program. In this type of program, you have to use the dreaded value π (pi). That's equal to 3.1415926 (and on and on). Because it never changes, you can create a constant named `pi` that is equal to that value.

Another example of a constant is a quoted string of text:

```
printf("%s","This is a string of text");
```

The text `"This is a string of text"` is a constant used with this `printf()` function. A variable can go there, though a string constant — a literal, quoted string — is used instead.

- A constant is used just like a variable, though its value never changes.
- A numeric constant is a number value, like π, that remains the same throughout your program.
- π is pronounced "pie." It's the Greek letter *p*. We pronounce the English letter *p* as *"pee."*
- A string constant is a bit of text that never changes, though that's really true of most text in a C language program. This chapter, therefore, concentrates primarily on numeric constants.

Dreaming up and defining constants

All this constant nonsense can seem silly. Then one day, you're faced with a program like SPEED.C — except that the program is much longer — and you truly come to realize the value of a C language constant and the nifty `#define` directive you read about later in this chapter:

```
#include <stdio.h>

int main()
{
      printf("Now, the speed limit here is %i.\n",55);
      printf("But I clocked you doin' %i.\n",55+15);
      printf("Didn't you see that %i MPH sign?\n",55);
      return(0);
}
```

Start over with a new slate in your editor. Carefully type the preceding source code. There's nothing new or repulsive in it. Save the file to disk as SPEED.C.

Compile it! Fix it (if you have to)! Run it!

The output is pretty plain; something like this example is displayed:

```
Now, the speed limit here is 55.
But I clocked you doin' 70.
Didn't you see that 55 MPH sign?
```

Eh? No big deal.

But what if the speed limit were really 45? That would mean that you would have to edit the program and replace `55` with `45` all over. Better still, what if the program were 800 lines long and you had to do that? Not only that, but what if you had to change several other instances in which constants were used, and using your editor to hunt down each one and replace it properly would take months or years? Fortunately, the C language has a handy way around this dilemma.

- You can easily argue that this isn't a problem. After all, most editors have a search-and-replace command. Unfortunately, searching and replacing numbers in a computer program is a dangerous thing to do! Suppose that the number is `1`. Searching and replacing it would change other values as well: 100, 512, 3.141 — all those would be goofed up by a search-and-replace.
- For all you Mensa people out there, it's true that the nature of the program changes if the speed limit is lowered to 45. After all, was the scofflaw doing 70 or 60? To me, it doesn't matter. If you're wasting your excess IQ points on the problem, you can remedy it on your own.

The handy shortcut

The idea in this section is to come up with a handy shortcut for using number constants in C. I give you two solutions.

The first solution is to use a variable to hold the constant value:

```
int speed=55;
```

This line works because the compiler sticks the value 55 into the speed integer variable, and you can then use speed rather than 55 all over your program. To change the speed, you have to make only one edit:

```
int speed=45;
```

Although this line works, it's silly because a variable is designed to hold a value that changes. The compiler goes to all that work, fluffing up the pillows and making things comfy for the variable, and then you misuse it as a constant. No, the true solution is to define the constant value as a *symbolic constant.* It's really cinchy, as the updated SPEED.C program shows:

```
#include <stdio.h>

#define SPEED 55

int main()
{
        printf("Now, the speed limit here is %i.\n",SPEED);
        printf("But I clocked you doin' %i.\n",SPEED+15);
        printf("Didn't you see that %i MPH sign?\n",SPEED);
        return(0);
}
```

Several changes are made here:

- The program's new, third line is another one of those doohickeys that begins with a pound sign (#). This one, #define, sets up a numeric constant that can be used throughout the program:

  ```
  #define SPEED 55
  ```

  As with the #include thing, a semicolon doesn't end the line. In fact, two big boo-boos with #define are using an equal sign and ending the line with a semicolon. The compiler will surely hurl error-message chunks your way if you do that.

- The shortcut word SPEED is then used in the program's three printf() statements to represent the value 55. There, it appears just like a number or variable in the printf statement.

Secretly, what happens is that the compiler sees the #define thing and all by itself does a search-and-replace. When the program is glued together, the value 55 is stuck into the printf() statements. The advantage is that you can easily update the constant values by simply editing the #define directive.

Carefully edit your SPEED.C source code so that it matches what you see listed here. Save the file to disk again and then recompile. It has the same output because your only change was to make the value 55 a real, live constant rather than a value inside the program.

- Again, the key is that it takes only one, quick edit to change the speed limit. If you edit Line 3 to read

  ```
  #define SPEED 45
  ```

  you have effectively changed the constant value 45 in three other places in the program. This change saves some time for the SPEED.C program — but it saves you even more time for longer, more complex programs that also use constant values.

- *Symbolic constant* is C technospeak for a constant value created by the `#define` directive.

The `#define` directive

The `#define` construction (which is its official name, though I prefer to call it a directive) is used to set up what the C lords call a *symbolic constant* — a shortcut name for a value that appears over and over in your source code. Here's the format:

```
#define SHORTCUT value
```

`SHORTCUT` is the name of the constant you're defining. It's traditional to name it like a variable and use ALL CAPS (no spaces).

`value` is the value the *`SHORTCUT`* takes on. It's replaced by that value globally throughout the rest of your source code file. The *`value`* can be a number, equation, symbol, or string.

No semicolon is at the end of the line, but notice that the line absolutely must begin with a pound sign. This line appears at the beginning of your source code, before the `main()` function.

You should also tack a comment to the end of the `#define` line to remind you of what the value represents, as in this example:

```
#define SPEED 55  /* the speed limit */
```

Here, `SPEED` is defined to be the value 55. You can then use `SPEED` anywhere else in your program to represent 55.

A string constant can be created in the same way, though it's not as popular:

```
#define GIRLFRIEND "Brenda"  /* This week's babe */
```

The only difference is that the string is enclosed in double quotes, which is a traditional C-string thing.

- The shortcut word is usually written in ALL CAPS so as not to confuse it with a variable name. Other than that, the rules that apply to variable names typically apply to the shortcut words. Keep 'em short and simple is my recommendation.
- You have to keep track of which types of constants you have defined and then use them accordingly, as shown in this example:

  ```
  printf("The speed limit is %i.\n",SPEED);
  ```

- And in this one:

  ```
  puts(GIRLFRIEND);
  ```

- These lines may look strange, but they're legit because the compiler knows what `SPEED` and `GIRLFRIEND` are shortcuts for.
- No equal sign appears after the shortcut word!
- The line doesn't end with a semicolon (it's not a C language statement)!
- You can also use escape-sequence, backslash-character things in a defined string constant.
- String constants that are set up with `#define` are rare. Only if the string appears many times over and over in your program is it necessary to make it a constant. Otherwise, most programs use `printf()` or `puts()` to display text on the screen.
- You can also use math and other strangeness in a defined numeric constant. This book doesn't go into that subject, but something as obnoxious as the following line is entirely possible:

  ```
  #define SIZE 40*35
  ```

  Here, the shortcut word `SIZE` is set up to be equal to `40*35`, whatever that figures out to be.
- Using the `#define` thing isn't required, and you're not penalized if you don't use it. Sure, you can stick the numbers in there directly. And, you can use variables to hold your constants. I won't pout about it. You won't go to C prison.

Real, live constant variables

Using #define to create a constant for use throughout your program is a handy thing to do. In fact, I recommend using it whenever you have something in your program that you figure may change. For example:

```
#define NUMBER_OF_USERS 3
#define COLUMN_WIDTH 80
#define US_STATES 50
```

Each of these examples makes it possible to change aspects of your entire program merely by editing a single #define declaration. But are they really constants — the opposite of variables?

No! That's because they have the const keyword, which converts a mild-mannered variable into an unyielding constant. To wit:

```
const int senses = 6;
```

The preceding statement creates a variable named senses, but fixes that variable's value at 6. The value cannot be changed or used for something else later in the program; if you try, a "read-only variable" error pops up.

Most often you don't see const used to create constant values. Instead, this statement is quite common:

```
const char prompt[] = "Your command:";
```

This statement creates the string variable prompt and sets its contents equal to Your command:. The const keyword ensures that this variable cannot be reused or its contents ever changed — a good idea for this type of variable.

Chapter 9

How to C Numbers

In This Chapter

- Using different variables for different numbers
- Understanding the `long` and `short` of `int`
- Knowing your `signed` and `unsigned` variables
- Floating a number
- Double floating a number
- Formatting a huge value

Put on your safety goggles, my greenhorn companion! I have danced around the flaming inferno of numbers far too long. It's time to dive headlong into that hellfire of values and digits. Far down from the comfy safety of the `int` lie numbers large and loathsome. Terrifying values you can gingerly place into your puny programs. Numbers lethal and toxic, but which you can also tame, as long as you obey my gentle advice in this chapter.

Fear not! Instead, don your asbestos suit and follow me. Watch your step.

There Are Numbers, and Then There Are Numbers

Welcome to what will soon be one of many new, frustrating aspects of the C programming language. It's known as the C Numeric Data Type Puzzle. Unlike in real life, where we can just pull any number out of the ethers and be joyously happy with it, in C you must pull numbers from specific parts of the ethers based on which type of number it is. This makes the frustration factor begin rising, with the logical question "What's a number type?"

Okay. It isn't a "number type." It's a *numeric data type,* which is how you say "number type" if you work at the Pentagon. You have to tell the C compiler which type of number you're using because it thinks about numbers differently from the way humans do. For example, you have to know the following things about the number:

- Is it a whole number — without a fraction or decimal part?
- How big is the number (as in value-large, not big-on-the-page-large)?
- If the number does have a fractional part, how precise must the number be? (Like to the thousandths, millionths, or gazillionths decimal place. Scientists have to know the precision when they send missiles to countries with opposing ideologies.)

I know that this stuff is all alien to you. What most programmers want to do is say "I need a number variable — just give me one, quick — before this value slips out the back of the computer and becomes a government statistic!" But you have to think a little more before you do that.

- The most common numeric data type is the integer.
- If you're going to work with decimal numbers, such as a dollar amount, you need the *floating-point* number.
- Keep reading.

Numbers in C

A number of different types of numbers are used in C — different numeric data types, so to speak. Table 9-1 lists them all, along with other statistical information. Flag the table with a sticky note. This table is something you refer to now and again because only the truly insane would memorize it.

Table 9-1 C Numeric Data Types

Keyword	*Variable Type*	*Range*
char	Character (or string)	–128 to 127
int	Integer	–32,768 to 32,767
short	Short integer	–32,768 to 32,767
short int	Short integer	–32,768 to 32,767

Keyword	***Variable Type***	***Range***
long	Long integer	–2,147,483,648 to 2,147,483,647
unsigned char	Unsigned character	0 to 255
unsigned int	Unsigned integer	0 to 65,535
unsigned short	Unsigned short integer	0 to 65,535
unsigned long	Unsigned long integer	0 to 4,294,967,295
float	Single-precision floating-point (accurate to 7 digits)	$\pm3.4 \infty 10^{38}$ to $\pm3.4 \infty 10^{-38}$
double	Double-precision floating-point (accurate to 15 digits)	$\pm1.7 \infty 10^{-308}$ to $\pm1.7 \infty 10^{308}$

- The *keyword* is the C language keyword used to declare the variable type. If you have been reading the chapters in this book in order, you have used `int`, `char`, and `float` already.
- The *variable type* tells you which type of variable the keyword defines. For example, `char` defines a character (or string) variable, and `int` defines integers. C has many variable types, each of which depends on the type of number or value being described.
- The *range* tells you how big of a number fits into the variable type. For example, integers range from –32,768 up to 0 and up again to 32,767. Other types of variables handle larger values. This value may be different on your compiler; use the values in Table 9-1 for reference only.

Table 9-1 isn't that complex. In all, C has really only four types of variables:

- `char`
- `int`
- `float`
- `double`

The `int` can be modified with either `short` or `long`, and both `char` and `int` are modified with `unsigned`. The `float` and `double` variables are both floating-point, though the values held by `double` are larger.

Why use integers? Why not just make every number floating-point?

Obviously, if you have a double-precision floating-point number that can handle, essentially, numbers up to one gazillion, why bother declaring any variables as integers? Heck, make everything a double-whammy floating point and be done with it! Sounds good. Is bad.

Integers are truly the handiest and most common types of numeric variables. Oftentimes, you need only small, whole-number values when you're programming. Floating-point numbers are okay, but they require more overhead from the computer and take longer to work with. By comparison, integers are far quicker. For this reason, God saw fit to create integers (which He did on the third day, by the way).

Integer types (short, long, wide, fat, and so on)

You have to concern yourself with only two types of integers: the normal integer — the `int` — and the long integer — the `long`. (The signed and unsigned aspects are chewed over slowly later in this chapter.)

The `int` (rhymes with "bent") is a whole-number value, normally ranging from –32,768 to 32,767. It's ideally put to use for small numbers without a fractional part. In some versions of C, you may see this value referred to as a `short` or `short int`.

The `long` is a whole-number value, ranging from –2,147,483,648 to 2,147,483,647 — a big range, but not big enough to encompass the national debt or Madonna's ego. This type of numeric variable is referred to as a `long`, or `long int` in some versions of C.

- You use the `int` and `long` keywords to declare integer variables. `int` is for smaller values; `long` is for larger values.
- The `%d` placeholder is used in the `printf()` function to display `int` variables. (You can also use the `%i` placeholder; refer to Table 24-2 in Chapter 24.)
- `int = short = short int`
- `long = long int`
- Integer variables (`int`) are shorter, faster, and easier for the computer to deal with. If `Soup for One` were a variable, it would be an `int`. Use an `int` whenever you need a small, whole numeric value.

- In some C compilers, the ranges for `int` and `long int` are the same. That's because the compiler (usually a 32-bit model) can more efficiently handle `long` values than it can handle smaller `int` values. It's merely technical junk; don't memorize it or let it otherwise ruin your day.
- Negative numbers — why bother? Sometimes, you need them, but most of the time you don't. See the next section.
- The `char` variable type can also be used as a type of integer, though it has an extremely small range. These variables are used mostly to store single characters (or strings), which is discussed somewhere else. (Give me a second to look.) Oh, it's in Chapter 10.

Signed or unsigned, or "Would you like a minus sign with that, Sir?"

I have this thing against negative numbers. They're good only when you play Hearts. Even so, that's justification because you may someday write a program that plays Hearts on the computer, in which case you will be in dire need of negative numbers (because you can write the program so that you always win).

When you declare a numeric variable in C, you have two choices: *signed* and *unsigned*. Everything is signed unless you specifically type **unsigned** before the variable type:

```
unsigned int shoot_the_moon = 26;
```

A signed type of number means that a variable can hold a negative value. The standard `int` variable can hold values from –32,768 up to 32,767. That's half negative numbers, from –32,768 to –1, and then half positive numbers, from 0 up to 32,767. (Zero is considered positive in some cults.)

An unsigned number means that the variable holds only positive values. This unsigned number moves the number range all up to the positive side — no negatives (the C language equivalent of Prozac). Your typical `unsigned int` has a range from 0 to 65,535. Negative numbers aren't allowed.

The `int` variable `elephants` holds the value 40,000. Try *that* with a signed `int`! Ha!

```
unsigned int elephants = 40000;
```

Table 9-2 illustrates the differences between the variable types as far as the values they can hold are concerned.

The whole painful spiel on why we have signed integers

The signed-unsigned business all has to do with how numbers are stored inside a computer. The secret is that everything, no matter how it looks on the screen or in your program, is stored in the binary tongue inside the computer. That's counting in base 2 (ones and zeroes).

Binary numbers are composed of *bits,* or *b*inary dig*its.* Suppose that your C language compiler uses two bytes to store an integer. Those two bytes contain 16 binary digits, or bits. (Eight bits are in a byte.) For example:

```
0111 0010 1100 0100
```

This value is written as 29,380 in decimal (the human counting system). In binary, the ones and zeroes represent various multiples of two, which can get quite complex before your eyes, but is like eating ice cream to the computer.

Look at this number:

```
0111 1111 1111 1111
```

It's the value 32,767 — almost a solid bank of ones. If you add 1 to this value, you get the following amazing figure:

```
1000 0000 0000 0000
```

How the computer interprets this binary value depends on how you define your variable. For a signed value, a `1` in the far left position of the number isn't a `1` at all. *It's a minus sign.* The preceding number becomes –32,768 in binary math. If the variable is an unsigned value, it's interpreted as positive 32,768.

The deal with signed and unsigned numbers all depends on that pesky first bit in the computer's binary counting tongue. If you're working with a signed number, the first bit is the minus sign. Otherwise, the first bit is just another droll bit in the computer, happy to be a value and not a minus sign.

Table 9-2 What Signed and Unsigned Variables Can Hold

Signed	*Range*	*Unsigned*	*Range*
char	–128 to 127	unsigned char	0 to 255
int	–32768 to 32,767	unsigned int	0 to 65,535
long	–2,147,483,648 to 2,147,483,647	unsigned long	0 to 4,294,967,295

- Floating-point numbers (numbers with a decimal part or fractions) can be positive or negative without regard to any signed or unsigned nonsense.
- Floating-point numbers are covered in the following section.
- Normally, the differences between signed and unsigned values shouldn't bother you.

- Signed variables can be maddening and the source of frustration as far as creepy errors are concerned. For example, I once wrote a program in which I added 1 to a signed integer variable and the result turned out to be negative! That's because of something called *overflow.* It can also happen with signed variables; when the variable's value exceeds what the variable is designed to hold, the results can be unpredictable.
- To use an unsigned variable and skirt around the negative-number issue, you must declare your variables by using either the `unsigned int` or `unsigned long` keyword. Your C compiler may have a secret switch that allows you to always create programs by using unsigned variables; refer to the online documentation to see what it is.

How to Make a Number Float

Two scoops of ice cream. . . .

Integer variables are the workhorses in your programs, handling most of the numeric tasks. However, when you have to deal with fractions, numbers that have a decimal part, or very large values, you need a different type of numeric variable. That variable is the *float.*

The `float` keyword is used to set aside space for a variable designed to contain a floating-point, or noninteger, value. Here's the format:

```
float var;
```

The keyword `float` is followed by a space or a tab, and then comes the variable name, *var.* The line ends in a semicolon.

Or, you can declare a `float` variable and give it a value, just as you can any other variable in C:

```
float var=value;
```

In this format, the variable *var* is followed by an equal sign and then a *`value`* to be assigned to it.

Float is short for floating point. That term somehow refers to the decimal point in the number. For example, the following number is a floating-point value:

```
123.4567
```

An integer variable wouldn't cut it for this number. It could be only 123 or 124. When you have a decimal, you need a floating-point variable.

The range for floating-point numbers is quite large. With most C compilers, you can store any number in the range $\pm 3.4 \times 10^{-38}$ to $\pm 3.4 \times 10^{38}$. In English, that's a value between negative 340 undecillion and positive 340 undecillion. An undecillion is a 1 with 36 zeroes after it. That's a true, Mr. Spock-size value, though most numbers you use as floats are far less.

- Rules for naming variables are in Chapter 8.
- Noninteger values are stored in `float` variables.
- Even though 123 is an integer value, you can still store it in a `float` variable. However. . . .
- `float` variables should be used only when you need them. They require more internal storage and more PC processing time and power than integers do. If you can get by with an integer, use that type of variable instead.

"Hey, Carl, let's write a floating-point number program!"

Suppose that you and I are these huge, bulbous-headed creatures, all slimy and green and from the planet Redmond. We fly our UFO all over the galaxy, drink blue beer, and program in C on our computers. I'm Dan. Your name is Carl.

One day, while assaulting cows in Indiana, we get into this debate:

> *Dan*: A light-year is 5,878,000,000,000 miles long! That's 5 trillion, 878 billion, plus change! I'm not walking that!
>
> *Carl*: Nay, but it's only a scant 483,400,000 miles from the sun to Jupiter. That is but a fraction of a light-year.
>
> *Dan*: How much of a fraction?
>
> *Carl*: Well, why don't you type the following C program and have your computer calculate the distance for you?
>
> *Dan*: Wait. I'm the author of this book. *You* type the program, JUPITER.C, and *you* figure it out. Sheesh.

```
#include <stdio.h>

int main()
{
    float lightyear=5.878E12;
    float jupiter=483400000;
    float distance;
```

```
    distance=jupiter/lightyear;

    printf("Jupiter is %f light years from the
        sun.\n",distance);

    return(0);
}
```

Enter this program into your text editor. Be careful! Check spelling, odd characters, other stuff. Save the file to disk as JUPITER.C.

Compile the program. If you see any errors, fix 'em up and recompile.

Run the program. The output looks something like this:

```
Jupiter is 0.000082 light years from the sun.
```

Carl: A mere stumble!

Dan: I'm still not walking it.

- You use the `float` keyword to declare a floating-point variable.
- In *scientific notation,* which is how scientists sneak around the requirement of typing zeroes and commas, the length of a light year is written as 5.878E12. That means that the decimal in 5.878 should be shifted to the right 12 times. (The next section covers this ugly E-notation thing.)
- The variable `jupiter` is set equal to the mean distance between Jupiter and the sun, which is 484 million miles. In the source code, that's 4834 followed by 5 zeroes. There's no need to mess with scientific notation here because the compiler can eat this relatively small-size number. (Anything over 100 billion usually requires the scientific E notation; you have to refer to your compiler's manual to check the size of its mouth.)
- The `distance` variable contains the result of dividing the distance between the sun and Jupiter by the length of a light-year — to find out how many light-years Jupiter is from the sun. The number is extremely small.
- The `%f` placeholder is used in the `printf()` function to display floating-point values.
- The `float` variables are used in this program for two reasons: because of the humongous size of the numbers involved and because division usually produces a noninteger result — a number with a decimal part.

The E notation stuff

When you deal with very large and very small numbers, the old scientific E notation stuff crops up. I assume that it's okay to discuss this subject, because if you're interested in programs that deal with these types of numbers, you probably already have one foot in the test tube.

E notation is required in C (or even in the Excel spreadsheet) when some numbers get incredibly huge. Those numbers are floating-point numbers — or the floats, as you have come to know them. Integers don't count.

When you get a number over about eight or nine digits long, it must be expressed in E notation or else the compiler doesn't eat it. For example, take the length of a light-year in miles:

```
5,878,000,000,000
```

That's 5 trillion, 878 billion. In C, you don't specify the commas, so the number should be written as follows:

```
5878000000000
```

That's 5878 followed by nine zeroes. The value is still the same; only the commas — conveniently added to break up large numbers for your human eyeballs — have been removed. And though this number is within the range of a float, if you were to compile it, the compiler would moan that it's too large. It's not the value that bugs the compiler — it's the number of digits in the number.

To make the compiler understand the value, you have to express it by using fewer digits, which is where scientific notation comes in handy. Here's the same value in E notation, as you specify it in the JUPITER.C program, from the preceding section:

```
5.878E12
```

Scientific, or E, notation uses a number in the following format:

```
x.xxxxEnn
```

The *x.xxxx* is a value; it's one digit followed by a decimal point and then more digits. Then comes big E and then another value (*nn*). To find out the number's true size, you have to hop the decimal point in the *x.xxxx* value to the right *nn* places. Figure 9-1 illustrates how this concept works with the light-year value.

5.878	E12
58.78	E11
587.8	E10
5878.	E9
58780.	E8
587800.	E7
5878000.	E6
58780000.	E5
587800000.	E4
5878000000.	E3
58780000000.	E2
587800000000.	E1
5878000000000.	E0
5,878,000,000,000	

Figure 9-1: Scientific notation and the light year.

When you enter E numbers in the compiler, use the proper E format. To display the numbers in E format with `printf()`, you can use the `%e` placeholder. To see how it works, replace the `%f` in the JUPITER.C program with `%e`, save the change to disk, recompile, and run the result. The output is in E notation, something like the following:

```
Jupiter is 8.223886e-05 light years from the sun.
```

If the E has a negative number in front of it, as shown in this example, you hop the decimal point to the left *nn* places, to indicate very small numbers. You would translate the preceding value into the following:

```
.00008223886
```

- Scientific, or E, notation is required when numbers contain too many digits for the C compiler to eat.
- A negative E number means that the value is very small. Remember to move the decimal point to the *left* rather than to the right when you see this type of number.
- Some compilers allow you to use the `%E` (big E) placeholder in `printf()` to display scientific-notation numbers with a big E in them.

Bigger than the Float, It's a Double!

For handling really huge numbers, C has a really huge data type, the `double`. These types of variables can contain absolutely huge values and should be used only when you must work with those outer-space-size values or when you require a mathematical operation that must be precise.

Double variables are declared by using the `double` keyword. *Double* comes from the term *double precision,* which means that the numbers are twice as accurate as floats, which are also known as single-precision numbers.

What's *precision?* It deals with how decimal numbers, fractions, and very small and huge numbers are stored in a computer. Keep in mind that the computer uses only ones and zeroes to store information. For integers, that's great. For non-integers, it means that some tomfoolery must take place. That tomfoolery works, but it tends to get inaccurate, or "fuzzy," after a time, especially on the details.

As an example, gawk at this number:

```
123.4567891234
```

That's a float if I ever saw one. But if you define that value as a `float` variable in C, the computer can store it only as a single-precision value. It can accurately hold only the first eight digits. The rest — it makes them up! To wit:

```
123.45678422231
```

The first eight digits are precise. The rest — eh? After the `8`, the value gets screwy. It's single precision in action. Double precision can be accurate to maybe 12 or 16 decimal places (but after that, it begins acting goofy as well).

The moral of this story is twofold: First, if you have to make float calculations with your computer, remember that the number can be only so accurate. After about eight digits or so, the rest of the output is meaningless. Second, if you need precise calculations, use the `double` type of variable. It still has its problems, but it's more precise than the `float`.

- You use the `double` keyword to declare a double-precision floating-point variable in your C programs.
- If you ever print a value — 123.456, for example — and the output you see is something like 123.456001, that extra `001` is the lack of precision the computer has when it's dealing with floating-point numbers. For the most part, any extra value that's added is insignificant, so don't let it bug you.

- Being accurate to eight digits is more than enough for most noninteger calculations. For sending people to Mars, however, I recommend the `double`. (I know that NASA reads these books intently.)
- Some compilers may offer quadruple-precision numbers with their own unique keywords and other rules and regulations.
- The greater the precision, the longer it takes the computer to deal with the numbers. Don't use more precision than you have to.

Formatting Your Zeroes and Decimal Places

Floating-point values can sure look gross when they're displayed by using the `%f` in the `printf()` function. Ugh. Now you have to plug your nose and plunge a little deeper into the murky waters of `printf()` formatting. Fortunately, this is about the only time you have to do that.

Between the `%` and the `f`, you can insert some special formatting characters. They control the `printf()` function's output and may help you get rid of some excess zeroes or trim up the number that is displayed.

The following few examples show you how to trim up your numbers with `printf()` and avoid the cavalcade of zeroes that appears sometimes when you're dealing with floats and doubles.

The following placeholder displays the float number by using only two decimal places. It's ideal for displaying dollar amounts. Without it, you may have $199.9500 displayed as a price — which doesn't appease your customer's sense of thrift any.

```
%.2f
```

If you need to display more decimal places, specify that number after the dot:

```
%.4f
```

This placeholder formats floating-point numbers to display four digits after the decimal point. If the value isn't that small, zeroes pad out the four decimal places.

The following format information tells `printf()` to display the number by using six digits — which includes the decimal point:

```
%6.f
```

No matter how big the number is, it's always displayed by using six digits. Rather than leading zeroes, the number is padded on the left with spaces. The number 123 is displayed as

```
  123.
```

This line begins with two spaces, or is indented two spaces, depending on how you look at it.

Sometimes the `%f` may display a number that looks like this:

```
145000.000000
```

In that case, you can trim up the number by using either `%.2f`, which displays only two zeroes after the decimal point, or something like `%6f`, which limits the output to only six digits.

- An alternative to messing with numbers and other characters between the `%` and little *f* is to use the `%e` placeholder. It displays numbers in scientific format, which is usually shorter than the `%f` placeholder's output.
- Then there's the `%g` placeholder. That thing displays a floating-point number in either the `%f` or `%e` (scientific) format, depending on which is shorter.

Yes, I know that this chapter is short on examples. But numbers are boring. So there.

Chapter 10

Cook That C Variable Charred, Please

In This Chapter

- Using the `char` declaration
- Assigning characters to variables
- Understanding `getchar()` and `putchar()`
- Treating `char` as a tiny integer variable

Too many C language books seem to fixate on numbers and avoid completely the other type of variable — the character, or string, variable. It's definitely more fun. Rather than hold values — values, bah! — character variables hold individual characters or letters of the alphabet and complete strings of text. This certainly opens the floodgates of creativity over pounding the sand with numbers.

This chapter rounds off your variable declaration journey with an official hello to the `char` variable, suited for storing both single characters and strings of text. In this chapter, it's only single characters you have to worry about.

The Other Kind of Variable Type, the `char`

Though I talk about both single-character and string variables, C language has only one variable type, the `char`, which is defined by the keyword `char`. And I think, though I'm not certain, that it's pronounced "care" and not "char," as in "charred beyond all recognition."

Single-character variables

Like a string of text, the single-character variable is declared by using the `char` keyword. Unlike a string, the single-character variable holds only one character — no more. In a way, the character variable is like a padded cell. The string variable is merely several padded cells one after the other — like an asylum.

The `char` keyword is used to set aside storage space for a single-character variable. Here's the format:

```
char var;
```

`char` is written in lowercase, followed by a space and then *var,* the name of the variable to be created.

In the following format, you can predefine a single-character value:

```
char var='c';
```

Typing those hard-to-reach characters

Some characters can't be typed at the keyboard or entered by using escape sequences. For example, the extended ASCII characters used on most PCs — which include the line-drawing characters, math symbols, and some foreign characters — require some extra effort to stuff into character variables. It's possible — just a little technical. Follow these steps:

1. Look up the character's secret code value — its ASCII or extended ASCII code number.
2. Convert that code number into base 16, the hexadecimal, or "hex," system. (That's why hexadecimal values are usually shown in the ASCII tables and charts.)
3. Specify that hex value, which is two digits long, after the `\x` escape sequence.
4. Remember to enclose the entire escape sequence — four characters long — in single quotes.

Suppose that you want to use the British pound symbol, £, in your program. That character's secret code number is 156. The hexadecimal value is 9C. (Hex numbers contain letters.) So you specify the following escape sequence in your program:

```
'\x9C'
```

Notice that it's enclosed in single quotes. The C, or any other hexadecimal letter, can be upper- or lowercase. When the escape sequence is assigned to a character variable, the C compiler takes the preceding number and converts it into a character — the £ — which sits snugly until needed.

`char` is followed by a space. The name of the variable you're creating, *var*, is followed by an equal sign and then a character in *single* quotes. The statement ends in a semicolon.

Inside the single quotes is a single character, which is assigned to the variable *var*. You can specify any single character or use one of the escape sequences to specify a nontypable character, such as a double-quote, a single quote, or the Enter key press. (See Table 24-1 in Chapter 24 for the full list of escape sequences; also see the nearby sidebar, "Typing those hard-to-reach characters.")

The single-character variable is ideal for reading one character (obviously) from the keyboard. By using miracles of the C language not yet known, you can compare that character with other characters and make your programs do wondrous things. This is how a menu system works, how you can type single-key commands without having to press Enter, and how you can write your own keyboard-reading programs. Oh, it can be fun.

Char in action

The following statement creates the character variable `ch` for use in the program (you can also predefine the variable if need be):

```
char ch;
```

This next statement creates the character variable `x` and assigns to it the character value `'X'` (big X):

```
char x='X';
```

When you assign a character to a single-character variable, you use single quotes. It's a must!

Some characters, you can't really type at the keyboard. For example, to predefine a variable and stick the Tab key into it, you use an *escape sequence:*

```
char tab='\t';
```

This statement creates the character variable `tab` and places in that variable the tab character, represented by the `\t` escape sequence.

- Single-character variables are created by using the `char` keyword.
- Don't use the square brackets when you're declaring single-character variables.

- If you predefine the variable's value with a character, enclose that character in single quotes. Don't use double quotes.
- You can assign almost any character value to the character variable. Special, weird, and other characters can be assigned by using the escape sequences.
- Information about creating string variables is presented in Chapter 4. This chapter deals primarily with single-character variables.

Stuffing characters into character variables

You can assign a character variable a value in one of several ways. The first way is to just stuff a character in there, similar to the way you stuff a value into a numeric variable or your foot into a sock. If `key` is a character variable, for example, you can place the character `'T'` in it with this statement:

```
key='T';
```

The `T`, which must be in single quotes, ladies and gentlemen, slides through the equal sign and into the key variable's single-character holding bin. The statement ends in a semicolon. (I assume that `key` was defined as a character variable by using the `char key;` statement, earlier in the program.)

In addition to single characters, you can specify various escape sequences (the `\`-character things), values, and whatnot. As long as it's only one character long, you're hunky-dory.

Another way to stick a character into a single-character variable is to slide one from another character variable. Suppose that both `old` and `new` are character variables. The following is acceptable:

```
old=new;
```

The character in `new` squirts through the equal sign and lands in the character variable `old`. After the preceding statement, both variables hold the same character. (It's a copy operation, not a move.)

- You can assign single characters to single-character variables. But. . . .
- You still cannot use the equal sign to put a string of text into a string variable. Sorry. It just can't be done.

Reading and Writing Single Characters

This book introduces you to two C language functions used to read text from the keyboard: `scanf()` and `gets()`. Both read text from the keyboard, usually as full sentences. However, `scanf()` can be used to read in single characters, which is part of its charm — and flexibility:

```
scanf("%c",&key);
```

In this format, `scanf()` reads the keyboard for a single character, specified by the placeholder `%c`. That value is stored in the `char` variable `key`, which you can assume was already declared earlier in the program. To wit:

```
#include <stdio.h>

int main()
{
    char key;

    puts("Type your favorite keyboard character:");
    scanf("%c",&key);
    printf("Your favorite character is %c!\n",key);
    return(0);
}
```

Carefully enter this source code into your editor. Save it to disk as FAVKEY1.C.

Compile and run. Here's the sample output:

```
Type your favorite keyboard character:
```

Press a key, such as **m** (or whatever your favorite is), and then press the Enter key. You see this:

```
M
Your favorite character is M!
```

The M key is read from the keyboard, stored in the `char` variable `key`, and then displayed by `printf()`.

- Yes, you have to press the Enter key to finish your input — that's the way the `scanf()` function works.
- You can type a whole string of text, but only the first character that's typed is read by `scanf()` as the favorite key.

The getchar() *function*

Fortunately, you're not stuck with scanf() for reading in individual keys from the keyboard. The C language also has a function named getchar(), which is used specifically to read a single character from the keyboard. Here's the format:

```
var=getchar();
```

var is an integer variable. It holds whatever character is typed at the keyboard. *var* is followed by an equal sign and then getchar and two parentheses hugging nothing. This function is a complete statement and ends with a semicolon.

The getchar() function causes your program to pause and wait for a key to be typed at the keyboard. getchar() sits and waits. Sits and waits. Sit. Wait. Sit. Wait. When a key is typed and then Enter is pressed, that character's "value" slides across the equal sign and is stored in the character variable.

The following is the update to the FAVKEY1.C program, this time replacing the sordid scanf() function with the better getchar() function:

```
#include <stdio.h>

int main()
{
    char key;

    puts("Type your favorite keyboard character:");
    key=getchar();
    printf("Your favorite character is %c!\n",key);
    return(0);
}
```

Edit the source code for FAVKEY1.C, changing only Line 8 and replacing the scanf() function with getchar(), as just shown. Save the new file to disk as FAVKEY2.C. Compile and run!

The output is the same as for the first version of the program; and you still have to press the Enter key to enter your favorite key value.

- Yes, it seems silly that you have to type Enter when entering a single character. That's just the way getchar() works. (And I hate it.)
- There are ways to read the keyboard more interactively, where pressing the Enter key isn't required. I cover these methods in my book *C All-in-One Desk Reference For Dummies* (Wiley).

The putchar() function

The putchar() function, pronounced "püt-care," for "put character," is the opposite of the getchar() function; getchar() reads in a character from the keyboard, and putchar() displays a character on the screen. Here's the format, though you probably could have guessed it:

```
putchar(c);
```

c can be either a single-character variable or a character constant in single quotes:

```
putchar('c');
```

The character 'c' is displayed on the screen.

The following program shows how putchar() can be put to use in tossing up characters on the screen:

```
#include <stdio.h>

int main()
{
    puts("Press Enter:");
    getchar();
    putchar('H');
    putchar('e');
    putchar('l');
    putchar('l');
    putchar('o');
    putchar('!');
    putchar('\n');
    return(0);
}
```

Enter this source code as PUTHELLO.C. Double-check for errors. Compile and run:

```
Press Enter.
```

Do so. Then:

```
Hello!
```

Note that getchar() is used here merely to read the Enter key press; any value returned by getchar() isn't stored. When used in this format, getchar() still returns a value, but because it's not stored in a variable, the value is "lost." That's perfectly okay.

Beyond the `getchar()` dilemma, the program uses seven `putchar()` functions to display `Hello!` (plus a newline character) to the screen. It's a rather silly use of `putchar()`, but it works.

- The `putchar()` function is used to display a single character on the screen.
- You can also specify a character as an escape sequence or a code value with `putchar()` (see the next section).

Character Variables As Values

If you want, you can live your life secure in the knowledge that the `char` keyword sets aside storage space for single-character variables and strings. That's all well and good, and it gets you an A on the quiz. You can stop reading now, if you want.

The horrible truth is that a single-character variable is really a type of integer. It's a tiny integer, but an integer nonetheless. The reason that it isn't obvious is that treating a `char` as an integer is really a secondary function of the single-character variable. The primary purpose of single-character variables is to store characters. But they can be used as integers. It's twisted, so allow me to explain in detail.

The basic unit of storage in a computer is the byte. Your computer has so many bytes (or megabytes) of memory, the hard drive stores so many gigabytes, and so on. Each one of those bytes can be looked at as storing a single character of information. A *byte* is a character.

Without boring you with the details, know that a byte is capable of storing a value, from 0 to 255. That's the range of an unsigned `char` integer: from 0 to 255 (refer to Table 9-1, in Chapter 9). Because a character is a byte, the `char` can also be used to store those tiny integer values.

When the computer deals with characters, it doesn't really know an A from a B. It does, however, know the difference between 65 and 66. Internally, the computer uses the number 65 as a code representing the letter *A*. The letter *B* is code 66. In fact, all letters of the alphabet, number characters, symbols, and other assorted jots and tittles each have their own character codes. The coding scheme is referred to as *ASCII,* and a list of the codes and characters is in Appendix B.

Essentially, when you store the character A in a `char` variable, you place the value 65 into that variable. Internally, the computer sees only the 65 and, lo, it's happy. Externally, when the character is "displayed," an A shows up. That satisfies you and me, supposing that an A is what we want.

This is how `char` variables can be both integers and characters. The truth is, they *are* integers. However, they are treated like characters. The following program, WHICH.C, reads a character from the keyboard and displays it by using the `printf()` function. The trick with WHICH.C is that the character is displayed as both a character and a numeric, integer value. Such duality! Can you cope?

```
#include <stdio.h>

int main()
{
    char key;

    printf("Press a key on your keyboard:");
    key=getchar();
    printf("You pressed the '%c' key.\n",key);
    printf("Its ASCII value is %d.\n",key);
    return(0);
}
```

Save the file to disk, naming it WHICH.C.

Compile WHICH.C. If you get any errors, double-check the source code, fix it up, and recompile.

Run the final program. If you press the A key (and then Enter), the output on your screen looks something like this:

```
Press a key on your keyboard:A
You pressed the 'A' key.
Its ASCII value is 65.
```

The second `printf()` statement displays the key variable by using the `%c` placeholder. This placeholder tells `printf()` to display the variable as a character. In the third `printf()` statement, the variable is displayed by using the `%d` placeholder. That one tells `printf()` to display the variable as an integer value — which it does.

- All letters of the alphabet, symbols, and number keys on the keyboard have ASCII codes.
- ASCII code values range from 0 to 127.
- Code values higher than 127 — from 128 to 255 — are called *extended* ASCII codes. Those characters aren't standard on all computers, though they're pretty consistent on Windows PCs. It's just a technical snit.
- Appendix B lists all the ASCII characters and their values.
- Chapter 13 shows you how to "compare" one letter or ASCII character with another. What's being compared is really the character's code value, not its aesthetics.

Part III

Giving Your Programs the Ability to Run Amok

The 5th Wave By Rich Tennant

"I'm sure there will be a good job market when I graduate. I created a virus that will go off that year."

In this part . . .

The programs illustrated in the first two parts of this book have been top-down. That is, they are executed one line after another, from top to bottom. They make no deviations and have no change in the pattern, no creativity, no choice. Boring! But computer programs can do more than that.

To really make a program run amok, you can place a decision machine inside of it. That decision machine lets the program do one thing or another based on a comparison, such as "If the user types L, then go left and get eaten by the hungry elf." It's not a choice that the computer makes; the computer is dumb. But it's an alternative, which means that the program is capable of more than just chomping through instructions, one after the other.

In addition to making decisions, the computer is good at doing things over and over — without complaining! Combine decision-making with this love of repetition, and pretty soon you have programs that spin off into alternative universes, taking control of the computer with them! It's run-amok time!

Chapter 11

C More Math and the Sacred Order of Precedence

In This Chapter

- Reviewing the C math operators
- Incrementing variables
- Understanding the order of precedence
- Introducing My Dear Aunt Sally
- Using parentheses to control your math

Beware ye the dreadful math chapter! Bwaa-ha-ha!

Math is so terrifying to some people that I'm surprised there isn't some math-themed horror picture, or at least a ride at Disneyland. Pirates. Ghosts. Screaming Dolls. Disneyland *needs* math in order to terrify and thrill children of all ages. Ludwig von Drake would host. But I digress.

This chapter really isn't *the* dreadful math chapter, but it's my first lecture that dwells on math almost long enough to give you a headache. Don't panic! The computer does all the work. You're only required to assemble the math in the proper order for the answers to come out right. And, if you do it wrong, the C compiler tells you and you can start over. No embarrassment. No recriminations. No snickering from the way-too-smart female exchange student from Transylvania.

An All-Too-Brief Review of the Basic C Mathematical Operators

Table 11-1 shows the basic C mathematical operators (or it could be arithmetic operators — whatever). These symbols and scribbles make basic math happen in a C program.

Table 11-1 C's Mathematical Doodads

Operator or Symbol	*What You Expect*	*As Pronounced by Sixth Graders*	*Task*
+	+	"Plus"	Addition
-	–	"Minus"	Subtraction
*	×	"Times"	Multiplication
/	÷	"Divided by"	Division

You use the symbols to do the following types of math operations:

- **Work with values directly:**

  ```
  total = 6 + 194;
  ```

  The integer variable `total` contains the result of adding 6 and 194.

  In this example:

  ```
  result = 67 * 8;
  ```

  the variable `result` (which can be either an integer or a float variable) contains the result of multiplying 67 by 8:

  ```
  odds = 45/122;
  ```

  The float variable `odds` contains the result of dividing 45 by 122:

  In all cases, the math operation to the right of the equal sign is performed first. The math is worked from left to right by the C compiler. The value that results is placed in the numeric variable.

- **Work with values and variables:**

  ```
  score = points*10;
  ```

  The variable `score` is set equal to the value of the variable `points` times 10.

- **Work with just about anything; functions, values, variables, or any combination:**

  ```
  height_in_cm = atoi(height_in_inches)*2.54;
  ```

  The variable `height_in_cm` is set equal to the value returned by the `atoi` function times 2.54. The `atoi()` function manipulates the variable `height_in_inches` (which is probably a string input from the keyboard).

- The math part of the equation is calculated first and is worked from left to right. The result is then transferred to the variable sitting on the left side of the equal sign.

The old "how tall are you" program

You can use "the power of the computer" to do some simple yet annoying math. As an example, I present the HEIGHT.C program, with its source code shown next. This program asks you to enter your height in inches and then spits back the result in centimeters. Granted, it's a typically dull C language program. But, bear with me for a few pages and have some fun with it. Enter this trivial program into your editor:

```
#include <stdio.h>
#include <stdlib.h>

int main()
{
    float height_in_cm;
    char height_in_inches[4];

    printf("Enter your height in inches:");
    gets(height_in_inches);
    height_in_cm = atoi(height_in_inches)*2.54;
    printf("You are %.2f centimeters tall.\n",height_in_cm);
    return(0);
}
```

Be careful with what you type; some long variable names are in there. Also, it's *height*, not *hieght*. (I mention it because I tried to compile the program with that spelling mistake — not once, but twice!) Save the file to disk as HEIGHT.C.

Compile the program. Watch for any syntax or other serious errors. Fix them if they crop up.

Run the HEIGHT program. Your output looks something like this:

```
Enter your height in inches:60
You are 152.40 centimeters tall.
```

If you're 60 inches tall (5 feet exactly), that's equal to 152.40 centimeters — a bigger number, but you're still hovering at the same altitude. The program is good at converting almost any length in inches to its corresponding length in centimeters.

- *Height.* It has *e* before *i.* It's another example of why English is the worst-spelled language on the planet. (It's your number-one typo possibility if you get a syntax error in the program.)
- The `atoi()` function reaches into the string you enter and pulls out an integer value. And, it's `atoi()`, not `atio()` (*another* reason, though invalid, to hate English spelling).
- The `atoi()` function translates the value held in the string variable, `height_in_inches`, into an integer. Then that value is multiplied by `2.54`. (The asterisk is used for multiplication.) The result is then slid through the equal sign and stored in the float variable, `height_in_cm`.
- The value `2.54` is obviously a float because it contains a decimal part. `height_in_inches` is an integer because that's the type of value the `atoi()` function returns. When you multiply an integer by a float, however, the result is a float. That's why the `height_in_cm` variable is a float.
- An inch has 2.54 centimeters in. It's not that this knowledge gets you anywhere, at least not in the United States. However, if you're on *Jeopardy!* and the Final Jeopardy answer is 2.54, you'll know the question. (By the way, an easy mnemonic device for remembering how many centimeters are in an inch is to scream "two-point-five-four centimeters per inch" at the top of your lungs 30 times.)
- A centimeter equals 0.39 inches. A centimeter is really about as long as your thumbnail is wide —as long as you don't have colossal thumbs, of course.

Unethical alterations to the old "how tall are you" program

Though I'm not standing behind you, I can clearly see the HEIGHT.C program source code sitting in your editor. Good. Change Line 11 as follows:

```
height_in_cm = atoi(height_in_inches)*2.54*1.05;
```

After the `2.54` and before the semicolon, insert ***1.05** ("times one point-oh-five"). This increases your height by five-hundredths of a centimeter for each centimeter you have in height. The result? Wait! Save the file and recompile it. Then run it again:

```
Enter your height in inches:60
You are 160.02 centimeters tall.
```

That may not mean much to you. But suppose that you're corresponding with some French person who's romantically interested in you. If so, you can tell him or her that, according to a program run on your computer, you're

160.02 centimeters tall. That means nothing to an American, but it means that you're three whole inches taller in France. If you were 5'10" (70 inches), the program would produce the following:

```
Enter your height in inches:70
You are 186.69 centimeters tall.
```

Now, you're 186.69 centimeters tall — or 6'1½" tall! They'll swoon!

And now, the confession:

The purpose of this discussion is not to tell you how to cheat when you're programming a computer, nor is there any value in deceiving the French. For the most part, people who run programs want accurate results. However, it does show you the following:

```
height_in_cm = atoi(height_in_inches)*2.54*1.05;
```

The variable *height_in_cm* is equal to the result of three mathematical operations: First, an integer is produced based on the value of the string variable `height_in_inches`. That's multiplied by 2.54, and the result is multiplied again by 1.05.

Having a long mathematical formula is perfectly okay in C. You can add, multiply, divide, and whatnot all the time. To ensure that you always get the result you want, however, you must pay special attention to something called the order of precedence. That's the topic of a section later in this chapter.

- An equation in C can have more than two items. In fact, it can have a whole chorus line of items in it. The items must all be on the right, after the equal sign.
- TECHNICAL STUFF: To increase the height value by .05 (five-hundredths, or 5 percent), the number must be multiplied by 1.05. If you just multiply it by .05, you decrease it by 95 percent. Instead, you want to increase it by 5 percent, so you multiply it by 105 percent, or 1.05. I stumbled on this knowledge accidentally, by the way.

The Delicate Art of Incrementation (Or, "Just Add One to It")

The mathematical concept of "just add 1 to it" is called *incrementation.* You move something up a notch by incrementing it — for example, shifting from first to second, racking up another point in Gackle Blaster, or increasing your compensation by a dollar an hour. These are examples of incrementation.

Increasing the value of a variable in C happens all the time. It involves using this funky equation:

```
i=i+1;
```

This math problem serves one purpose: It adds 1 to the value of the variable *i*. It looks funny, but it works.

Suppose that i equals 3. Then i+1 (which is 3 + 1) equals 4. Because the right side of the equal sign is worked out first in C, the value 4 is slid over and put into the *i* variable. The preceding statement *increments* the value of the *i* variable by 1.

You can also use the equation to add more than 1 to a value. For example:

```
i=i+6;
```

This equation increments the value of the *i* variable by 6. (Purists will argue, though, that the word *increment* means strictly to "add one to." Then again, true purists wouldn't put any dressing on their salad, so what do they know anyway?)

- To add 1 to a variable — *i*, in this instance — you use the following C language mathematical-statement thing:

  ```
  i=i+1;
  ```

  This is known as incrementation.
- No, that's not *incrimination.* Different subject.
- Some examples of incrementing values are altitude as a plane (or space-ship) climbs; miles on an odometer; your age before and after your birthday; the number of fish the cat has eaten; and your weight over the holidays.
- Incrementation — i=i+1 — works because C figures out what's on the right side of the equal sign first. i+1 is done first. Then it replaces the original value of the *i* variable. It's when you look at the whole thing all at once (from left to right) that it messes with your brain.

Unhappily incrementing your weight

The following program is LARDO.C, a rather rude interactive program that uses math to increment your weight. You enter what you weigh, and then LARDO calculates your newfound bulk as you consume your holiday feast:

```
#include <stdio.h>
#include <stdlib.h>

int main()
{
    char weight[4];
    int w;

    printf("Enter your weight:");
    gets(weight);
    w-atoi(weight);

    printf("Here is what you weigh now: %d\n",w);
    w=w+1;
    printf("Your weight after the potatoes: %d\n",w);
    w=w+1;
    printf("Here you are after the mutton: %d\n",w);
    w=w+8;
    printf("And your weight after dessert: %d pounds!\n",w);
    printf("Lardo!\n");
    return(0);
}
```

Type the preceding source code into your text editor. The only truly new material in this example is the `w=w+1` equation, which increments the value of the *w* variable by one. The final equation, `w=w+8`, adds eight to the value of the *w* variable.

Check your typing and be mindful of semicolons and double quotes. Save the file to disk as LARDO.C.

Compile LARDO.C. Fix any errors, if need be.

The following sample of the program's final run uses 175 as the user's weight:

```
Enter your weight:175
Here is what you weigh now: 175
Your weight after the potatoes: 176
Here you are after the mutton: 177
And your weight after dessert: 185 pounds!
Lardo!
```

- This program doesn't need to be insulting — but what the hey! The idea in this example is to show how the `w=w+1` equation is used to add 1 to the value of a variable. It's called *incrementation.* (It's what God does to your weight every morning that you lug your pudgy legs onto the scale.)
- Yeah, 175 pounds! I'm sure that you typed an equally modest value rather than something more representative of your true girth.

Bonus program! (One that may even have a purpose in life)

Monopoly is perhaps one of the greatest board games ever invented, and it can be terrific fun — especially when you own rows of hotels and your pitiful opponents land on them like witless flies on a discarded all-day sucker. The only problem at that point is drawing the Community Chest card that proclaims the following:

> You are assessed for street repairs — $40 per house, $115 per hotel.

You count up all your houses and multiply that number by $40 and all the hotels by $115 (which is a strange number), and then you add the two values. It's a terrible thing to do to one's brain in the middle of a Monopoly game. But the mental drudgery can be easily abated by a simple computer program, one such as ASSESSED.C:

```
#include <stdio.h>
#include <stdlib.h>

int main()
{
      int houses, hotels, total;
      char temp[4];

      printf("Enter the number of houses:");
      gets(temp);
      houses=atoi(temp);

      printf("Enter the number of hotels:");
      gets(temp);
      hotels=atoi(temp);

      total=houses*40+hotels*115;

      printf("You owe the bank $%d.\n",total);
      return(0);
}
```

Carefully type this program into your editor on a new screen. Double-check your semicolons, parentheses, and quotes. Then save it to disk as ASSESSED.C.

Compile! Fix any errors, if need be. Then run the program. Suppose that you have nine houses and three hotels. Here's what your output looks like:

```
Enter the number of houses:9
Enter the number of hotels:3
You owe the bank $705.
```

Amazing how easy the computer could figure that out! Of course, at this point in the game, you can easily afford the $705 in funny money. All you need is for some poor sap to land on St. Charles Place with its hotel, and you make the money back jiffy pronto.

- Notice how the `temp` variable is used to hold and help convert two different strings into numbers? This example illustrates how variables can change and, well, be variable.
- The mathematical computation in Line 17 works because of something called the Sacred Order of Precedence, which is covered in the very next section.
- You may think, and rightly so, that the total displayed by the program should be a float variable. After all, dollar amounts usually have a decimal part: $705.00 rather than $705. But, in this case, because all the values are integers, it just makes more sense to stick with a `total` integer variable. Keep in mind that integers are faster, which is especially apparent in larger programs.

The Sacred Order of Precedence

Precedence refers to what comes first. The fact that the theater is on fire, for example, takes precedence over the fact that you'll miss the second act if you leave in a hurry.

The *order of precedence* is a double redundancy (which in itself is redundant several times over). It refers to which of the mathematical operators has priority over the others. For example, a plus sign just can't march into the middle of a group of numbers and expect to add things the way it wants to. In C, other mathematical operations are done before addition. It's just proper.

A problem from the pages of the dentistry final exam

Witness with your own eyes the following long and complex mathematical equation that may one day slink into one of your C programs:

```
answer = 100 + 5 * 2 - 60 / 3;
```

This question is one of those tough math questions from the dentistry final exam. Yes, most dentists would rather be pulling teeth — even their own. The preceding problem isn't really a problem for you, though. The computer figures the answer. But what is it?

Is the answer 50? One hundred plus 5 is 105; times 2 is 210; minus 60 is 150; divided by 3 is 50. Does the compiler force the computer to do that for you automatically? Or should the value 90 be placed into the `answer` variable?

Ninety? Yes, the value of the `answer` variable is 90. This all has to do with My Dear Aunt Sally and the order of precedence. Before getting into that, I show you the following program, DENTIST.C, which you can type to prove that the answer is 90 and not 50:

```
#include <stdio.h>

int main()
{
    printf("%d",100+5*2-60/3);
    return(0);
}
```

Enter this short and sweet program into your editor. Compile it. Run it. It's a `printf()` statement, with only `%d` in double quotes. That's followed by a comma and then the math question from the dentistry final.

Run the program. The result should shock you:

```
90
```

- The order of your mathematical equations is important. Not knowing how the C compiler works out its math means that you may not get the answer you want. That's why you have to know the order of precedence and, more importantly, My Dear Aunt Sally.
- When the DENTIST.C program runs, the computer works on the equation `100+5*2-60/3` first in the `printf()` function. The result is then passed over to the fill-in-the-blanks `%d` and is displayed on the screen.
- I could have expanded DENTIST.C to declare the `answer` integer variable, assign the value to that variable, and then use `printf()` to display the variable's contents. But, naaah. That would be too long of a program. The C language is full of short ways to do things. The `printf()` statement in DENTIST.C is just one example of a scrunched-up C program.

What's up, Sally?

My Dear Aunt Sally is a mnemonic device, or "a silly thing we say to remember something we would forget otherwise, which isn't saying much because we nearly always forget our own phone number and family birthdays." In this case, My Dear Aunt Sally is a mnemonic for

Multiplication

Division

Addition

Subtraction

MDAS is the order in which math is done in a long C language mathematical equation — the order of precedence.

The compiler scopes out an entire equation — the whole line — and does the multiplication first and then the division and then the addition and subtraction. Things just aren't from left to right any more. Figure 11-1 illustrates how the mathematical example in the preceding section figures out to be 90.

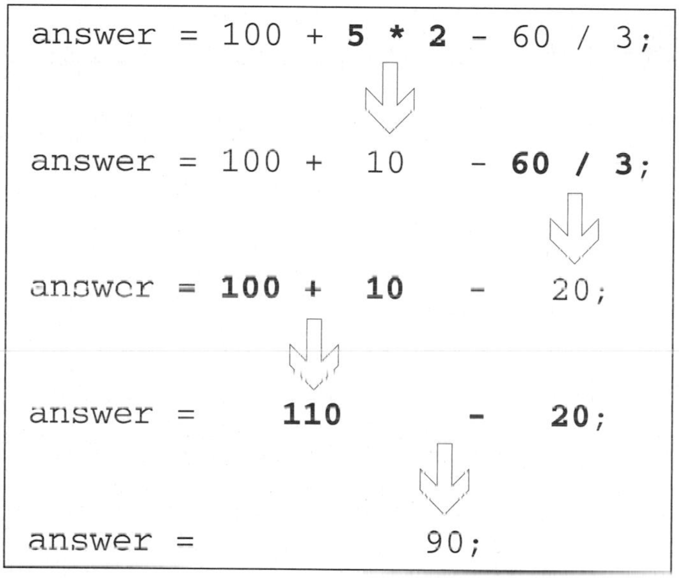
answer = 100 + 5 * 2 - 60 / 3;
answer = 100 + 10 - 60 / 3;
answer = 100 + 10 - 20;
answer = 110 - 20;
answer = 90;

Figure 11-1: How the C compiler figures out a long math function.

Here's another puzzle:

```
answer = 10 + 20 * 30 / 40;
```

In this statement, the multiplication happens first and then the division and then the addition. When the multiplication and division are next to each other, as in the preceding line, it goes from left to right.

When the computer is finished counting its thumbs and the preceding statement is resolved, the `answer` variable contains the value `25`. You can prove it by editing the DENTIST.C program and replacing the math that's already there, in the preceding math equation. Recompile and run the program to confirm that the answer is 25. Or, just trust me and let it go at that.

- *My Dear Aunt Sally. M*ultiplication (*), *d*ivision (/), *a*ddition (+), and *s*ubtraction (–) are done in that order in the C language's long mathematical equations.
- The reason that the order of precedence is important is that you must organize your mathematical equations if you expect the proper answer to appear.
- The ASSESSED.C program, from the preceding section, also takes advantage of the order of precedence:

  ```
  total=houses*40+hotels*115;
  ```

  The number of houses times 40 is worked out first, and then `hotels` times 115 is done second. The last step is to add the two.
- A way to control the order of precedence is by using parentheses, as discussed in the obviously named section "Using parentheses to mess up the order of precedence," later in this chapter.

The confounding magic-pellets problem

I hated those math-class story problems when I was a kid. In fact, I still do. In any event, here I am, in my adulthood, making up something like the following:

Suppose that you have 100 of these magic pellets. They double in quantity every 24 hours. After a day, you have 200. But, first you have to give 25 to the butcher in exchange for three dozen lamb's eyeballs for a casserole you want to surprise your spouse with. If so, how many magic pellets would you have the next day?

Don't bother stewing over the problem. The equation is

```
100 - 25 * 2;
```

That's 100 magic pellets minus 25 for the eyeballs and then times 2 (doubled) the next day. In your head, you can figure that 100 minus 25 is 75. Multiply 75 by 2 and you have 150 magic pellets the next day. But in C, this just wouldn't work; the order of precedence (that Sally person) would multiply 25 by 2 first. That would calculate to 50 magic pellets the next day. What a gyp!

The following C program, PELLETS.C, illustrates how the magic-pellet problem is confounded by C's order of precedence. This program is a somewhat more complex version of the basic DENTIST.C program, presented earlier in this chapter:

```
#include <stdio.h>

int main()
{
    int total;

    total=100-25*2;
    printf("Tomorrow you will have %d magic
          pellets.\n",total);
    return(0);
}
```

Enter this program in your editor. Double-check everything. Save the file to disk as PELLETS.C.

Compile PELLETS.C. Fix any errors.

Run the PELLETS program. Your output looks like this:

```
Tomorrow you will have 50 magic pellets.
```

Uh-huh. Try explaining that to the IRS. Your computer program, diligently entered, tells you that there are 50 pellets, when tomorrow you will really have 150. The extra 100? They were lost to the order of precedence. In the PELLETS.C program, addition must come first. The way that works is by using parentheses.

Using parentheses to mess up the order of precedence

My Dear Aunt Sally can be quite overbearing. She's insistent. Still, even though she means well, she goofs up sometimes. In the PELLETS.C program, for example, she tells the C compiler to multiply 25 by 2 first and then subtract the result from 100. Anyone who reads the problem knows that you must subtract 25 from 100 first and then multiply what's left by 2. The problem is convincing the C compiler — and Aunt Sally — how to do that.

REMEMBER

You can circumvent the order of precedence by using parentheses. When the C compiler sees parentheses, it quickly darts between them, figures out the math, and then continues with multiplication, division, addition, and subtraction, in that order, from left to right, outside the parentheses.

To fix the PELLETS.C program, you have to change the seventh line to read:

```
total=(100-25)*2;
```

The C compiler does the math in the parentheses first. So, at once, 25 is subtracted by 100, to equal 75. Then, the rest of the math is done: 75 times 2 is 150 — the correct number of magic pellets.

I beg of you to make the preceding change to Line 7 in your PELLETS.C program. Stick the left parenthesis before `100`, and insert the right one after `25`. Save the changes to disk, recompile, and then run the program. The result should please you:

```
Tomorrow you will have 150 magic pellets.
```

- The math that appears in the parentheses is always done first. It doesn't matter whether it's addition, subtraction — whatever. It's always done first in the equation.
- Inside the parentheses, the math is still worked from left to right. Also, multiplication and division still have priority inside the parentheses. It's just that whatever is in the parentheses is done before whatever is outside. Here's a summary for you:
  1. Work inside the parentheses first.
  2. Multiplication and division first, and addition and subtraction second.
  3. Work from left to right.
- If you have ever worked with complex spreadsheet equations, you're familiar with the way parentheses can be used to force some math operations to be done before others. And, if you don't use spreadsheets, then, hey — you have read about something in a C book that you can apply to your spreadsheeting. Such value.
- Yeah, you can even put parentheses inside parentheses. Just make sure that they match up; rogue parentheses produce syntax errors, just like missing double quotes and absent curly braces do.
- It doesn't matter where the parentheses are in the math equation; what's in them is always done first. For example:

```
total=2*(100-25);
```

In this statement, 100 minus 25 is calculated first. The result, 75, is then multiplied by 2. This holds true no matter how complex the equation gets — though I'm afraid that you may run away or faint if I show you a more complex example.

Chapter 12

C the Mighty `if` Command

In This Chapter

- Using the `if` statement
- Comparing values with `if`
- Formatting the `if` statements
- Handling exceptions with `else`
- Making multiple decisions

Okay, `if` isn't a command. It's *another* keyword in the C programming language, one that you can use in your program to make decisions — although it really makes comparisons, not decisions. It's the program that decides what to do based on the results of the comparison.

This chapter is about adding decision-making power to your programs by using the `if` command.

REMEMBER

Keep in mind that the computer doesn't decide what to do. Instead, it follows a careful path that you set down for it. It's kind of like instructing small children to do something, though with the computer, it always does exactly what you tell it to and never pauses eternally in front of the TV set or wedges a Big Hunk into the sofa.

If Only. . . .

The idea behind the `if` command is to have the computer handle some predictable yet unknown event: A choice is made from a menu; the little man in some game opens the door with the hydra behind it; or the user types something goofy. These are all events that happen, which the computer must deal with.

The `if` keyword allows you to put these types of decisions into your programs. The decisions are based on a comparison. For example:

- If the contents of variable *X* are greater than variable *Y*, scream like they're twisting your nose.
- If the contents of the variable *calories* are very high, it must taste very good.
- If it ain't broke, don't fix it.
- If Doug doesn't ask me out to the prom, I'll have to go with Charley.

All these examples show important decisions, similar to those you can make in your C programs by using the `if` keyword. However, in the C programming language, the `if` keyword's comparisons are kind of, sort of — dare I say it? — mathematical in nature. Here are more accurate examples:

- If the value of variable `A` is equal to the value of variable `B`
- If the contents of variable `ch` are less than 132
- If the value of variable `zed` is greater than 1,000,000

These examples are really simple, scales-of-justice evaluations of variables and values. The `if` keyword makes the comparison, and if the comparison is true, your program does a particular set of tasks.

- `if` is a keyword in the C programming language. It allows your programs to make decisions.
- `if` decides what to do based on a comparison of (usually) two items.
- The comparison that `if` makes is mathematical in nature: Are two items equal to, greater than, less than — and so on — to each other? If they are, a certain part of your program runs. If not, that part of the program doesn't run.
- The `if` keyword creates what is known as a *selection statement* in the C language. I wrote this topic down in my notes, probably because it's in some other C reference I have read at some time or another. *Selection statement.* Impress your friends with that term if you can remember it. Just throw your nose in the air if they ask what it means. (That's what I do.)

The computer-genie program example

The following program is GENIE1.C, one of many silly computer guess-the-number programs you write when you find out how to program. Computer scientists used to play these games for hours in the early days of the computer. They would probably drop dead if we could beam a Sony PlayStation back through time.

What GENIE1.C does is to ask for a number, from 0 through 9. You type that number at the keyboard. Then, using the magic of the `if` statement, the computer tells you whether the number you entered is less than 5. This program was a major thigh-slapper when it was first written in the early 1950s.

Enter the following source code into your text editor. The only new stuff comes with the `if` statement cluster, near the end of the program. Better double-double-check your typing.

```
#include <stdio.h>
#include <stdlib.h>

int main()
{
    char num[2];
    int number;

    printf("I am your computer genie!\n");

    printf("Enter a number from 0 to 9:");
    gets(num);
    number=atoi(num);

    if(number<5)
    {
        printf("That number is less than 5!\n");
    }

    printf("The genie knows all, sees all!\n");
    return(0);
}
```

Save the file to disk as GENIE1.C.

Compile GENIE1.C. If you see any errors, run back to your editor and fix them. Then recompile.

Run the final program. You see these displayed:

```
I am your computer genie!
Enter a number from 0 to 9:
```

Type a number, somewhere in the range of 0 through 9. For example, you can type 3. Press Enter and you see:

```
That number is less than 5!
The genie knows all, sees all!
```

- The `#include <stdlib.h>` part is necessary because the program uses the `atoi()` function.
- The `if` command is followed by parentheses, which contain the comparison that the `if` keyword tests.
- The comparison that `if` makes tests the value of the variable `number` with `5`. The `<` symbol between them means "less than." The test reads "If the value of the variable `number` is less than 5." If this is true, the cluster of statements following the `if` keyword is executed. If the test proves false, the cluster of statements is skipped.
- Remember the `<` — less than — from school? Good!
- Notice that the `if` test isn't followed by a semicolon! Instead, it's followed by a statement enclosed in curly braces. The statements (there can be more than one) "belong" to the `if` command and are executed only *if* the condition is true.
- If you see only the line `The genie knows all, sees all!`, you probably typed a number greater than 4 (which includes 5 and higher). The reason is that the `if` statement tests only for values *less than* 5. If the value is less than 5, `That number is less than 5!` is displayed. The next section elaborates on how it all works.
- No, the computer genie doesn't know all and see all if you type a number 5 or greater.
- Did you notice the extra set of curly braces in the middle of this program? That's part of how the `if` statement works. Also notice how they're indented.

The `if` keyword, up close and impersonal

It's unlike any other C language word you have seen. The `if` keyword has a unique format, with plenty of options and room for goofing things up. Yet, it's a handy and powerful thing that you can put in your programs — something you use a lot.

The `if` keyword is used to make decisions in your programs. It makes a comparison. If the result is true, the rest of the `if` statement is executed. If the comparison isn't true, the program skips over the rest of the `if` statement, as shown in Figure 12-1.

The `if` statement is a statement "block" that can look like this:

```
if(comparison)
{
        statement;
        [statement;...]
}
```

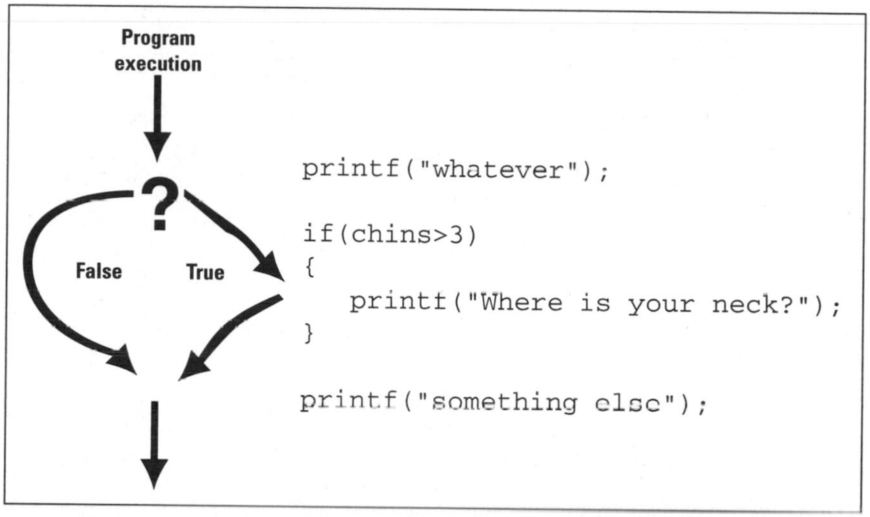
Program execution
?
False
True
printf("whatever");
if(chins>3)
{
printf("Where is your neck?");
}
printf("something else");

Figure 12-1: How `if` affects a program.

`if` is followed by a set of parentheses in which a *comparison* is made. The comparison is mathematical in nature, using the symbols shown in Table 12-1. What's being compared is usually the value of a variable against a constant value, or two variables against each other. (See Table 12-1 for examples.)

If the result of the comparison is true, the *statement* (or group of statements) between the curly braces is executed. If the result is false, the stuff in the curly braces is conveniently skipped over — ignored like a geeky young lad at his first high school dance and with a zit the size of Houston on his chin.

Yes, the curly braces that follow `if` can contain more than one statement. And, each of the statements ends with a semicolon. All are enclosed in the curly braces. It's technically referred to as a *code block*. It shows you which statements "belong" to `if`. The whole darn thing is part of the `if` statement.

Table 12-1 Operators Used in `if` Comparisons

Comparison	*Meaning or Pronunciation*	*"True" Examples*
<	Less than	1 < 5
		8 < 9
==	Equal to	5 == 5
		0 == 0

(continued)

Table 12-1 *(continued)*

Comparison	*Meaning or Pronunciation*	*"True" Examples*
>	Greater than	8 > 5
		10 > 0
<=	Less than or equal to	4 <= 5
		8 <= 8
>=	Greater than or equal to	9 >= 5
		2 >= 2
!=	Not equal to	1 != 0
		4 != 3.99

The GENIE1 program, from the preceding section, uses this `if` statement:

```
if(number<5)
{
    printf("That number is less than 5!\n");
}
```

The first line is the `if` keyword and its comparison in parentheses. What's being compared is the value of the numeric variable `number` and the constant value `5`. The comparison is "less than." Is `number` less than 5? If so, the statement in curly braces is executed. If not, the whole deal is skipped over.

Consider these modifications:

```
if(number==5)
{
    printf("That number is 5!\n");
}
```

Now, the comparison is `number==5`? (Is the number that is entered equal to five?) If it is, the `printf()` statement displays `That number is 5!`

These changes compare the value of `number` with `5` again:

```
if(number>=5)
{
    printf("That number is more than 4!\n");
}
```

This time, the test is greater than *or* equal to: Is the number that is entered 5 or more than 5? If the number is greater than or equal to 5, it must be more than 4, and the `printf()` statement goes on to display that important info on the screen.

The following modification to the GENIE1.C program doesn't change the `if` comparison, as in the previous examples. Instead, it shows you that more than one statement can belong to `if`:

```
if(number<5)
{
    printf("That number is less than 5!\n");
    printf("By goodness, aren't I smart?\n");
}
```

Everything between the curly braces is executed when the comparison is true. Advanced C programs may have lots of stuff in there; as long as it's between the curly braces, it's executed only `if` the comparison is true. (That's why it's indented — so that you know that it all belongs to the `if` statement.)

- The comparison that `if` makes is usually between a variable and a value. It can be a numeric or single-character variable.
- `if` cannot compare strings. For information on comparing strings, refer to my book *C All-in-One Desk Reference For Dummies* (Wiley).
- Less than and greater than and their ilk should be familiar to you from basic math. If not, you should know that you read the symbols from left to right: The > symbol is *greater than* because the big side comes first; the < is *less than* because the lesser side comes first.
- The symbols for less than or equal to and greater than or equal to always appear that way: <= and >=. Switching them the other way generates an error.
- The symbol for "not" in C is the exclamation point. So, != means "not equal." What is !TRUE (not-true) is FALSE. "If you think that it's butter, but it's !." No, I do ! want to eat those soggy zucchini chips.
- When you're making a comparison to see whether two things are equal, you use *two* equal signs. I think of it this way: When you build an `if` statement to see whether two things are equal, you think in your head "is equal" rather than "equals." For example:

  ```
  if(x==5)
  ```

  Read this statement as "If the value of the `x` variable *is equal* to `5`, then. . . ." If you think "equals," you have a tendency to use only one equal sign — which is very wrong.

- If you use one equal sign rather than two, you don't get an error; however, the program is wrong. The nearby Technical Stuff sidebar attempts to explain why.
- If you have programmed in other computer languages, keep in mind that the C language has no `2ewd` or `fi` word. The final curly brace signals to the compiler that the `if` statement has ended.
- Also, no `then` word is used with `if`, as in the `if-then` thing they have in the BASIC or Pascal programming language.

A question of formatting the `if` statement

The `if` statement is your first "complex" C language statement. The C language has many more, but `if` is the first and possibly the most popular, though I doubt that a popularity contest for programming language words has ever been held (and, then again, `if` would be great as Miss Congeniality but definitely come up a little thin in the swimsuit competition).

Though you probably have seen the `if` statement used only with curly braces, it can also be displayed as a traditional C language statement. For example, consider the following — one of the modifications from the GENIE1 program:

```
if(number==5)
{
    printf("That number is 5!\n");
}
```

In C, it's perfectly legitimate to write this as a more traditional type of statement. To wit:

```
if(number==5) printf("That number is 5!\n");
```

This line looks more like a C language statement. It ends in a semicolon. Everything still works the same; if the value of the number variable is equal to `5`, the `printf()` statement is executed. If `number` doesn't equal `5`, the rest of the statement is skipped.

Although all this is legal and you aren't shunned in the C programming community for using it, I recommend using curly braces with your `if` statements until you feel comfortable reading the C language.

Clutter not thy head with this comparison nonsense

The comparison in the `if` statement doesn't have to use any symbols at all! Strange but true. What the C compiler does is to figure out what you have put between the parentheses. Then it weighs whether it's true or false.

For a comparison using <, >, ==, or any of the horde in Table 12-1, the compiler figures out whether the comparison is true or false. However, you can stick just about anything — any valid C statement — between the parentheses and the compiler determines whether it works out to true or false. For example:

```
if(input=1)
```

This `if` statement doesn't figure out whether the value of the `input` variable is equal to 1. No, you need *two* equal signs for that. Instead, what happens between these parentheses is that the numeric variable `input` is given the value `1`. It's the same as

```
input=1;
```

The C compiler obeys this instruction, stuffing 1 into the `input` variable. Then, it sits back and strokes its beard and thinks, "Does that work out to be true or false?" Not knowing any better, it figures that the statement must be true. It tells the `if` keyword, and the cluster of statements that belong to the `if` statement are then executed.

The final solution to the income-tax problem

I have devised what I think is the fairest and most obviously well-intentioned way to decide who must pay the most in income taxes. You should pay more taxes if you're taller and more taxes if it's warmer outside. Yessir, it would be hard to dodge this one.

This problem is ideal for the `if` keyword to solve. You pay taxes based on either your height or the temperature outside, multiplied by your favorite number and then 10. Whichever number is higher is the amount of tax you pay. To figure out which number is higher, the program TAXES.C uses the `if` keyword with the greater-than symbol. It's done twice — once for the height value and again for the temperature outside:

```
#include <stdio.h>
#include <stdlib.h>

int main()
{
    int tax1,tax2;
    char height[4],temp[4],favnum[5];

    printf("Enter your height in inches:");
    gets(height);
    printf("What temperature is it outside?");
    gets(temp);
    printf("Enter your favorite number:");
    gets(favnum);

    tax1 = atoi(height) * atoi(favnum);
    tax2 = atoi(temp) * atoi(favnum);

    if(tax1>tax2)
    {
        printf("You owe $%d in taxes.\n",tax1*10);
    }
    if(tax2>=tax1)
    {
        printf("You owe $%d in taxes.\n",tax2*10);
    }
    return(0);
}
```

This program is one of the longer ones in this book. Be extra careful when you're typing it. It has nothing new in it, but it covers almost all the information I present in the first several chapters. Double-check each line as you type it into your editor.

Save the file to disk as TAXES.C.

Compile TAXES.C. Fix any errors you see.

Run the program:

```
Enter your height in inches:
```

Type your height in inches. Five feet is 60 inches; six feet is 72 inches. The average person is 5'7" tall or so — 67 inches. Press Enter.

```
What temperature is it outside?
```

Right now, in the bosom of winter in the Pacific Northwest, it's 18 degrees. That's Fahrenheit, by the way. Don't you dare enter the smaller Celsius number. If you do, the IRS will hunt you down like a delinquent country music star and make you pay, pay, pay.

```
Enter your favorite number:
```

Type your favorite number. Mine is 11. Press Enter.

If I type 72 (my height), 18, and 11, for example, I see the following result, due April 15:

```
You owe $7920 in taxes.
```

Sheesh! And I thought the old system was bad. I guess I need a smaller favorite number.

- The second `if` comparison is "greater than or equal to." This catches the case when your height is equal to the temperature. If both values are equal, the values of both the `tax1` and `tax2` variables are equal. The first `if` comparison, "`tax1` is greater than `tax2`," fails because both are equal. The second comparison, "`tax1` is greater than or equal to `tax2`," passes when `tax1` is greater than `tax2` or when both values are equal.
- TIP: If you enter zero as your favorite number, the program doesn't say that you owe any tax. Unfortunately, the IRS does not allow you to have zero — or any negative numbers — as your favorite number. Sad, but true.

If It Isn't True, What Else?

Hold on to that tax problem!

No, not the one the government created. Instead, hold on to the TAXES.C source code introduced in the preceding section. If it's already in your text editor, great. Otherwise, open it in your editor for editing.

The last part of the TAXES.C program consists of two `if` statements. The second `if` statement, which should be near Line 23 in your editor, really isn't necessary. Rather than use `if` in that manner, you can take advantage of another word in the C language, `else`.

Change Line 23 in the TAXES.C program. It looks like this now:

```
if(tax2>=tax1)
```

Edit that line: Delete the `if` keyword and the comparison in parentheses and replace it with this:

```
else
```

That's it — just `else` by itself. No comparison and no semicolon, and make sure that you type it in lowercase.

Save the file back to disk.

Compile TAXES.C. Run the final result. The output is the same because the program hasn't changed (and assuming that it hasn't gotten any warmer and you haven't grown any taller in the past few moments). What you have done is to create an `if-else` *structure,* which is another way to handle the decision-making process in your C programs.

- The `else` keyword is a second, optional part of an `if` cluster of statements. It groups together statements that are to be executed when the condition that `if` tests for isn't true.
- Or else what?
- Alas, if you enter the same values as in the old program, you still owe the same bundle to Uncle Sam.

Covering all the possibilities with `else`

The `if-else` keyword combination allows you to write a program that can make either-or decisions. By itself, the `if` keyword can handle minor decisions and execute special instructions if the conditions are just so. But when `if` is coupled with `else`, your program takes one of two directions, depending on the comparison `if` makes. Figure 12-2 illustrates how this can happen.

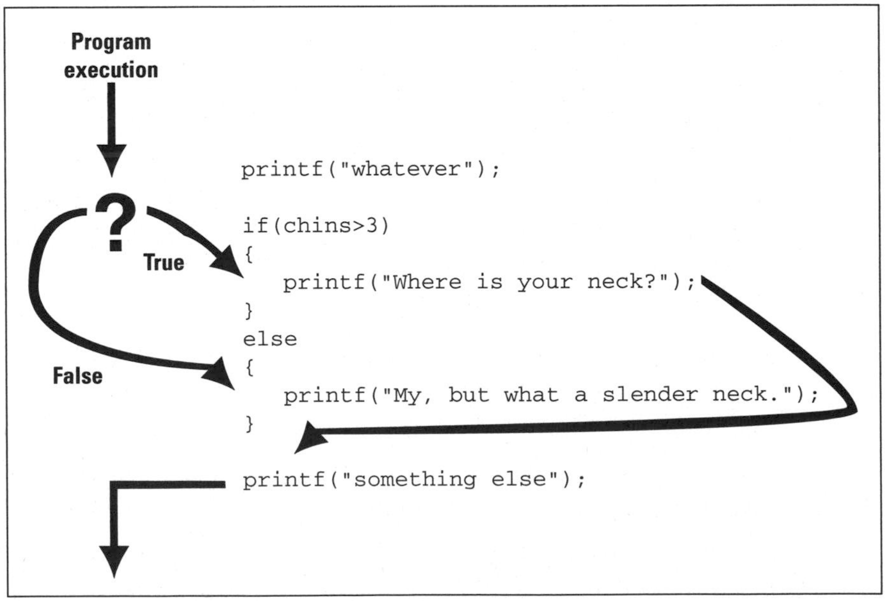

Figure 12-2: How `if` and `else` affect a program.

If the comparison is true, the statements belonging to the if statement are executed. But, if the comparison is false, the statements belonging to the else are executed. The program goes one way or the other, as illustrated in Figure 12-2. Then, after going its own way, the statement following the else's final curly brace is executed, like this: "You guys go around the left side of the barn, we'll go around the right, and we'll meet you on the other side."

The if *format with* else

The else keyword is used in an if statement. The keyword holds its own group of statements to be executed (okay, "obeyed") when the if comparison isn't true. Here's the format:

```
if(comparison)
{
        statement(s);
}
else
{
        statement(s);
}
```

The if keyword tests the comparison in parentheses. If it's a true comparison — no foolin' — the statements that appear in curly braces right after the if statement are executed. But, if the comparison is false, those statements following the else keyword and enclosed in curly braces are executed. One way or another, one group of statements is executed and the other isn't.

The else keyword, like all words in the C language, is in lowercase. It isn't followed by a semicolon. Instead, a set of curly braces follows the else. The curly braces enclose one or more statements to be run when the comparison that if makes isn't true. Notice that those statements each must end in a semicolon, obeying the laws of C first etched in stone by the ancient Palo Altoites.

The statements belonging to the else keyword are executed when the condition that the if keyword evaluates is false. Table 12-2 illustrates how it works, showing you the opposite conditions for the comparisons that an if keyword would make.

Table 12-2 `if` Comparisons and Their Opposites

`if` *Comparison*	`else` *Statement Executed By This Condition*
<	>= (Greater than or equal to)
==	!= (Not equal to)
>	<= (Less than or equal to)
<=	> (Greater than)
>=	< (Less than)
!=	== (Is equal to)

- I don't know about you, but I think that all those symbols in Table 12-2 would certainly make an interesting rug pattern.
- The `else` keyword is used only with `if`.
- Both `if` and `else` can have more than one statement enclosed in their curly braces. `if`'s statements are executed when the comparison is true; `else`'s statements are executed when the comparison is false.
- To *execute* means to run. C programs execute, or run, statements from the top of the source code (the first line) to the bottom. Each line is executed one after the other unless statements like `if` and `else` are encountered. In that case, the program executes different statements, depending on the comparison that `if` makes.
- When your program doesn't require an either-or decision, you don't have to use `else`. For example, the TAXES program has an either-or decision. But, suppose that you're writing a program that displays an error message when something doesn't work. In that case, you don't need `else`; if an error doesn't occur, the program should continue as normal.
- If you're the speaker of another programming tongue, notice that the C language has no `end-else` word in it. This isn't smelly old Pascal, for goodness' sake. The final curly brace signals the end of the `else` statement, just as it does with `if`.

The strange case of `else-if` *and even more decisions*

The C language is rich with decision making. The `if` keyword helps if you need to test for only one condition. True or false, `if` handles it. And, if it's true, a group of statements is executed. Otherwise, it's skipped over. (After the `if`'s group of statements is executed, the program continues as before.)

Silly formatting trivia

The `if-else` structure need not be heavy-laden with curly braces. Just as you can abbreviate an `if` statement to one line, you can also abbreviate `else`. I don't recommend it, which is why I'm terribly brief and don't ever show a program that illustrates examples this crudely:

```
if(tax1>tax2)
{
     printf("You owe $%i in
    taxes.\n",tax1*10);
}
else
{
     printf("You owe $%i in
    taxes.\n",tax2*10);
}
```

In this example, you see the meat and potatoes of the TAXES.C program: the `if-else` structure. Because both `if` and `else` have only one statement belonging to them, you can abbreviate the source code this way:

```
if(tax1>tax2)
     printf("You owe $%i in
    taxes.\n",tax1*10);
else
     printf("You owe $%i in
    taxes.\n",tax2*10);
```

This format keeps the indenting intact, which is one way to see what belongs to what (and also to easily identify the `if-else` structure). The following format is also possible, though it makes the program hard to read:

```
if(tax1>tax2) printf("You owe
    $%i in taxes.\n",tax1*10);
else printf("You owe $%i in
    taxes.\n",tax2*10);
```

Everything is scrunched up on two lines; the `if` statement has its own line, and the `else` has its own line. Both lines end with a semicolon, which is how this works as two statements in the C language. But, look-it. It's gross! Please don't write your programs this way.

You can do this trick — eliminating the curly braces — whenever only one statement appears with an `if` or `else` keyword. If multiple statements must be executed, you're required by law to use the curly braces. That's why I recommend them all the time: No sense risking prison over brevity. To wit:

```
if(tax1>tax2)
     printf("You owe $%i in
    taxes.\n",tax1*10);
else
{
     printf("You owe $%i in
    taxes.\n",tax2*10);
     printf("It pays to live
    where it's cold!\n");
}
```

Because two `printf` statements belong to the preceding `else`, the curly braces are required.

Either-or conditions are the daily bread of the `if-else` duo. Either way, one set of statements is executed and not the other, depending on the comparison made by `if`.

What about "one, two, or the third" types of decisions? For them, you need the miraculous and overly versatile `else-if` combination. It really drives you batty, but it's handy.

The following program is a modification of the GENIE1.C source code, as shown earlier in this chapter. This time, the `else-if` combination is used to allow the computer genie to accurately report whether the number is less than 5, equal to 5, or greater than 5:

```
#include <stdio.h>
#include <stdlib.h>

int main()
{
    char num[2];
    int number;

    printf("I am your computer genie!\n");

    printf("Enter a number from 0 to 9:");
    gets(num);
    number=atoi(num);

    if(number<5)
    {
        printf("That number is less than 5!\n");
    }
    else if(number==5)
    {
        printf("You typed in 5!\n");
    }
    else
    {
        printf("That number is more than 5!\n");
    }

    printf("The genie knows all, sees all!\n");
    return(0);
}
```

Start working on this source code by loading the GENIE1.C source code I show you how to create earlier in this chapter. Make modifications so that the latter part of the program looks like the new, GENIE2.C source code that was just listed.

Watch your indenting. Pay attention to everything; two equal signs are in the `else-if` comparison. Pay attention to where semicolons go and where they don't go.

After inserting the new lines, save the file to disk as GENIE2.C.

Compile GENIE2.C. If the error monster rears its ugly head, reedit the source code and then recompile.

Run the final result and see how much more clairvoyant the computer genie has become. Type **3** and see `That number is less than 5!` Type **9** and see `That number is more than 5!` Type **5** and the genie knows: `You typed in 5!`

- The `else-if` comparison resembles combined `else` and `if` statements. The second `if` comes right after `else` and a space. Then, it has its own comparison statement, which is judged either true or false.
- In GENIE2.C, the `else-if` comparison is `number==5`, testing to see whether the value of the `number` variable is `5`. Two equal signs are used for this comparison.
- You can do `else-if`, `else-if`, `else-if` all day long, if you want. However, the C language has a better solution in the `select-case` structure. I cover this topic in this book's companion volume, *C All-in-One Desk Reference For Dummies* (Wiley).

Bonus program! The really, really smart genie

A solution always exists. If you wanted to, you could write a program that would `if`-compare any value, from zero to infinity and back again, and the "computer genie" would accurately guess it. But, why bother with `if` at all?

Okay, the `if` keyword is the subject of this section, along with `if-else` and `else-if` and so on. But, the following source code for GENIE3.C doesn't use `if` at all. It cheats so that the genie always guesses correctly:

```
#include <stdio.h>

int main()
{
        char num;

        printf("I am your computer genie!\n");

        printf("Enter a number from 0 to 9:");
        num = getchar();

        printf("You typed in %c!\n",num);

        printf("The genie knows all, sees all!\n");
        return(0);
}
```

You can create this source code by editing either GENIE1.C or GENIE2.C. Make the necessary modifications and then save the source code to disk as GENIE3.C.

Compile the program. Fix any errors that you (hopefully) don't get. Run the result:

```
I am your computer genie!
Enter a number from 0 to 9:8
You typed in 8!
The genie knows all, sees all!
```

Run the program again and again with different numbers. Hey! That genie knows exactly what you typed! I wonder how that happened? It must be your deftness with the C language. Tame that computer!

- The problem with GENIE3.C? It doesn't make a decision. The genie isn't smart at all — it's just repeating what you already know. The purpose behind `if`, `else`, and the others is that they allow you to make a decision in your program.
- Refer to Chapter 10 for more information about the `getchar()` function.

Chapter 13

What If C==C?

In This Chapter

- Comparing characters with `if`
- Understanding standard input
- Fixing the flaws of `getchar()`
- Making a yes-or-no decision

Apologies are in order for the preceding chapter. Yes, I definitely drift into Number Land while introducing the virtues of the `if` command. Computer programs aren't all about numbers, and the judgment that the `if` keyword makes isn't limited to comparing dollar amounts, ecliptic orbits, subatomic particle masses, or calories in various fudgy cookie snacks. No, you can also compare letters of the alphabet in an `if` statement. That should finally answer the mystery of whether the *T* is "greater than" the *S* and why the dollar sign is less than the minus sign. This chapter explains the details.

The World of `if` without Values

I ask you: How can one compare two letters of the alphabet? Truly, this subject is right up there with "How many angels can dance on the head of a pin?" and "Would it be a traditional dance, gavotte, rock, or perhaps heavenly hokey-pokey?"

Yet, comparing letters is a necessary task. If you write a menu program, you have to see whether the user selects option A, B, or C. That's done by using the handy `if` keyword. For example:

```
if(key=='A')
```

Here, `key` is a single-character variable holding input from the keyboard. The comparison that `if` makes is to see whether the content of that variable *is equal to* (two equal signs) the letter *A,* which is enclosed in single quotes. This comparison is legitimate. Did the user type an A?

- To compare a single-character variable with a character — letter, number, or symbol — you must enclose that character in single quotes. Single character, single quotes.
- When `if` tests to see whether two things are equal, two equal signs are used. Think "is equal to" rather than "equals."
- When you compare a variable — numeric or single character — to a constant, the variable always comes first in the comparison.
- On a good day, 4.9E3 angels can dance on the head of a pin, given the relative size of the pin and the size of the angels and whether they're dancing all at once or taking turns.
- When you compare two letters or numbers, what you're 'really comparing are their ASCII code values. This is one of those weird instances when the single-character variable acts more like an integer than a letter, number, or symbol.

Which is greater: S or T, $ or –?

Is the T greater than the S? Alphabetically speaking, yes. *T* comes after *S.* But, what about the dollar sign and the minus sign? Which of those is greater? And, why should *Q* be lesser than *U,* because everyone knows that *U* always follows *Q?* Hmmm.

Computers and math (do I even have to remind you to skip this stuff?)

Sad to say, too much about computers does deal with math. The computer evolved from the calculator, which has its roots in the abacus, which is somehow related to human fingers and thumbs. After all, working with numbers is called *computing,* which comes from the ancient Latin term *computare.* That word literally means "hire a few more accountants and we'll never truly know what's going on."

Another word for *compute* is *reckon,* which is popular in the South as "I reck'n." Another word for *compute* is *figure,* which is popular in the !South (not-South) as "I figure." Computers reckon. Go figure.

To solve this great mystery of life, I list next the source code for a program, GREATER.C. It asks you to enter two single characters. These characters are compared by an `if` statement as well as by `if-else`. The greater of the two is then displayed. Although this program doesn't lay to rest the angels-on-the-head-of-a-pin problem, it soothes your frayed nerves over some minor alphabetic conundrums:

```
#include <stdio.h>

int main()
{
    char a,b;

    printf("Which character is greater?\n");
    printf("Type a single character:");
    a=getchar();
    printf("Type another character:");
    b=getchar();

    if(a > b)
    {
        printf("'%c' is greater than '%c'!\n",a,b);
    }
    else if (b > a)
    {
        printf("'%c' is greater than '%c'!\n",b,a);
    }
    else
    {
        printf("Next time, don't type the same character
           twice.");
    }
    return(0);
}
```

Enter the source code for GREATER.C into your editor. Make sure that you enter all the proper curly braces, confirm the locations of semicolons, watch your double quotes, and pay attention to the other minor nuances (or nuisances) of the C language.

Save the file to disk as GREATER.C.

Compile GREATER.C.

Run the final program. You're asked this question:

```
Which character is greater?
Type a single character:
```

Type a character, such as the **$** (dollar sign). Press Enter after typing the character.

Uh-oh! What happened? You see something like this:

```
Type another character:'$' is greater than '
'$
```

```
What? What? What?
```

You bet! A problem. Right in the middle of the chapter that talks about comparing single-character variables, I have to totally pick up the cat and talk about something else vital in C programming: properly reading single characters from the keyboard.

The problem with getchar()

Despite what it says in the brochure, `getchar()` *does not* read a single character from the keyboard. That's what the `getchar()` function *returns,* but it's not what the function does.

Internally, `getchar()` reads what's called *standard input.* It grabs the first character you type and stores it, but afterward it sits and waits for you to type something that signals "the end."

Two characters signal the end of input: The Enter key is one. The second is the EOF, or end-of-file, character. In Windows, it's the Ctrl+Z character. In the Unix-like operating systems, it's Ctrl+D.

Run the GREATER program, from the preceding section. When it asks for input, type **123** and then press the Enter key. Here's what you see for output:

```
Which character is greater?
Type a single character:123
Type another character:'2' is greater than '1'
```

When you're first asked to type a single character, you provide standard input for the program: the string `123` plus the press of the Enter key.

The `getchar()` function reads standard input. First, it reads the `1` and places it in the variable *a* (Line 9 in GREATER.C). Then, the program uses a second `getchar()` function to read again from standard input — but it has already been supplied; `2` is read into the variable *b* (refer to Line 11).

The 3? It's ignored; there's no place to store it. But, the Enter key press signifies to the program that standard input was entered and the program continued, immediately displaying the result, all on the final line:

```
Type another character:'2' is greater than '1'!
```

You may think that one way around this problem is to terminate standard input by pressing the Enter key right after entering the first character. After all, Enter ends standard input. But, it doesn't work that way.

Run the GREATER program again — this time, entering **$** and pressing the Enter key at the first prompt. Here's the output:

```
Which character is greater?
Type a single character:$

Type another character:'$' is greater than '
'!
```

This matches what you probably saw the first time you entered the program. See the Enter key displayed? It's what separates the ' at the end of the third line and the ' at the beginning of the fourth line.

In this case, the Enter key itself is being accepted as standard input. After all, Enter is a key on the keyboard and a proper character code, just like anything else. That rules out Enter as a proper way to end standard input. That leaves you with the EOF character.

Run the GREATER program one more time:

```
Which character is greater?
Type a single character:
```

In Windows, type **$** and then press Ctrl+Z and Enter.

In Unix, type **$** and then pressCtrl+D.

```
Type another character:
```

Then you can type **2** and press Enter:

```
'2' is greater than '$'!
```

The program finally runs properly, but only after you brute-force the end of standard input so that `getchar()` can properly process it. Obviously, explaining something like that to the users who run your programs would be bothersome. You have a better solution. Keep reading.

- In Windows, the end-of-file (EOF) character is Ctrl+Z. That's ASCII code 27.
- In Unix (Linux, FreeBSD, Mac OS, and so on), the end-of-file (EOF) character is Ctrl+D. That's ASCII code 4.
- To properly enter Ctrl+Z in Windows, you must press Ctrl+Z and then the Enter key. In Unix, the Ctrl+D combo works instantly.
- Be careful when you press Ctrl+D at your Unix command prompt! In many instances, Ctrl+D is also the key that terminates the shell, logging you off.

Fixing GREATER.C to easily read standard input

The easy way to fix GREATER.C is to ensure that all standard input is cleared out — purged or flushed — before the second `getchar()` function reads it. That way, old characters hanging around aren't mistakenly read.

The C language function `fflush()` is used to clear out information waiting to be written to a file. Because C treats standard input as a type of file, you can use `fflush()` to clear out standard input. Here's the format:

```
fflush(stdin);
```

You can insert this statement into any program at any point where you want to ensure that no leftover detritus can accidentally be read from the keyboard. It's a handy statement to know.

To fix the GREATER.C source code, you need to stick the `fflush()` function in after the first `getchar()` function — at Line 10. This code snippet shows you how the fixed-up source code should look:

```
printf("Type a single character:");
a=getchar();
fflush(stdin);
printf("Type another character:");
b=getchar();
```

Add the new Line 10, as shown here, to your source code for GREATER.C. Save the changes to disk. Compile and run the result. The program now properly runs — and you can continue reading about comparing characters with the `if` command.

TIP

If using `fflush(stdin)` doesn't work, replace it with this function:

```
fpurge(stdin);
```

The `fpurge()` function specifically erases text waiting to be read. I have noticed that it's required for Unix, Linux, and Mac OS programs.

"Can I get `getchar()` to read only one character?"

Alas, the `getchar()` function isn't a keyboard-reading function *per se.* What it really does is read standard input, which for nearly all computers I have used is text typed at the keyboard.

To read the keyboard, you need a specific function. Some versions of GCC for Windows use the `getch()` and `getche()` functions, which can read text directly from the keyboard and lack the standard input problems of `getchar()`. The problem with illustrating these functions in this book is that they don't have a Unix counterpart.

To read the keyboard directly in Unix, you have to access the *terminal* being used and then interpret which keyboard codes are being generated. Another solution is to use the Curses programming library.

Alas, this book doesn't have room to describe all these keyboard-reading functions. Instead, I recommend that you pick up this book's companion, *C All-in-One Desk Reference For Dummies* (Wiley).

Meanwhile, back to the GREATER problem

Now that you may have ironed out the problem with `getchar()` in the GREATER program, it's time to examine the output. Run the program again, just for old time's sake. Try to see whether the '–' character is greater than the '$'.

```
Which character is greater?
Type a single character:-

Type another character:$
'-' is greater than '$'!
```

And, why is that?

You see, the `if` command doesn't know squat about letters, numbers, or symbols. Rather than compare the character's physique, `if` compares the character's corresponding ASCII code values.

The ASCII code value for the minus sign is 45. The code value for the dollar sign is 36. Because 36 is less than 45, the computer thinks that the `'-'` is greater than the `'$'`. This also holds true for letters of the alphabet and their ASCII code values.

In real life, rarely do you compare one letter to another. Instead, you compare whatever keystroke was entered with a known, desired choice. I cover this topic in the next section.

- See Appendix B for a gander at ASCII values.
- Run the program again and try typing these two letters: **a** (little *a*) and **Z**. The big Z is less than the little *A*, even though *A* comes before *Z* in the alphabet. The reason is that the ASCII code has two alphabets: one for uppercase letters and another for lowercase. The uppercase letters have smaller values than the lowercase letters do, so `"a-z"` always is greater than `"A-Z"`.

Severely boring trivia on the nature of "alphabetical order"

So why is it A, B, C first, and why does Z come last? The answer is buried in the bosom of trivia, which most computer junkies are also fond of memorizing. Because I was curious, I thought I would look it up. And, lo, here's what I found.

Our alphabet is based on ancient alphabets, which in turn are based on even older, dinosaur-age alphabets. Back in those days, the letters they used were based on symbols for various things they encountered in everyday life, and the symbols were often named after those things as well: The letter *A* was named after and shaped like the ox, an important beast. B was named after a house and shaped like a door. And so on for all the letters. That's how it was for most of the early Semitic languages, which used phonics rather than pictographs or ideographs.

The Greeks borrowed their alphabet from the Semites. The Romans stole their alphabet from the Greeks (the Romans stole just about everything). But the Romans didn't really steal all of Greek. They left out a few sounds they didn't think they needed: (theta), U, V, X, Y, and Z. Eventually, they realized that the sounds were important, so they added them to the end of their alphabet in the order in which they were accepted. (The theta was never added by the Romans, though some middle English scripts used a Y symbol to represent it. That's why, for example, you have "Ye Old Shop" for "The Old Shop.")

That sort of explains how the alphabet got to be in alphabetical order. The ASCII numbering scheme came about from the early teletype days as a way to encode numbers, common symbols, and secret codes. There's probably a story to tell there, but at this stage in the book, I'm just too lazy to look it up.

Another, bolder example

About the most common use of the `if` command to compare characters is in answer to the old yes-or-no question. Here's an example:

```
#include <stdio.h>

int main()
{
    char c;

    printf("Would you like your computer to explode?");
    c=getchar();
    if(c=='N')
    {
        printf("Okay. Whew!\n");
    }
    else
    {
        printf("OK: Configuring computer to explode now.\n");
        printf("Bye!\n");
    }
    return(0);
}
```

Oh! Such jocularity!

Enter the preceding source code. Save it to disk as BLOWUP1.C.

Compile and run. Here's what you see:

```
Would you like your computer to explode?
```

Thanks to your years of computer training, you know that the answer is *No*. What can the user type? Who cares! As the programmer you know that you type a big N to make the computer *not* explode. Any other key makes it go Boom. Type **N** and press Enter:

```
Okay. Whew!
```

Run the program again and type any other key except N. (Even little N works.) Boom! There goes the computer!

- Only if the user types a capital N does the computer not explode.
- Well, the computer doesn't explode, which you should have figured out by now.

- Even to compare a single character variable with a single character, *two* equal signs are used.
- Yes, this program has its limitations. Most of them are covered in Chapter 14.

Using the `if` Keyword to Compare Two Strings

The `if` keyword cannot be used to compare strings. It can be used only to compare single-character variables.

- If you try to use `if` to compare two strings, the result is, as they say, unpredictable. The program is compiled without any errors (maybe), but it definitely doesn't run the way you anticipated.
- *C All-in-One Desk Reference For Dummies* (Wiley) has information about comparing strings.

Chapter 14

Iffy C Logic

In This Chapter

- Helping your program make sense
- Using logical comparisons in an `if` statement
- Understanding logical `OR`, `||`
- Understanding logical `AND`, `&&`

There's more to the `if` command than you can C, or than you may have seen in earlier chapters in this book. That extra stuff involves good old-fashioned Mr. Spock-like logic.

Unlike with math, most people don't go running and screaming from logic. That's because people don't have the foggiest idea what logic really is. If they did, no one would ever play the lottery or visit Las Vegas. That's because it's illogical to assume that odds of 1 in 80 million *mean* anything. But I digress.

You can apply two types of logic in a computer program. First is the logic of properly laying out the decision that `if` makes: whether to use < or > — and other silly things like that. But beyond that is the logic of either-or and and-both and various mixtures of each one. It's enough to drive you insane! This chapter helps prevent that.

Exposing Flaws in Logic

Sometimes, programmers get so involved in whether their programs run that they forget about *using* the programs.

Once upon a time, a study was done on the "usability" of a particular program. In the program, users were asked a vital question and had to respond by pressing the Tab key. Normally, it's the Enter key that users expect to press, but with that one program, pressing the Enter key caused something odd to happen, which required three or four steps to undo and returned users to the original question.

The odd thing is that the users tended to blame themselves for pressing Enter rather than Tab. They blamed themselves rather than assume that the program behaved in an illogical way. Had the programmer been using logic, the program would have used the Enter key rather than Tab. But, as the budding programmer you're becoming, even you know that such a thing is really easy to change.

Take a moment to review the flow of the BLOWUP1.C program, which I show you how to create in Chapter 13. The program asks a vital question:

```
Would you like your computer to explode?
```

I believe that it's safe to assume in most cases that the user *would not* want their computer to explode. Yet the program was written so that only the N key press — one key of many possible keys — prevents the computer from blowing up. This is a great example of misapplied logic.

When giving the user a choice and one option is better than another, make it very easy for them to accidentally select the best option. In the case of the BLOWUP1.C program, the code should probably look like this:

```
    printf("Would you like your computer to explode?");
    c=getchar();
    if(c=='Y')
    {
        printf("OK: Configuring computer to explode now.\n");
        printf("Bye!\n");
    }
    else
    {
        printf("Okay. Whew!\n");
    }
```

The only option in this example that truly blows up the computer is pressing the Y key. Any other key causes the computer *not* to blow up — the better option.

Of course, the best option is to limit input precisely. To do that, you need to know a few more `if` command tricks, which are introduced starting in the next section.

- You may have noticed this illogic in Chapter 13, when you first ran the BLOWUP1 program. Pressing even the little N key causes the blow-up message to be displayed.
- Most Yes or No questions wait for either Y or N to be pressed and ignore any other key (except for maybe Esc).

If, And, Or, But

The BLOWUP1.C program also presents an interesting problem. No, not *how* to blow up the computer. That's easy! Instead, I mean what about the little Y key?

In the preceding section, when the program runs, the user can only press the Y key to blow up the computer. But, how can you be certain that a capital Y is pressed rather than a baby Y? Or vice versa: What if only the little Y is being checked for?

A solution (but not the best one)

This section shows modified source code for BLOWUP1.C:

```
#include <stdio.h>

int main()
{
    char c;

    printf("Would you like your computer to explode?");
    c=getchar();
    if(c=='Y')
    {
        printf("OK: Configuring computer to explode now.\n");
        printf("Bye!\n");
    }
    else if(c=='y')
    {
        printf("OK: Configuring computer to explode now.\n");
        printf("Bye!\n");
    }
    else
    {
        printf("Okay. Whew!\n");
    }
    return(0);
}
```

Edit the original source code for BLOWUP1.C and make the changes shown in this example. Primarily, you're checking for Y to begin with, and an `else if` block is added to confirm checking for baby Y. Oh, and the `printf()` statements are all switched around from the first program example to improve the program's overall logic.

Save the modified source code to disk as BLOWUP2.C.

Compile and run.

Anything you type, other than a Y or a (highlight), is "safe." But, if you type a **Y** or a **y**, the computer blows up (supposedly).

- Why check for both upper- and lowercase? Logic! You never know whether the user has the Caps Lock key turned on.
- By making the program specifically check for the Y/y key press, you make every other key on the keyboard a No selection. That's wise. Logical, even.
- For another improvement, tell users about their options. For example, the following modification to Line 7 adds a common key-choice gizmo to the question:

  ```
  printf("Would you like your computer to explode? (Y/N)");
  ```

  This line lets users know that they can press Y or N. (This is fine despite the fact the program doesn't specifically check for N; you don't need to!)

A better solution, using logic

I want to believe that there's no right or wrong way to program a computer, but there are more efficient ways. For example, the BLOWUP2.C source code has several statements that are repeated:

```
{
    printf("OK: Configuring computer to explode now.\n");
    printf("Bye!\n");
}
```

Whenever you see repetition like that in a program, it generally means that you have a better way to do things. In this case, the problem lies with the two `if` commands: one to look for `'Y'` and the other to look for `'y'`. A better option is to use the `OR` logical operator so that the `if` command reads like this:

```
If variable a is equal to 'Y' or if variable a is equal to
        'y'
```

which becomes

```
if(a=='Y' OR a=='y')
```

Then, all you need to know is that, in C, the logical operator for `OR` is two pipe characters: `||`. The equation becomes

```
if(a=='Y' || a=='y')
```

This line reads as just described: "If variable a is equal to 'Y' or if variable a is equal to 'y'." If either one is true, the set of statements belonging to the if command is executed.

Here's your updated source code:

```
#include <stdio.h>

int main()
{
    char c;

    printf("Would you like your computer to explode?");
    c=getchar();
    if(c=='Y' || c=='y')
    {
        printf("OK: Configuring computer to explode now.\n");
        printf("Bye!\n");
    }
    else
    {
        printf("Okay. Whew!\n");
    }
    return(0);
}
```

The major modification is with the if condition, which now compares two operations with a logical OR. That cuts down on the program's redundancy.

Save the changes to disk as BLOWUP3.C. Compile. Fix any errors. Then run it:

It's logically cured twice!

- The pipe character is also known as the *vertical bar*. It's on the same key as the backslash character, usually right above the Enter or Return key, on the main part of the keyboard.
- Sometimes the pipe character has a break in the middle, and sometimes it's a solid line.
- Two pipe characters mean OR in the C language, a logical choice between two different conditions.
- A condition must be on either side of the ||, logical OR, comparison.
- The || means that either condition specified must be true for the if command to be true. Each condition must be its own comparison, using the operators in Table 12-1, over in Chapter 12.

The `if` command's logical friends

You can use the logical operators `&&` and `||` to help the `if` command make multiple decisions in one statement:

The `&&` is the logical `AND` operator.

The `||` is the logical `OR` operator.

Table 14-1 explains both.

Table 14-1 Logical Operators Used in `if` Comparisons

Operator	*Meaning*	*"True" Examples*
||	Or	true || true
		true || false
		false || true
&&	And	true || true

The logical operator is used on two standard `if` command comparisons. For example:

```
if(temperature>65 && temperature<75)
{
    printf("My, but it's nice weather outside\n");
}
```

In this example, the `if` command makes two comparisons: `temperature>65` and `temperature<75`. If both are true, the `&&`, logical `AND` condition is also true and the entire statement passes; the `printf()` function then displays the string. Table 14-2 shows the possibilities of how you can figure it out.

Table 14-2 Figuring Out a Logical AND Operation

Temperature	*temperature>65*	*(and)*	*temperature<75*	*Logical AND result*
45	45>65		45<75	
	FALSE	&&	TRUE	FALSE
72	72>65		72<75	

Temperature	*temperature>65*	*(and)*	*temperature<75*	*Logical AND result*
	TRUE	&&	TRUE	TRUE
90	90>65		90<75	
	TRUE	&&	FALSE	FALSE

According to Tables 14-1 and 14-2, both conditions that `if` evaluates must be true for the logical `AND` to work. (Not shown, and not possible in the given program, is when both conditions are FALSE. In that case, the `AND` test also fails.)

Here's a logical `OR` puzzle, which is used in an `if` statement to test two conditions:

```
if(score>100 || cheat code=='Y')
{
    printf("You have defeated the level boss!\n");
}
```

The logical `OR` tests two different conditions — making two utterly different comparisons. That's fine; as long as they're valid `if` command comparisons, they'll work. Table 14-3 plods through the potential results.

Table 14-3 Figuring Out a Logical OR Operation

Score, cheat_code	*score>100*	*(or)*	*cheat_code=='Y'*	*Logical OR result*
50,Z	50>100		'Z'=='Y'	
	FALSE	||	FALSE	FALSE
200,Z	200>100		'Z'=='Y'	
	TRUE	||	FALSE	TRUE
50,Y	50>100		'Y'=='Y'	
	FALSE	||	TRUE	TRUE
200,Y	200>100		'Y'=='Y'	
	TRUE	||	TRUE	TRUE

Table 14-3 shows how the logical `OR` judges comparisons. If only one of them is TRUE, the entire statement is proven true. Unlike the logical `AND`, where both (or all) conditions must be true, it takes only one comparison to make the entire `if` statement true.

Most of the time, you probably compare only two conditions with `&&` or `||`. You can, however, compare more than one. It works, though it can look sloppy. All the following examples are legal, though they may take some mental work to figure out:

```
if(key=='A' || key=='B' || key=='C')
```

In the preceding line, the `if` statement is true if the value of the character variable key is either `A`, `B`, or `C`. Any one that's true works.

In the following example, all three conditions must work out `TRUE` for the entire statement to be true: The `temperature` value must be greater than `70` *and* the value of `sun` must equal the value of `shining` *and* the value of `weekend` must equal the constant `YES`. If all three are true, the statement is true.

```
if(temperature>70 && sun==shining && weekend==YES)
```

The next one takes a little brain grease:

```
if(status==1 || user==ROOT && timer<MAX)
```

Logical statements read from left to right. Each condition is evaluated as you read it: `status` can be `1`, or the `user` can be `ROOT` — either one must be true. But then that is evaluated against `timer` being less than `MAX`, which must be true for the entire statement to be true. Whew!

- Yeah: If you're brain is fried now, please do take a break.
- You can easily remember that the `&&` means "logical `AND`" because the ampersand character is used to mean "and" in English.
- It's not easy to remember that `||` means "logical `OR`."

- Multiple `&&` and `||` conditions are evaluated from *left to right* (just like you read). Any single condition that fails the text makes the entire statement false.
- There's a difference between `&&` and `&` (a single ampersand). The `&` serves a different purpose in C, so be sure to use `&&` when making logical decisions in an `if` statement. The same goes for `||` and `|`; use `||` in an `if` statement.

- The `|` and `&` are bit-wise operators, performing logical operations on bits. These may or may not be covered in this book's companion, *C All-in-One Desk Reference For Dummies* (Wiley).
- The ampersand itself is a contraction of the Latin *et,* which means *and.* The `&` character is simply a stylized combination of an *e* and a *t.*

A logical AND *program for you*

The following source code demonstrates how a logical AND operation works. It's another — the final — modification to the BLOWUP series of programs:

```
#include <stdio.h>

int main()
{
    char c,d;

    printf("Enter the character code for self-destruct?");
    c=getchar();
    fflush(stdin);           /* use fpurge(stdin) in unix */

    printf("Input number code to confirm self-destruct?");
    d=getchar();

    if(c=='G' && d=='0')
    {
        printf("AUTO DESTRUCT ENABLED!\n");
        printf("Bye!\n");
    }
    else
    {
        printf("Okay. Whew!\n");
    }
    return(0);
}
```

Start editing with the source code from BLOWUP3.C if you like, or just enter this code on a blank slate. Save the final result to disk as BLOWUP4.C.

Compile. Fix any errors. Run.

You know the codes from entering the source code: Big G and Zero. Both must be typed at the keyboard to properly authorize the computer to blow up. Cinchy.

- This program uses the `fflush(stdin)` command (in Line 9) to clear input from the first `getchar()` function. Refer to Chapter 13 for more information on why this command is needed.
- If you're using a Unix-like operating system, substitute `fpurge(stdin)` for Line 9. Again, refer to Chapter 13.
- The logical AND operator `&&` ensures that both variables `c` and `d` must equal the proper values for that part of the `if` statement to be true.

- You can also test for a little G by making the following change to Line 14 in your editor:

```
if(c=='G' || c=='g' && d=='0')
```

  First, variable `c` is compared with either `G` or `g` — either one can be true. Then, that result is compared with `d==0`, which must be true. If either of the first comparisons is false, or if the last comparison is false by itself, the entire statement is false. Funky.

Chapter 15

C You Again

In This Chapter

- Understanding the loop
- Repeating chunks of code with `for`
- Using a loop to count
- Displaying an ASCII table by using a loop
- Avoiding the endless loop
- Breaking a loop with `break`

One thing computers enjoy doing more than anything else is repeating themselves. Humans? We think that it's punishment to tell a kid to write "*National Geographic* films are not to be giggled at" 100 times on a chalkboard. Computers? They don't mind a bit. They *enjoy* it, in fact.

Next to making decisions with `if`, the power in your programs derives from their ability to repeat things. The only problem with that is getting them to stop, which is why you need to know how `if` works before you progress into the *looping* statements. This chapter begins your looping journey by introducing you to the most ancient of the loopy commands, `for`.

- To find out about the `if` statement, refer to Chapters 12 though 14.
- It may behoove you to look at Table 12-1, in Chapter 12, which contains comparison functions used by both the `if` and `for` commands.

For Going Loopy

Doing things over and over is referred to as *looping*. When a computer programmer writes a program that counts to one zillion, he writes a loop. The *loop* is called such because it's a chunk of programming instructions — code — that is executed a given number of times. Over and over.

As an example of a loop, consider the common Baby-Mother interaction program:

```
Baby picks up spoon.
Baby throws spoon on floor; Baby laughs.
Mommy picks up spoon from floor.
Mommy places spoon before Baby.
Repeat.
```

This primitive program contains a loop. The loop is based on "Repeat," which tells you that the entire sequence of steps repeats itself.

Unfortunately, the steps in the preceding primitive program don't contain any stopping condition. Therefore, it's what is known as an *endless loop*. Most looping statements in computer programming languages have some sort of condition — like an `if` statement — that tells the program when to stop repeating (or that, at least, such a thing is desired.)

A simple modification to the program can fix the endless loop situation:

```
Repeat until Mommy learns not to put spoon before Baby.
```

Now, the program has a stopping condition for the loop.

In conclusion, loops have three parts:

- A start
- The middle part (the part that is repeated)
- An end

These three parts are what make up a loop. The start is where the loop is set up, usually some programming-language instruction that says "I'm going to do a loop here — stand by to repeat something." The middle part consists of the instructions that are repeated over and over. Finally, the end marks the end of the repeating part or a condition on which the loop ends ("until Mommy learns," in the preceding example).

- The C language has several different types of loops. It has `for` loops, which you read about in this chapter; `while` loops and `do-while` loops; and the ugly `goto` keyword, covered elsewhere in this book and in more detail in its companion book, *C All-in-One Desk Reference For Dummies* (Wiley).
- The instructions held within a loop are executed a specific number of times, or they can be executed until a certain condition is met. For example, you can tell the computer, "Do this a gazillion times" or "Do this until your thumb gets tired." Either way, several instructions are executed over and over.

- After the loop has finished going through its rounds, the program continues. But while the loop is, well, "looping," the same part of the program is run over and over.

Repetitive redundancy, I don't mind

The following source code is for OUCH.C, a program which proves that computers don't mind doing things over and over again. No, not at their expense. Not while you sit back, watch them sweat, and laugh while you snarf popcorn and feast on carbonated beverages.

What this program does is to use the `for` keyword, one of the most basic looping commands in the C language. The `for` keyword creates a small loop that repeats a single `printf()` command five times:

```
#include <stdio.h>

int main()
{
    int i;

    for(i=0 ; i<5 ; i=i+1)
    {
        printf("Ouch! Please, stop!\n");
    }
    return(0);
}
```

Enter this source code into your editor.

The new deal here is the `for` keyword, at Line 7. Type what happens in there carefully. Notice that the line which begins with `for` doesn't end with a semicolon. Instead, it's followed by a set of curly braces — just like the `if` statement. (It's exactly like the `if` statement, in fact.)

Save the file as OUCH.C.

Compile OUCH.C by using your compiler. Be on the lookout for errors. A semicolon may be missing in `for`'s parentheses.

Run the final program. You see the following displayed:

```
Ouch! Please, stop!
Ouch! Please, stop!
Ouch! Please, stop!
Ouch! Please, stop!
Ouch! Please, stop!
```

See? Repetition doesn't hurt the PC. Not one bit.

- The `for` loop has a start, a middle, and an end. The middle part is the `printf()` statement — the part that gets repeated. The rest of the loop, the start and end, are nestled within the `for` keyword's parentheses. (The next section deciphers how this stuff works.)
- Just as with the `if` structure, when only one statement belongs to the `for` command, you could write it like this:

  ```
  for(i=0 ; i<5 ; i=i+1)
      printf("Ouch! Please, stop!\n");
  ```

  The curly braces aren't required when you have only one statement that's repeated. But, if you have more than one, they're a must.
- The `for` loop repeats the `printf()` statement five times.
- Buried in the `for` loop is the following statement:

  ```
  i=i+1
  ```

  This is how you add 1 to a variable in the C language. It's called *incrementation,* and you should read Chapter 11 if you don't know what it is.
- Don't worry if you can't understand the `for` keyword just yet. Read through this whole chapter, constantly muttering "I *will* understand this stuff" over and over. Then go back and reread it if you need to. But read it all straight through first.

For doing things over and over, use the `for` keyword

The word *for* is one of those words that gets weirder and weirder the more you say it: for, for, fore, four, foyer. . . . For he's a jolly good fellow. These are for your brother. For why did you bring me here? An eye for an eye. For the better to eat you with, my dear. Three for a dollar. And on and on. For it can be maddening.

In the C programming language, the `for` keyword sets up a loop, logically called a `for` loop. The `for` keyword defines a starting condition, an ending condition, and the stuff that goes on while the loop is being executed over and over. The format can get a little deep, so take this one step at a time:

```
for(starting; while_true; do_this)
    statement;
```

After the keyword `for` comes a set of parentheses. Inside the parentheses are three items, separated by two semicolons. A semicolon doesn't end this line.

The first item is `starting`, which sets up the starting condition for the loop. It's usually some variable that is initialized to a value. In OUCH.C, it's `i=0`.

The second item is `while_true`. It tells `for` to keep looping; as long as the condition specified by `while_true` is true, the loop is repeated. Typically, `while_true` is a comparison, similar to one found in an `if` command. In OUCH.C, it's `i<5`.

The final item, `do_this`, tells the `for` keyword what to do each time the loop is executed once. In OUCH.C, the job that is done here is to increment variable `i` one notch: `i=i+1`.

The `statement` item is a statement that follows and belongs to the `for` keyword. `statement` is repeated a given number of times as the `for` keyword works through its loops. This `statement` must end with a semicolon.

If more than one *statement* belongs to the `for` structure, you must use curly braces to corral them:

```
for(starting; while_true; do_this)
     {
     statement;
     statement;
     /* etc. */
     }
```

Note that the statements are optional. You can have a `for` loop that looks like this:

```
for(starting; while_true; do_this)
     ;
```

In this case, the single semicolon is the "statement" that `for` repeats.

- One of the most confusing aspects of the `for` keyword is what happens to the three items inside its parentheses. Take heart: It confuses both beginners and the C lords alike (though they don't admit to it).
- The biggest mistake with the `for` loop? Using commas rather than semicolons. Those are semicolons inside them thar parentheses!
- Some C programmers leave out the `starting` and `do_this` parts of the `for` command. Although that's okay for them, I don't recommend it for beginners. Just don't let it shock you if you ever see it. Remember that *both* semicolons are always required inside `for`'s parentheses.

Tearing through OUCH.C a step at a time

I admit that the `for` loop isn't the easiest of C's looping instructions to understand. The problem is all the pieces. It would be easier to say, for example:

```
for(6)
{
 /* statements */
}
```

and then repeat the stuff between the curly braces six times. But what that does is limit the *power* of the `for` command's configuration.

To help you better understand how `for`'s three parentheses' pieces' parts make sense, I use the following `for` statement from OUCH.C as an example:

```
for(i=0 ; i<5 ; i=i+1)
```

The `for` loop uses the variable `i` to count the number of times it repeats its statements.

The first item tells the `for` loop where to begin. In this line, that's done by setting the integer variable `i` equal to 0. This plain old C language statement stuffs a variable with a value:

```
i=0
```

The value `0` slides through the parentheses into the integer variable `i`. No big deal.

The second item is a condition — like you would find in an `if` statement — that tells the `for` loop how long to keep going; to keep repeating itself over and over as long as the condition that's specified is true. In the preceding code, as long as the statement `i<5` (the value of the variable `i` is less than 5) is true, the loop continues repeating. It's the same as the following `if` statement:

```
if (i<5)
```

If the value of variable `i` is less than `5`, keep going.

The final item tells the `for` loop what to do each time it repeats. Without this item, the loop would repeat forever: `i` is equal to 0, and the loop is repeated as long as `i<5` (the value of `i` is less than `5`). That condition is true, so `for` would go on endlessly, like a federal farm subsidy. However, the last item tells `for` to increment the value of the `i` variable each time it loops:

```
i=i+1
```

The compiler takes the value of the variable `i` and adds 1 to it each time the `for` loop is run through once. (Refer to Chapter 11 for more info on the art of incrementation.)

Altogether, the `for` loop works out to repeat itself — and any statements that belong to it — a total of five times. Table 15-1 shows how it works.

Table 15-1 How the Variable i Works Its Way through the `for` Loop

Value of i	*Is i<5 true?*	*Statement*	*Do This*
i=0	Yes, keep looping←	`printf()...`(1)	i=0+1
i=1	Yes, keep looping←	`printf()...`(2)	i=1+1
i=2	Yes, keep looping←	`printf()...`(3)	i=2+1
i=3	Yes, keep looping←	`printf()...`(4)	i=3+1
i=4	Yes, keep looping←	`printf()...`(5)	i=4+1
i=5	No — stop now!		

In Table 15-1, the value of the variable `i` starts out equal to 0, as set up in the `for` statement. Then, the second item — the comparison — is tested. Is `i<5` true? If so, the loop marches on.

As the loop works, the third part of the `for` statement is calculated and the value of `i` is incremented. Along with that, any statements belonging to the `for` command are executed. When those statements are done, the comparison `i<5` is made again and the loop either repeats or stops based on the results of that comparison.

- The `for` loop can be cumbersome to understand because it has so many parts. However, it's the best way in your C programs to repeat a group of statements a given number of times.
- The third item in the `for` statement's parentheses — `do_this` — is executed only once for each loop. It's true whether `for` has zero, one, or several statements belonging to it.

- Where most people screw up with the `for` loop is the second item. They remember that the first item means "start here," but they think that the second item is "end here." It's not! The second item means "keep looping while this condition is true." It works like an `if` comparison. The compiler doesn't pick up and flag it as a boo-boo, but your program doesn't run properly when you make this mistake.

- Don't forget to declare the variable used in `for`'s parentheses. This common mistake is another one made by just about everyone. Refer to Chapter 8 for more information about declaring variables.
- Here's a handy plug-in you can use for loops. Just substitute the big *X* in the following line for the number of times you want the loop to work:

  ```
  for(i=1 ; i<=X ; i=i+1)
  ```

  You must declare `i` to be an integer variable. It starts out equal to `1` and ends up equal to the value of `X`. To repeat a loop 100 times, for example, you use this command:

  ```
  for(i=1 ; i<=100 ; i=i+1)
  ```

Having fun whilst counting to 100

This section has the source code for a program named 100.C. This program uses a `for` loop to count to 100 and display each number on the screen. Indeed, it's a major achievement: Early computers could count up to only 50 before they began making wild and often inaccurate guesses about what number came next. (Refer to your phone bill to see what I mean.)

The core of 100.C is similar to OUCH.C. In fact, the only reason I have tossed it in here is that `for` loops are so odd to some folks that you need two program examples to drive home the point:

```
#include <stdio.h>

int main()
{
    int i;

    for(i=1 ; i<=100 ; i=i+1)
        printf("%d\t",i);
    return(0);
}
```

Type this source code into your editor. Watch your indentations; it's traditional in the C language to indent one statement belonging to another (as shown in the example), even when the curly braces are omitted.

In the `for` statement, the `i` variable starts out equal to 1. The `while_true` condition is `i<=100` — which means that the loop works, although the value of variable `i` is less than or equal to 100. The final part of the statement increments the value of `i` by 1 each time the loop works.

The printf statement displays the value of the integer variable i by using the %d placeholder. The \t escape sequence inserts a tab into the output, lining up everything by nice, neat columns.

Save the file to disk as 100.C. (It's a chess-club joke; C in Roman numerals is 100. Hardy-har-har.)

Compile the program and run it. You see 10 rows of 10 columns and numbers 1 through 100 neatly displayed. It's amazing how fast the computer can do that.

- The output shows you the value of the variable i as the for loop works, repeating the printf() statement 100 times and incrementing the value of the i variable 100 times as well.
- Change the for statement in Line 5 of your 100.C source code to make the loop go up to 10,000. Use your editor to make it read

  ```
  for(i=1 ; i<=10000 ; i=i+1)
  ```

  Just insert 2 extra zeroes after the 100 that are already there. Save the change to disk and recompile. It doesn't take the computer that much longer to count to 10,000; but it does take longer to display all those numbers.

I'm Bustin' Outta Here!

Loops are one of the handiest things you can toss into a program — like rich, creamy, high fat dressing on top of dull (yet cold and crisp) lettuce. It's only by using loops that programs become useful. Just about anything useful a computer can do for you is accomplished by using a loop: sorting, searching, listing, getting "hung" up. It's all thanks to loops.

I save the completely loopy lessons for Chapter 17. My task in this section is to round out coverage of the lovely yet foreboding for keyword and show you some interesting anti-loop devices, designed to let you foil the attempts of even the most (over)diligent computer program.

At last — the handy ASCII program

This section has the source code for ASCII.C — which I proudly proclaim as the first useful program in this book. What ASCII.C does is to display the ASCII characters and their corresponding codes, from Code 32 on up to Code 127.

This program proves handy because you can more easily type ASCII at the DOS prompt to see the codes than keep looking them up in appendixes. (If you program for any length of time, you look up ASCII codes almost hourly.)

```
#include <stdio.h>

int main()
{
    unsigned char a;

    for(a=32;a<128;a=a+1)
        printf("%3d = '%c'\t",a,a);
    return(0);
}
```

Enter this source code into your editor. It contains a basic `for` loop that repeats a `printf()` statement several dozen times.

After double-checking your work, save the source code to disk as ASCII.C.

Compile the program by using your compiler.

When you run the final result, you see a 5-column display on your screen, illustrating the ASCII characters and their codes, from Code 32 (the "space" character) up to Code 127, which looks like a little house but is really supposed to be the Greek letter Delta (as in Δ Burke).

- I use this program all the time to quickly scope out ASCII code values.
- The `for` loop in the ASCII.C program starts with the value `32`. It increments (by 1) up to the value `127`, which is the last stop before `a<128`. The incrementation is done by the handy `a=a+1` equation in the `for` keyword's parentheses.
- Notice how the `printf()` function uses the character variable `a` twice — once as an integer and again as a character. To avoid duplicate output, however, both the `%d` and `%c` placeholders are used in `printf()`'s format string.
- The number `3` in `printf()`'s `%3d` placeholder directs `printf()` to always display three characters when it prints the integer value. When you set the display width to three characters, all the code values line up right-justified (a space is inserted before the 2-digit numbers).
- TECHNICAL STUFF: Here's a secret: The `a` variable in ASCII.C can be either an integer or a character variable. Whichever way you declare it, the program works. That's because in the `for` loop, `a` is used as a value, and in the `printf()` function, it's used as both a character and a value. This type of duplicity works for both `int`s and `char`s, as long as the value never rises higher than 255 (the largest "value" you can store in a `char` variable).

- Here's another secret: The variable `a` must be declared as an `unsigned` character. By being `unsigned`, the possibility of the program dealing with negative numbers is eliminated. If variable `a` were just a `char` variable, the loop would repeat endlessly; adding 1 to `a` when it equals `127` gives a value of `-127`, and the loop just repeats forever. (To prove it, edit out the word `unsigned` in the ASCII.C source code and recompile, and then the program runs forever, which probably isn't what you want.)
- Speaking of looping forever. . . .

Beware of infinite loops!

Some things are eternal. Love, they say. Diamonds, of course. Death and taxes, yup. And, some loops can be eternal, though you don't really want them to be. *Eternal* is too endearing a term. Moody programmers prefer the term *infinite,* as in "It goes on forever and never stops." Yes, it's kind of like the Energizer bunny.

The *infinite loop* is a repeating section of your program that is repeated without end. I can think of no practical application for this. In fact, the infinite loop is usually an accident — a bug — that pops up in a well-meaning program. You don't really know that it's there until you run the program. Then, when the program just sits there and doesn't do anything or when something is splashed on the screen again and again, with no hint of stopping, you realize that you have created an infinite loop. Everybody does it.

The following program is FOREVER.C, an on-purpose infinite loop that you can type and try out. Using a misguided `for` command, the program repeats the `printf()` statement *ad infinitum:*

```
#include <stdio.h>

int main()
{
    int i;

    for(i=1;i=5;i=i+1)
        printf("The computer has run amok!\n");
    return(0);
}
```

Type this source code into your text editor. It's similar to the first `for`-loop program in this chapter, OUCH.C. The difference is in the `for` loop's "while true" part and the message that is repeated. Save the source code to disk with the name FOREVER.C.

Compile the program. Even though the `for` statement contains a deliberate infinite loop, no error message is displayed (unless you goofed up and typed something else). After all, the compiler may think that you're attempting to do something forever as part of your master plan. How would it know otherwise?

When you run the program, forever, you see the following messages scrolling madly up your screen:

```
The computer has run amok!
```

Indeed, it has! Press Ctrl+C to stop the madness.

- Most loops are designed with a *condition* on which they end. In an endless loop, either they don't have a condition or the condition is set up in some fashion as to be unobtainable. That's bad.
- Infinite loops are insidious! Often, you don't detect them until the program runs, which is a great argument for testing every program you create.
- The Ctrl+C keyboard combination works in both Windows and Unix to cancel a command that is producing standard output, which is what FOREVER.C is doing (over and over). Other types of programs with infinite loops, particularly those that don't produce standard output, are much harder to stop. If Ctrl+C doesn't work, often you have to use your operating system's abilities to kill off the program run amok.
- In the olden days, you often had to restart the entire computer to regain control from a run-amok endlessly looping program.
- The program loops forever because of a flaw in the `for` loop's "while true" part — the second item in the parentheses:

  ```
  for(i=1;i=5;i=i+1)
  ```

  The C compiler sees `i=5` and figures, "Okay, I'll put 5 into the `i` variable." It isn't a true-false comparison, like something you find with an `if` statement, which was expected, so the compiler supposes that it's true and keeps looping — no matter what. Note that the variable `i` is always equal to 5 for this reason; even after it's incremented with `i=i+1`, the `i=5` statement resets it back to `5`.
- Here's what the `for` statement should probably look like:

  ```
  for(i=1;i<=5;i=i+1)
  ```

  This line repeats the loop five times.
- Some compilers may detect the "forever" condition in the `for` statement and flag it as an infinite loop. If so, you're lucky. For example, the old Borland C++ compiler flagged FOREVER.C as having a `Possibly incorrect assignment` error. The compiler still produces the finished (and flawed) program, though.

Breaking out of a loop

Loops aren't infinite if you have a way to break out of them. For most loops, that escape clause is provided in the looping statement itself. In the `for` statement, the escape condition is the middle item, as in

```
for(a=32;a<128;a=a+1)
```

The escape clause is `a<128`, which is the condition on which the loop ends.

Some loops, however, are designed without an end. That's because the condition that ends the loop happens elsewhere. In that case, the loop is designed to be eternal — which is fine, as long as some condition elsewhere eventually breaks the loop.

As an example, most word processors work with an infinite loop hidden inside their programs. The loop sits and scans the keyboard, over and over, waiting for you to type a command. Only when you type the proper "I want to quit" command does the thing stop and you return to DOS. It's like a controlled infinite loop — it's not really infinite because you have a way out.

The following program is TYPER1.C, a first stab at a word processor, though you can do nothing in the program except type and see what you type on the screen. The program is set up with an on-purpose infinite `for` loop. The `break` keyword is then used with the `if` command to bust out of the loop when you press the ~ (tilde) key:

```
#include <stdio.h>

int main()
{
    char ch;

    puts("Start typing");
    puts("Press ~ then Enter to stop");

    for(;;)
    {
        ch=getchar();
        if(ch=='~')
        {
            break;
        }
    }
    printf("Thanks!\n");
    return(0);
}
```

This program wins the award for having the most indentation and curly braces to this point in this book. Be careful as you type it into your editor. Save the file to disk as TYPER1.C.

Compile TYPER1.C.

Run the resulting program, which works somewhat like a typewriter. You can type away and fill the screen with text.

When you're done typing, press the tilde (~) key and then Enter. (This is TYPER's only "command.") You're done.

- The `for(;;)` statement doesn't error. The reason is that the semicolons are required, but what's between them isn't (a peculiarity of the `for` keyword).
- I read the `for(;;)` command aloud as "for ever."
- The `for` loop in TYPER1.C is infinite because its "while true" condition is missing. Gone! The compiler therefore assumes that the condition is true all the time and that the program loops infinitely.
- The first and last parts of the `for` statement's items aren't included either, though the semicolons inside the parentheses are still required in order to meet the demands of C etiquette.
- Because several statements belong to the `for` loop, they're enclosed in curly braces.
- The `getchar` function waits for a key to be pressed on the keyboard and displays that character. The character is then saved in the `ch` variable.
- The `if` statement tests the `ch` variable to see whether it's equal to the ~ (tilde) character. Note that two equal signs are used. If the comparison is true, indicating that the user pressed the ~ key, the `break` command is executed. Otherwise, `break` is skipped and the loop is repeated, reading another character from the keyboard.

The `break` keyword

The `break` keyword gets you out of a loop — any loop in C, not just a `for` loop. No matter what the loop's ending condition is, `break` immediately issues a "parachute out of this plane" command. The program continues with the next statement after the loop:

```
break;
```

The `break` keyword is a C language statement unto itself and must end properly with a semicolon.

The loop that `break` breaks you out of doesn't have to be an endless loop. `break` can stop any loop, at any time. It's often used with an `if` statement to test some condition. Based on the results of the test, the loop is stopped by using `break` (just as was done with TYPER1.C in the preceding section).

- `break` stops only the loop it's in. It doesn't break out of a nested loop, or a loop within a loop. See Chapter 18 for more information on nested loops.
- If you use `break` outside of a loop — when there's nothing to break out of — the compiler goes berserk and generates an error.
- It's funny how the word is `break` and not *brake*. The same twisted logic applies to the Break key on your keyboard.

Chapter 16

C the Loop, C the Loop++

In This Chapter

- Incrementing variables with ++
- Decrementing variables with --
- Using other math operator shortcuts

Looping is a core part of programming, just as compromising your principles is central to getting ahead in politics. And, closely tied to looping is a concept you have already been exposed to: *incrementation,* which I'm not certain is a real word, but it means to increment something.

Just as loops flip through various iterations, variables are incremented or decremented to help the computer keep track of things. In fact, the concepts of looping and incrementation are so closely linked that it was tough to write the preceding chapter about the `for` command while utterly avoiding the issue. The time has come for your full exposure to that ancient art and mysterious practice of incrementation.

The Art of Incrementation

When a `for` loop repeats something seven times, a variable somewhere gets incremented seven times. For example:

```
for(i=0;i<7;i=i+1)
```

This `for` statement sets up a loop that is repeated seven times, from `i=0` and up by 1 seven times as long as the value of `i` is less than 7 (`i<7`).

If you find the concept of starting the loop at `0` strange, the following `for` statement performs the same trick, working itself out, over and over, seven times:

```
for(i=1;i<=7;i=i+1)
```

In this example, `i` increments from `1` up to `7`. The C lords prefer to start loops with the counting variable at `0` because that's where the computer itself starts counting internally. Either way, incrementing is central to the idea of looping.

Keep in mind that the `for` statement is merely a frame for a loop. It repeats a group of statements a given number of times. The `for` statement itself only controls the looping.

Cryptic C operator symbols, Volume I: The `inc` operator (++)

The art of incrementation involves taking a variable and adding 1 to its value. So, no matter what the original value of the variable `count`, it's 1 greater after this equation:

```
count=count+1;
```

Face it: This equation is an awkward thing to look at. Yet, no loop happens without it, which means that incrementing happens frequently in C programs. Even so, few C programmers use the preceding statement. Instead, they resort to a shortcut, the incrementation operator, which is two plus signs holding hands:

```
count++;
```

The incrementation operator, ++, works like other mathematical operators you may have seen in other horrid math chapters: the +, `-`, *, and / for addition, subtraction, multiplication, and division, respectively. The difference here is that ++ works without an equal sign. It just tells the compiler, "Yo! Add 1 to the value of this variable. Thank you. Thank you very much." It's quick and tidy, but a bit cryptic (which is why I didn't throw it at you right away).

- Yes, you can say "plus plus" in your head when you see ++ in a program.
- Yes, that's why C++ is called "See plus plus." It's also the punch line of the joke: C++ is "one more" than regular C.
- You don't need an equal sign when you use ++. Just stick it at the end of a variable and that variable is incremented by 1.
- The equation `i++` is the same as `i=i+1`.
- Here we go:

```
var=3;              /* the variable var equals three */
var++;              /* Oops! var is incremented here */
                    /* From here on, var equals four */
```

- The ++ operator is used this way in a `for` statement:

  ```
  for(i=0;i<7;i++)
  ```

  This line means that variable `i` is incremented every iteration of the loop.

- This area is where the C language begins to get truly cryptic. Given the separate pieces of a `for` loop, most knowledgeable humans can detect that `i=1` means "`i` equals 1" and that `i<7` means "`i` is less than 7," and even that `i=i+1` is "`i` equals `i` plus 1." But toss `i++` at them and they think "`i` plus plus? Weird."

Another look at the LARDO.C program

Chapter 11 touches on the idea of incrementing a variable in a program. That program is LARDO.C, which I'm certain is near and dear to your heart and has impressed many a friend and family member. Unfortunately, now that you know the ++ thing, the program would really be an embarrassment if you showed it to a C guru. Seriously, all those gauche `w=w+1` things need to be properly changed to `w++` commands. Short. Sweet. Cryptic. It's what computers are all about!

The following program is an update to the LARDO.C source code, which is probably still sitting on your hard drive somewhere. Load that old file into your editor and make the necessary changes so that the program looks like the source code listed here:

```
#include <stdio.h>
#include <stdlib.h>

int main()
{
    char weight[4];
    int w;

    printf("Enter your weight:");
    gets(weight);
    w=atoi(weight);

    printf("Here is what you weigh now: %i\n",w);
    w++;
    printf("Your weight after the potatoes: %i\n",w);
    w++;
    printf("Here you are after the mutton: %i\n",w);
    w=w+8;
    printf("And your weight after dessert: %i pounds!\n",w);
    printf("Lardo!\n");
    return(0);
}
```

Edit your source code. The only changes are to Lines 14 and 16.

Save the file to disk again, using the same name, because this program is so much more superior to the original. Then compile.

Fix any errors if you got 'em. Otherwise, the program runs the same as it did before. The only true difference? You took advantage of the incrementation operator, ++, and earned the clever wink of sophisticated C language programmers worldwide.

TIP

Notice that the `w=w+8` statement wasn't modified. The reason is that the variable `w` is increased by 8, not just by 1. Yes, I have a shortcut for that, but you aren't exposed to it until the end of this chapter.

The Mysterious Practice of Decrementation

Loops don't necessarily have to go forward. They can also count down, which is definitely more dramatic and required in some occupations — such as launching spacecraft and many other common things you find yourself doing every day.

Consider OLLYOLLY.C, a program that counts backward. And, that's about all it's good for:

```
#include <stdio.h>

int main()
{
        int count;

        for(count=10;count>0;count=count-1)
             printf("%d\n",count);

        printf("Ready or not, here I come!\n");
        return(0);
}
```

Start off your editor with a new slate and carefully type this source code. The only strange stuff you encounter is in the `for` loop's parentheses, which may look a little funky — but it's counting backward! Will the loop work? Will the computer explode? Is Jane really cheating on Ralph? How can this be happening?

Quit pondering and type.

Save the file to disk as OLLYOLLY.C. Compile it. Run it.

The output looks like this:

```
10
9
8
7
6
5
4
3
2
1
Ready or not, here I come!
```

Yes, indeed, the computer can count backward. And, it did it in a `for` loop with what looks like a minimum of fuss — but still a little techy. The following section discusses the details.

- To prove that you're not going crazy, refer to Chapter 15's 100.C program. It counted from 1 to 100 using a `for` loop. The only difference now, aside from the `printf()` statements, is that the loop worked itself backward.
- Backward-counting loops in C are rare. Most of the time, whenever you have to do something 10 times, you do it forward, from 0 through 9 or from 1 through 10 or however you set up your `for` loop.

O, to count backward

Counting backward or forward makes no difference to the computer. You just have to tell the C language in which direction you want to go.

To count forward, you increment a variable's value. So, if you have the variable `f`, you do this:

```
f=f+1;
```

or even this:

```
f++;
```

Either way, the value of variable `f` is 1 greater than it was before; it has been incremented.

To count backward, you subtract 1 from a variable's value, which is exactly the way you do it in your head: 10, 9, 8, 7, and so on. It looks identical to the incrementing statement, except for the minus sign:

```
b=b-1;
```

The value of variable b is 1 less than it was before. If b came in with a value of 5, this statement sets b's value to 4. This process is known as *decrementing* a variable's value.

- Decrementing, or subtracting 1 (or any number) from a variable's value is just common subtraction. The only big deal here is that decrementing is done in a loop, which makes the loop count backward.
- Incrementing means adding (1) to a variable's value.
- Decrementing means subtracting (1) from a variable's value.
- Decrementing works because C first figures out what's on the right side of the equal sign:

  ```
  b=b-1;
  ```

  First comes b-1, so the computer subtracts 1 from the value of variable b. Then, that value is slid through the equal signs, back into the variable b. The variable is decremented.

How counting backward fits into the for loop

Take another look at Line 7 from the OLLYOLLY.C program:

```
for(count=10;count>0;count=count-1)
```

It's basic for loop stuff. The loop has a starting place, a while-true condition, and a do-this thing. The parts are listed in Table 16-1.

Table 16-1 How the for Loop Counts Backward

Loop Part	*Condition*
Starting	count=10
While-true	count>0
Do-this	count=count-1

Everything in the backward-counting `for` loop works per specifications. The loop begins by setting the value of the `count` variable equal to 10. And, it loops as long as the value of the `count` variable is greater than 0 (`count>0`). But, each time the loop repeats, the value of the `count` variable is decremented. It works backward.

Again, you have no reason to loop backward — except that the `printf()` statement belonging to the loop displays the numbers 10 through 1 in a countdown manner. Normally (which means about 99 percent of the time), you only loop forward. It's not only easier to do in your head, but it's also less likely to be a source for programming boo-boos than when you try to loop backward.

REMEMBER

- Most loops count forward. The backward-counting loop in C is possible but rarely used, mostly because counting is counting and it's just easier (for humans) to do it forward.
- You can't do a backward loop without decrementing the loop's variable.
- Other than decrementing the loop's variable, the only difference is in the loop's while-true condition (the one in the middle). That requires a little more mental overhead to figure out than with normal `for` loops. It's another reason that this type of loop is rare.
- Okay. The question arises: "Why bother?" Because you have to know about decrementing and the cryptic `--` operator, covered in the next section.

Cryptic C operator symbols, Volume II: The `dec` operator (--)

Just as C has a shortcut for incrementing a variable's value, there is also a shortcut for decrementing a variable's value. (If you read the first half of this chapter, you saw this coming from a mile back, most likely.) As a quick review, you can add 1 to a variable's value — *increment* it — by using the following C language statement:

```
i=i+1;
```

Or, if you're cool and remember the shortcut, you can use the cryptic ++ operator to do the same thing:

```
i++;
```

Both examples add 1 to the value of variable `i`.

Consider this example:

```
d=d-1
```

This statement subtracts 1 from the value of variable d, decrementing it. Here's the whiz-bang, cryptomic shortcut:

```
d--;
```

The -- is the decrement operator, which subtracts 1 from a variable's value.

Just like the incrementation operator, ++, the decrementing operator, --, works like other mathematical operators in the C language. In keeping with the theme of being cryptic, however, there is no equal sign. The -- tells the compiler to subtract 1 from the associated variable's value and — *poof!* — it's done.

- I pronounce -- as "deck deck," though I may be the only one in the world who does so. I haven't heard anyone say "minus-minus" — at least not aloud.
- The equation d-- is practically the same as d=d-1.
- You suffer no penalty for using d=d-1 if you forget about the -- thing.
- Don't bother with an equal sign when you use the decrementing operator, --. Glue it to the end of the variable you want to decrement and you're done.
- Here we go (again):

```
var=3;              /* the value of variable var is three */
var--;              /* Whoa! var is decremented here */
                    /* Now the value of var equals two */
```

- The -- operator is used this way in a for looping statement:

```
for(d=7;d>0;d--)
```

  The d-- replaces the d=d-1, as I demonstrate in the past few sections.

A final improvement to OLLYOLLY.C

Now that you know about --, you can improve the awkward and potentially embarrassing OLLYOLLY.C program, by spiffing it up with the decrementation operator.

Load OLLYOLLY.C into your editor again (if it's not there right now) and clickety-clack the down-arrow key to Line 7, where the for loop starts. Edit the for statement there, replacing the count=count-1 part with the cryptic, though proper, count-- thing. Here's how that line should look when you're done editing:

```
for(count=10;count>0;count--)
```

Save the source code file back to disk and then recompile it.

The program runs the same, but your C programming buddies will nod their heads in amazement at your deft use of the decrementation operator.

More Incrementation Madness

Incrementation and looping go hand in hand like (this week's) Hollywood's hottest couple.

Looping is an important part of programming — doing things over and over, like a famous actor rehearses his lines. (Make that famous *stage* actor.) In C, that can be done only with the `for` loop if you increment (or decrement) a variable's value.

Tied in with looping are the ++ and `--` operators, which you can also use independently from looping to increase or decrease a variable's value — like some actresses increase their bust size through various surgical techniques, and their age via bald-faced lying.

Given that, you should still keep in mind that incrementing and decrementing don't have to be done one tick at a time. For example, the LARDO.C program boosts the `w` variable's value by 8 by using the following statement in Line 18:

```
w=w+8;
```

The value of the variable `w` is increased by 8. The following statement decreases `w` by 3:

```
w=w-3;
```

This is still a form of incrementing and decrementing, though values larger than 1 are used. It's perfectly legit. And — as a bonus — you can use these types of incrementing or decrementing in loops. An example is coming forthwith.

- Although you can increment a variable by a value larger than 1, the ++ operator increases a variable's value by only 1. The same holds true for `--`, which always decreases a variable's value by 1.
- Fortunately, the C language lacks a +++ or `---` operator. Forget about it!

Leaping loops!

After losing or wining the game, the kids get together as a team and chant:

2, 4, 6, 8, who do we appreciate?

This chant is followed by the other team's name. It's a nice, polite, all-American athletic chant that means either "You sad sacks were easy to beat and, if we were unsupervised, we would be vandalizing your bicycles by now" or "You defeated us through treachery and deceit and, if we were unsupervised, we would be pummeling your heads with our aluminum bats."

Anyway, the following program uses a `for` loop to generate the "2, 4, 6, 8" part of the chant. It's a `for` loop that, yes, skips a bit as it counts. It's what I call a leaping loop:

```
#include <stdio.h>

int main()
{
    int i;

    for(i=2;i<10;i=i+2)
        printf("%d ",i);
    printf("who do we appreciate? GNU!\n");
    return(0);
}
```

Choose New in your editor and type the preceding source code. In the `printf()` statement in the `for` loop, note the space after the `%d`. It goes "double quote, percent sign, little *d,* space, double quote." Save the file to disk as CHANT.C.

Compile and run the program. Here's what your output should look like:

```
2 4 6 8 who do we appreciate? GNU!
```

- The loop starts at 2 and increments up to 10 by using the `i=i+2` formula. The loop reads like this: "Start with `i` equal to 2, and while the value of `i` is less than 10, repeat the following, adding 2 to variable `i` each time you loop."
- You can change Line 7 of the program to have the loop count by even numbers to any value. For example:

  ```
  for(i=2;i<1000;i=i+2)
  ```

  This modification makes the computer count by twos from 2 to 998. It doesn't do much for the chant, but it works. (Indeed, it would take forever to get to The Pizza Place if that were the case.)

Counting to 1,000 by fives

The following program is an update to the old 100.C program, from Chapter 15. In this case, the program counts to 1,000 by fives — a task that would literally take days without a computer:

```
#include <stdio.h>

int main()
{
    int i;

    for(i=5;i<=1000;i=i+5)
        printf("%d\t",i);
    return(0);
}
```

Start off with a new, clean slate in your editor. Type the preceding source code. It's nothing fancy. Indeed, it's just a take-off from the old 100.C program. Save the file to disk as 1000.C.

Compile 1000.C and run the result. Your screen fills with values from `5` to `1000`, all lined up in rows and columns.

- This leaping loop counts by fives because of the `i=i+5` part of the `for` statement. The `i=i+5` operation keeps increasing the value of the `i` variable by 5.
- The loop begins counting at 5 because of the `i=5` part of the `for` loop. It stops counting at 1,000 because of the `i<=1000` part of the loop. That's "less than or equal to 1000," which is how you get to 1,000.

Cryptic C operator symbols, Volume III: The madness continues

C is full of shortcuts, and mathematical operations are where you find most of them clustered like bees over a stray Zagnut bar. I feel that the two most cryptic shortcuts are for changing a variable's value by 1: ++ to increment and `--` to decrement. But there are more!

To add 5 to a variable's value, for example, such as in the 1000.C program, you use the following:

```
i=i+5
```

The cryptic C language shortcut for this operation is

```
i+=5
```

This line means "Increase the value of variable `i` by five." Unfortunately, it just doesn't *look* like that's what it means.

Although I can swallow ++ to increment and -- to decrement, the += thing seriously looks like a typo. Sad news: It's not. Even sadder: There are more of them, one each for adding, subtracting, multiplying, or dividing a variable's value by a certain amount (or by another variable). Table 16-2 lists the lot of them.

Table 16-2 Cryptic Shortcuts for Common Math Operations

Long, Boring Way	*Cryptic Shortcut*
var=var+5	var+=5
x=x+y	x+=y
var=var-5	var-=5
x=x-y	x-=y
var=var*5	var*=5
x=x*y	x*=y
var=var/5	var/=5
x=x/y	x/=y

In Table 16-2, you see two examples for each cryptic shortcut. The first one uses the variable *var,* which is modified by a constant value, `5`. The second uses two variables; the first one, *x,* is modified by another variable, *y*.

Yes, the shortcuts for incrementing, decrementing, or changing a variable are cryptic. You don't have to use them. You suffer no penalty for forgetting about them. I refer to them here for two reasons: It can be done, and C gurus love tossing this stuff into programs; so don't let the shortcuts scare you when you see them.

On your own: Modify the preceding two programs, CHANT.C and 1000.C. Replace the long math condition in the `for` loop with a shortcut version. Answers are provided at the end of this chapter.

TIP

- Technically, these doojabbies are referred to as *assignment operators.* Don't memorize that term. Even I had to look it up.
- Hey: It's a good idea to stick a sticky note on Table 16-2 or flag it by dog-earing the page. These cryptic shortcuts aren't easy to remember.
- One way to remember that the operator (+, -, *, or /) comes first is to look at the wrong way for subtraction:

  ```
  var=-5
  ```

  This is not a shortcut for `var=var-5`. Instead, it sets the value of variable *var* equal to negative-five. Ipso fasto, `var-=5` must be the proper way to do it.
- Remember that these mathematical-shortcut cryptic operators aren't necessarily limited to use in `for` loops. Each of them can be a C language statement unto itself, a mathematical operation to somehow pervert a variable's value. To wit:

  ```
  term+=4;
  ```

  This statement increases the value of the variable `term` by 4.

The answers

In CHANT.C, modify Line 7 to read:

```
for(i=2;i<10;i+=2)
```

In 1000.C, modify Line 7 to read:

```
for(i=2;i<10;i+=5)
```

In both cases, you change the longer equation `i=i+x` to its shorter variation, `i+=x`.

Chapter 17

C You in a While Loop

In This Chapter

- Using a `while` loop
- Choosing between `for` and `while`
- Making infinite `while` loops
- Beating a dead horse

When it comes time to create a loop, the C language gives you a choice. You can go with the complex `for` loop, which has all the gizmos and options to make most programmers happy, or you can choose the more exotic, free-wheeling `while` loop for your programs. Whereas `for` is more official and lays out all its plans in one spot, `while` is fanciful and free — like those care-free days of youth when Mommy would kiss your boo-boos and make them better and Daddy paid for everything.

This chapter introduces you to the happy-go-lucky `while` loop. Looping is a concept you should already be familiar with if you have been toiling with `for` loops for the past few chapters. But, I have good news! `while` loops are a heck of a lot simpler to understand. Ha-ha! Now, I tell you. . . .

The Lowdown on `while` Loops

`While` loops shouldn't be strange to you. Consider the following:

> While the light is red, keep your foot on the brake.

This simple example shows a `while` loop in real life. It means, roughly, "While this thing is true, keep repeating this action" (that is, a loop). Your foot is stepping on the brake as long as the light is red — a loop. Easy enough.

If you want to rewrite this instruction by using a C-like syntax and a `while` loop, it could look like this:

```
while(light==RED)
{
    foot_on_brake();
    light = check_light();
}
```

`light==RED` is a condition that can be either TRUE or FALSE — as in an `if` statement. While that condition is TRUE, the statements held in the `while` loop's curly braces are repeated.

One of the statements in the `while` loop checks the condition the loop repeats on: `light=check_light()` updates the status of the `light` variable. When it changes to something not `RED`, the `while` statement becomes FALSE, the block of statements is skipped, and the next part of the program is run. This is the essence of a `while` loop in C.

Whiling away the hours

As in a `for` loop, you can set up a `while` loop to repeat a chunk of statements a given number of times. Unlike a `for` loop, the `while` loop's controls (the doojabbies that tell the loop when to start and where to finish) are blasted all over the place. This is good because it doesn't mean that everything is crammed into one line, as with a `for` loop. This is bad because, well, I get into that in the next section. For now, busy yourself by typing the source code for HEY.C, a brilliant C program shown right next:

```
#include <stdio.h>

int main()
{
    int i;

    i=1;
    while(i<6)
    {
        printf("Ouch! Please stop!\n");
        i++;
    }
    return(0);
}
```

Type this program, which is essentially an update of the OUCH.C program, from Chapter 15. Both programs do the same thing, in fact, but by using different types of loops. Save the file to disk as HEY.C.

Compile. Run.

Here's what the output looks like:

```
Ouch! Please stop!
Ouch! Please stop!
Ouch! Please stop!
Ouch! Please stop!
Ouch! Please stop!
```

Brilliant. Simply brilliant.

- A loop in the C language requires three things: a start, a middle part (the part that is repeated), and an end. This information is from Chapter 15.
- With a `for` loop, the looping-control information is found right in the `for` command's parentheses.
- With a `while` loop, the looping-control information is found before the loop, in the `while` command's parentheses, and inside the `while` loop itself.
- In HEY.C, the variable `i` is set up (or *initialized*) before the loop. Then, it's incremented inside the loop. The `while` statement itself cares only when `i` is less than 6.
- The statements belonging to the `while` — those lines clutched by the curly braces — are repeated only as long as the condition in parentheses is TRUE. If the condition is FALSE (suppose that the variable `i` was already greater than 6), those statements are skipped (as in an `if` statement).
- `While` loops are easy targets for the infinite-loop boo-boo. For this reason, you have to check extra hard to make sure that the condition that `while` tests for eventually becomes FALSE, which makes the loop stop repeating.
- For a `while` loop to quit, something must happen inside the loop that changes the condition that `while` examines.
- This is probably the first time you have seen two different programs tackle the same problem: OUCH.C uses a `for` loop, and HEY.C uses a `while` loop. Neither one is better than the other. See the section "Deciding between a `while` loop and a `for` loop," later in this chapter, for more information.

The while keyword (a formal introduction)

The while keyword is used in the C language to repeat a block of statements. Unlike the for loop, while only tells the computer when to end the loop. The loop must be set up before the while keyword, and when it's looping, the ending condition — the sizzling fuse or ticking timer — must be working. Then, the loop goes on, la-de-da, until the condition that while monitors suddenly becomes FALSE. Then, the party's over, and the program goes on, sadder but content with the fact that it was repeating itself for a while (sic).

Here's the rough format:

```
starting;
while(while_true)
{
        statement(s);
        do_this;
}
```

First, the loop must be set up, which is done with the *starting* statement. For example, this statement (or a group of statements) may declare a variable to be a certain value, to wait for a keystroke, or to do any number of interesting things.

while_true is a condition that while examines. If the condition is TRUE, the *statements* enclosed in curly braces are repeated. while examines that condition after each loop is repeated, and only when the statement is FALSE does the loop stop.

Inside the curly braces are *statements* repeated by the while loop. One of those *statements, do_this,* is required in order to control the loop. The *do_this* part needs to modify the *while_true* condition somehow so that the loop eventually stops or is broken out of.

While loops have an advantage over for loops in that they're easier to read in English. For example:

```
while(ch!='~')
```

This statement says "While the value of variable ch does not equal the tilde character, repeat the following statements." For this to make sense, you must remember, of course, that ! means *not* in C. Knowing which symbols to pronounce and which are just decorations is important to understanding C programming.

- The `while true` condition that the `while` loop examines is the same as you find in an `if` comparison. The same symbols used there are used with `while`, including ==, <, >, and !=. You can even use the logical dojabbies && (AND) or || (OR), to evaluate multiple comparisons.
- When you apply the language of the `while` loop's format to HEY.C, you get this:

Starting	Line 7	`i=1`
While_true	Line 8	`i<6`
Do_this	Line 11	`i++`

- Notice that, like the `for` keyword, `while` lacks a proper semicolon. It's just followed with a group of statements in curly braces.
- If the `while` loop contains only one statement, you can do without the curly braces:

```
starting;
while(while_true)
        do_this;
```

- Some `while` loops can even be constructed to have no statements. This is rather common:

```
while((do_this)==TRUE)
     ;
```

In this example, the semicolon is the "statement" that belongs to the `while` loop.

Deciding between a `while` loop and a `for` loop

A `while` loop and a `for` loop have many similarities — so much so that you would almost seem kooky to use `while` if you're fond of `for` and vice versa. As an example, here's the basic `for` loop from the program 100.C, over in Chapter 15:

```
for(i=1;i<=100;i=i+1)
        printf("%d\t",i);
```

This loop counts from 1 to 100 and displays each number.

Here's the same loop à la `while`:

```
i=1;
while(i<=100)
{
	printf("%d\t",i);
	i=i+1;
}
```

See how the `for` loop was broken up and placed into the `while` loop? It's easier to see if I replace the pieces' parts with big, bold letters. Take a look at this:

```
for(A;B;C)
	printf("%d\t",i);
```

It becomes

```
A;
while(B)
{
	printf("%d\t",i);
	C;
}
```

Everything is there, but it looks as though the `while` loop involves even more typing. You could say that if your fingers are tired, you can use a `for` loop. I like `while` loops because everything isn't jammed into one line. It's easier to see the different parts. Also, you can control the "C" part of the loop in different ways, which I get into in later lessons.

Another advantage of the `while` loop is that it looks more graceful. That's especially true when you're replacing what I think are those ugly `for(;;)` structures. Speaking of which. . . .

Replacing those unsightly `for(;;)` loops with elegant `while` loops

Do you remember the following line?

```
for(;;)
```

This `for` loop is repeated forever. Indefinitely. Beyond when the cows come home. Of course, nestled within the loop is a `break` statement that halts it short, such as when some condition is met. But, meeting a condition to halt a loop — doesn't that sound like a natural job for a `while` loop?

Without going through a lot of effort, load the TYPER1.C program into your editor. This program is introduced in Chapter 15 to demonstrate the `break` keyword, among other things. The bulk of the program is the following `for` loop:

```
for(;;)
{
    ch=getchar();
    if(ch=='~')
    {
        break;
    }
}
```

This example reads "For*ever* do the following statements." A character, `ch`, is read from the keyboard and then checked to see whether a tilde was typed. If so (if TRUE), the loop stops with a `break` statement.

Go ahead and delete all those lines. Yank! Yank! Yank!

Replace them with these:

```
while(ch!='~')
{
        ch=getchar();
}
```

Oh, this is too easy! The `for` statement is gone, replaced by a `while` statement that says to repeat the following statement (or statements) as long as the value of the `ch` variable doesn't equal the tilde character. As long as that's the case, the statement is repeated. And, that sole statement simply reads characters from the keyboard and stores them in the `ch` variable.

Save the changed source code to disk as TYPER2.C. Compile it and run.

After you see the `Press ~ then Enter to stop` message, type away. La-la-la. Press the tilde key to stop.

- This example shows a `while` loop elegantly replacing an ugly `for` loop.
- There's no need for a `break` statement in this loop because `while` automatically halts the loop when `ch` equals a tilde.
- The condition checked for by the `while` loop is negative. It means to keep looping as long as `ch` does *not* equal the tilde character. If you had `while(ch=='~')`, the loop would be repeated only as long as someone kept pressing the tilde key on the keyboard.
- REMEMBER: The comparison for *does not equal* is `!=`, an exclamation point (which means *not* in C) and an equal sign.
- Remember to use single quotes when you're comparing character constants.

- Not that it's worth mentioning, but the endless `while` loop setup, equivalent to `for(;;)`, is written `while(1)`. In either case, the statements belonging to the loop are repeated indefinitely or until a `break` statement frees things up.

C from the inside out

Although C can be a strict language, it can also be flexible. For example, just because a function returns a value doesn't mean that you have to store that value in a variable. You can use the value immediately inside another function.

As an example, consider the `getchar()` function, which returns a character typed at the keyboard. You can use that character immediately and not store it in a variable. That's what I call "using C inside out." It's one of the more flexible things you can do with C.

The TYPER2.C program is a useful one to illustrate the example of C code being written from the inside out. Here's what I mean:

```
while(ch!='~')
      ch=getchar();
```

The variable *ch* is set by the `getchar()` function. Or, put another way, the `getchar()` function generates the key press. The `ch` is just a holding place, and using `ch` to store that value is merely an intermediate step. To wit:

```
while(getchar()!='~')
      ;
```

The drawback is that the character generated by `getchar()` isn't saved anywhere. But, it does illustrate a nifty aspect of both the C language and the `while` loop.

Reedit the TYPER2.C source code so that it looks like this:

```
#include <stdio.h>

int main()
{
    puts("Start typing.");
    puts("Press ~ then Enter to stop");

    while(getchar() != '~')
        ;
    printf("Thanks!\n");
    return(0);
}
```

There's no longer a need to declare the variable *ch*, so that line is gone, as are the curly braces belonging to `while`.

Save the changes to disk as TYPER3.C. Compile and run.

The output behaves the same — no surprises there. But, the code is much tighter (albeit a little less readable).

TIP

- Despite this trick, it's often better to write your code in several steps rather than combine things on one line, "inside out." By illustrating the several steps, you make your code more readable.
- Write things out long-ways first. Then, after you're certain that the code works, think about recoding from the inside out.
- If you do use this trick at any length, be sure to make use of comments to describe what your thinking is. That helps later, in case you ever need to debug your code.

Not to Beat a Dead Horse or Anything. . . .

It has come to this — your first inane programmer joke in C:

```
while(dead_horse)
    beat();
```

Drawing on your vast knowledge of C, you can now appreciate what humor there is in the "no use beating a dead horse" cliché translated into the C programming language. Here are the specifics — if you can hold your sides in long enough:

- `dead_horse` is the name of a variable whose value is either TRUE or FALSE. While `dead_horse` is TRUE, the loop repeats.
- I have also seen the first line written this way:

  ```
  while(horse==dead)
  and also
  while(!alive)
  ```

  In other words, "While it's a dead horse. . . ."
- The `beat()` function is repeated over and over as long as the value of `dead_horse` is TRUE (or as long as `horse==dead`, in the alternative form).
- You don't have to enclose `beat()` in curly braces because it's the only statement belonging to the loop.
- Yuck. Yuck. Yuck.

Chapter 18

Do C While You Sleep

In This Chapter

- Introducing the `do-while` loop
- Using a delay loop
- Nesting loops
- Creating a grid
- Understanding the `continue` keyword

You're not done looping!
You're not done looping!
You're not done looping!
You're not done looping!

The `for` and `while` commands may be an odd couple, and they may be the official looping keywords of the C language, but that's not the end of the story. No, there's more than one way to weave a loop, particularly a `while` loop. This chapter covers this oddity of nature, even showing you a few situations where the mythical "upside-down" while loop becomes a necessity.

The Down-Low on Upside-Down `do-while` Loops

A `while` loop may not repeat — no, not ever. If the condition it examines is false before the loop starts, the block of statements designed to repeat is skipped over like so many between-meal snacks would be if you really knew what's in them.

Witness the cold, cruel `while` statement:

```
while(v==0)
```

If v doesn't equal 0, the statements clinging to the underside of the while loop are skipped, just as though you had written this:

```
if(v==0)
```

There's an exception, of course — a kind of loop you can fashion that always executes *at least once*. It's the upside-down while loop, called a do-while loop. This type of loop is rare, but it has the charming aspect of always wanting to go through with it once.

The devil made me do-while *it!*

The following program contains a simple do-while loop that counts backward. To add some drama, you supply the number it starts at:

```
/* An important program for NASA to properly launch
America's spacecraft. */

#include <stdio.h>

int main()
{
    int start;

    printf("Please enter the number to start\n");
    printf("the countdown (1 to 100):");
    scanf("%d",&start);

/* The countdown loop */

    do
    {
        printf("T-minus %d\n",start);
        start--;
    }
    while(start>0);

    printf("Zero!\nBlast off!\n");
    return(0);
}
```

Type this source code into your editor. Save the file to disk as COUNTDWN.C.

Compile. Fix any errors. Notice that a semicolon is required after the end of the do-while loop. If you forget it, you get an error.

Run the program.

```
Please enter the number to start
the countdown (1 to 100):
```

Be a traditionalist and type **10**. Press Enter:

```
T-minus 10
T-minus 9
et cetera . . .
T-minus 1
Zero!
Blast off!
```

- The `do while` loop executes once, no matter what.
- In a `do-while` loop, a semicolon is required at the end of the monster, after `while`'s condition (see Line 21 in the program).
- Don't forget the ampersand (`&`), required in front of the variable used in a `scanf` statement. Without that `&` there, the program *really* screws up.

`do-while` *details*

A `do-while` loop has only one advantage over the traditional `while` loop: It always works through once. It's as though `do` is an order: "Do this loop once, no matter what." It's guaranteed to repeat itself. If it doesn't, you're entitled to a full refund; write to your congressman for the details.

The `do` keyword belongs to `while` when the traditional `while` loop stands on its head. The only bonus is that the `while` loop always works through once, even when the condition it examines is false. It's as though the `while` doesn't even notice the condition until after the loop has wended its way through one time.

Here's the standard format thing:

```
do
{
        statement(s);
}
while(condition);
```

The *condition* is a true-or-false comparison that `while` examines — the same type of deal you find in an `if` comparison. If the *condition* is true, the *statements* in the loop are repeated. They keep doing so until the *condition* is false, and then the program continues. But, no matter what, the statements are always gone through once.

An important thing to remember here is that the `while` at the end of the loop requires a semicolon. Mess it up and it's sheer torture later to figure out what went wrong.

One strange aspect of the `do-while` loop is that it seriously lacks the *starting, while-true,* and *do-this* aspects of the traditional `while` and `for` loops. It has no starting condition because the loop just dives right into it. Of course, this sentence doesn't mean that the loop would lack those three items. In fact, it may look like this:

```
starting;
do
{
        statement(s);
        do_this;
}
while(while_true);
```

Yikes! Better stick with the basic `while` loop and bother with this jobbie only when something needs to be done once (or upside down).

- The condition that `while` examines is either TRUE or FALSE, according to the laws of C, the same as a comparison made by an `if` statement. You can use the same symbols used in an `if` comparison, and even use the logical doodads (`&&` or `||`) as you see fit.
- This type of loop is really rare. It has been said that only a mere 5 percent of all loops in C are of the `do-while` variety.
- You can still use `break` to halt a `do-while` loop. Only by using `break`, in fact, can you halt the statements in the midst of the loop. Otherwise, as with a `while` or `for` loop, all the statements within the curly braces repeat as a single block.

A flaw in the COUNTDWN.C program

Run the COUNTDWN program again. When it asks you to type a number, enter **200**.

There isn't a problem with this task; the program counts down from 200 to 0 and blasts off as normal. But, 200 is out of the range the program asks you to type.

TIP

Use your operating system's scroll-back buffer to view the lines that have scrolled off the screen. Hopefully, the DOS prompt or terminal window that you're using has this feature.

What about typing 0 or a negative number? Try that now; run the program and type **–5**. You see something like this:

```
T-minus -5
Zero!
Blast off!
```

The `do while` loop is executed at least once, so the `-5` is displayed. Ack! It isn't one of the great boo-boos of modern programming history, but it's bound to startle the astronauts, who are expecting a leisurely though suspenseful takeoff sequence.

The way to guard against this faux pas is to write a special loop to ensure that the value that is typed is kosher. Yes, it's a kosher number loop. That is handled quite brilliantly by `do-while`.

The always kosher number-checking `do-while` *loop*

One thing you should do in all your programs is — and I have put this on a separate line for emphasis:

TIP

Check your input bounds!

This advice makes sense only if you know what *input bounds* are. Okay: They're the range of numbers or letters or whatever that your program is looking for. In COUNTDWN.C, they're numbers from 1 to 100. In some database programs, they're the "type 40 or fewer character" limits. Stuff like that.

You want to ensure that users cannot type a wrong, or "illegal," value — one that would screw up your program. You have to make sure that they type only 40 or fewer characters. Any more than that, and your program may die a strange death. You must guard against this situation — and you can, if you write your program correctly.

Traditionally, this type of defensive programming is known as *bulletproofing*. It protects the program from this type of error in advance. That's why you check everything the user types, to see whether it's kosher. If not, you can either ask politely for input again or just print a rude error message.

To make the COUNTDWN.C program bulletproof, you have to have the program ask for input again whenever the value that's entered is either less than 1 or greater than 100. A do-while loop does that job nicely, and I'm willing to argue that on two points:

- The first argument for do-while is that it repeats itself once, no matter what. That way, you can ask the question the first time and it has to be repeated only when the value that's entered is out of range.
- The second argument is that the while part of the loop checks to see whether the value that's entered (the start variable) is less than 1 or greater than 100.

You don't have to change COUNTDWN.C very much. Just modify the first part of the program to read:

```
do
{
        printf("Please enter the number to start\n");
        printf("the countdown (1 to 100):");
        scanf("%d",&start);
}
while(start<1 || start>100);
```

The do-while loop asks the same question the program asked earlier. But, after a user types a value, the while part of the loop checks to see whether the value of the start variable is less than 1 OR greater than 100. If either condition is true, the loop repeats, asking the same question over and over until a proper value is entered.

Save the changed COUNTDWN.C source code to disk. Compile the program. Run it:

```
Please enter the number to start
the countdown (1 to 100):
```

Type **0** and press Enter.

Ha! The program asks again. Type **101** and press Enter.

Golly, this program is smart! Any value outside the range from 1 to 100 causes the program to ask again and again for the proper number to be pressed. That's all made possible with a nifty do-while loop.

- Bounds checking like this is done in just about every professional program. Whenever you're asked to type a value in a certain range or to type fewer than so-many letters, a loop is in there, making sure that you're doing it right.

- Most of the problems Microsoft has had with critical or fatal errors in its software are caused by a *lack* of this type of bounds checking.
- Refer to Chapter 14 for more information about the logical `||` (OR) comparison.
- You may want to insert the following comment into your source code, just above the first loop:

```
/* This loop ensures they type in
a proper value */
```

Nested Loops and Other Bird-Brained Concepts

Glorious loops within loops, wheels within wheels, spinning 'round like some nauseating amusement park ride with a drugged-out, tattooed guy named Craig asleep at the controls. But that's another subject. In the C programming language, spinning two loops is a cinchy and practical thing to do. It's called making a *nested loop,* or with one loop inside another.

Adding a tense, dramatic delay to the COUNTDWN.C program

What's missing from the COUNTDWN.C program is a little tension. In case you haven't noticed, typing any value from 1 to 100 doesn't really affect the speed at which the countdown is displayed; after you press Enter, the text *zips* on up the screen. No suspense!

To help slow down the display, you can insert a delay loop into the program. The purpose of the delay loop is merely to spin the computer's CPU, burning up clock cycles to slow down the program at a certain point. Yes, you do it on purpose.

Modify the second `do while` loop in the COUNTDWN.C program to read:

```
do
{
    printf("T-minus %d\n",start);
    start--;
    for(delay=0;delay<100000;delay++);   /* delay loop */
}
while(start>0);
```

And, because the program would puke if it encountered the delay variable without its first being declared, add the following line just below the `int` start statement, at the top of the source code:

```
long delay;
```

Here's the entire, updated source code, including changes added in the previous sections:

```
/* An important program for NASA to properly launch
America's spacecraft. */

#include <stdio.h>

int main()
{
    int start;
    long delay;
    do
    {
        printf("Please enter the number to start\n");
        printf("the countdown (1 to 100):");
        scanf("%d",&start);
    }
    while(start<1 || start>100);


/* The countdown loop */

    do
    {
        printf("T-minus %d\n",start);
        start--;
        for(delay=0;delay<100000;delay++);   /* delay loop */
    }
    while(start>0);

    printf("Zero!\nBlast off!\n");
    return(0);
}
```

Ensure that your source code for COUNTDWN.C resembles this source code, which now has a nested loop, for purposes of delaying the text display and output.

Save. Compile. Run.

If the output still runs too fast, change the value in the `for` loop from 100,000 to 1,000,000 (written like this: `1000000`). If that still doesn't work, try 2,000,000. (If you need to go to 4,000,000, you need to declare the delay variable as an `unsigned long`.)

- Having a `for` loop inside a `while` loop is referred to as a *nested loop.* Note that both loops don't need to be of the same type (two `for` loops or two `while` loops).
- A nested loop is basically one loop spinning 'round inside another loop.
- The first loop, or outside loop, ticks off first. Then, the inside loop ticks off, looping as many times as it does. After that, the outside loop ticks off another one, and then the inside loop is repeated entirely again. That's how they work.
- Keep separate the variables associated with one loop or another. For example, the following two `for` loops are nested improperly:

```
for(x=0;x<5;x++)
      for(x=5;x>0;x--);
```

  Because `x` is used in both loops, these nested loops don't behave as you expect. This loop is infinite, in fact, because both are manipulating the same variable in different directions.

- This disaster probably isn't apparent to you. You write some huge program and nest two `for` loops miles apart without thinking about it, by using your favorite variable `x` (or `i`) in each one. Those kind of bugs can wreck your day.
- The way to avoid messing up nested loops is to use different variables with each one — for example, `a` or `b`, or `i1` and `i2`, or even something descriptive, such as `start` and `delay`, as used in the COUNTDWN.C example.
- That nested `for` loop in COUNTDWN.C ends with a semicolon, indicating that it doesn't "own" any statements that are repeated. Here's another way you could format it:

```
for(delay=0;delay<100000;delay++)
      ;
```

  This example shows you that the `for` loop doesn't have any statements worth repeating. It just sits and spins the microprocessor, wasting time (which is what you want).

- Although delay loops, such as the one shown in COUNTDWN.C, are common, a better way exists. That is to use the computer's internal clock to time a delay of a specific duration. I show you an example in *C All-in-One Desk Reference For Dummies* (Wiley).
- My first IBM PC — some 20 years ago — required a *delay* loop that counted to only 10,000 for about a half-second pause between each line displayed. Today's computers are much, much faster — obviously!

TIP

Sleepy time!

The C language does have a built-in delay function, so you really have no need to program a delay loop — as long as you can stand the wait!

The `sleep()` function is used to pause a program for a given number of seconds. Yes — I said *seconds.* You specify the seconds to wait in `sleep()`'s parentheses:

```
sleep(40);
```

You can catch 40 winks — or 40 seconds — of wait time while a program is running.

You can replace the for delay loop in COUNTDWN.C with

```
sleep(1);
```

This line adds a dramatic pause between each line's output — a slow, dramatic, and often maddening pause. But, it works.

Note that in some implementations of GCC, the `sleep()` function apparently uses milliseconds, not seconds, as its argument. To delay one second, for example, you use this command in COUNTDWN.C:

```
sleep(1000);
```

Keep in mind that this implementation of the `sleep()` function is nonstandard.

The nitty GRID.C of nested loops

Nested loops happen all the time. Most often, they happen when you're filling in a grid or an array. In that case, you work on rows and columns, filling up the columns row-by-row, one after the other, or vice versa. An example of how it's done is shown in the GRID.C program, which displays a grid of numbers and letters:

```
#include <stdio.h>

int main()
{
    int a;
    char b;

    printf("Here is thy grid...\n");

    for(a=1;a<10;a++)
    {
        for(b='A';b<'K';b++)
        {
            printf("%d-%c ",a,b);
        }
        putchar('\n');  /* end of line */
    }
    return(0);
}
```

This program creates a 10-by-9 square (okay — *grid*) of numbers and letters by using a nested-loop arrangement.

Enter the source code into your editor. Save your efforts to disk as GRID.C.

Compile the program. Notice that putting two `for` statements together doesn't cause the compiler to spew errors at you (unless you made a typo somewhere).

Run. Here's what the output should look like:

```
Here is thy grid...
1-A 1-B 1-C 1-D 1-E 1-F 1-G 1-H 1-I 1-J
2-A 2-B 2-C 2-D 2-E 2-F 2-G 2-H 2-I 2-J
3-A 3-B 3-C 3-D 3-E 3-F 3-G 3-H 3-I 3-J
4-A 4-B 4-C 4-D 4-E 4-F 4-G 4-H 4-I 4-J
5-A 5-B 5-C 5-D 5-E 5-F 5-G 5-H 5-I 5-J
6-A 6-B 6-C 6-D 6-E 6-F 6-G 6-H 6-I 6-J
7-A 7-B 7-C 7-D 7-E 7-F 7-G 7-H 7-I 7-J
8-A 8-B 8-C 8-D 8-E 8-F 8-G 8-H 8-I 8-J
9-A 9-B 9-C 9-D 9-E 9-F 9-G 9-H 9-I 9-J
```

Wow. Such efficiency should please any government bureaucracy.

- The first, outer `for` loop counts from 1 to 10.
- The inner `for` loop may seem strange, but it's not. It's only taking advantage of the dual-number/-character nature of letters in a computer. The character variable `b` starts out equal to the letter *A* and is incremented one letter at a time, up to the letter *K*. What happens is that `b` is set equal to the letter *A*'s ASCII value, which is 65. The variable `b` then increments up to the letter *K*'s ASCII value, which is 75. It's sneaky, but doable.
- The `printf()` function displays the numbers and letters as the inner loop spins. You can see this process on your screen: The outer loop stays at one number while the letters *A* through *K* are printed. Then, the outer loop is incremented, and the next row of letters is printed.
- Note that the `printf()` function has a space after the `%c` character. That's what keeps the columns in the grid from running into each other.
- The `putchar()` function displays a single character on the screen. In GRID.C, it's used to display a `\n` newline character at the end of each row.

Break *the Brave and* Continue *the Fool*

Two C language keywords can be used to directly control loops in your programs. The keywords are `break` and `continue`. The `break` keyword should be familiar to you, having been introduced in Chapter 15 and tossed at you every now and again since then. The `continue` keyword is a new beast, but it plays an important role — one that you may even find handy.

What `continue` does is to instantly repeat a loop. It works like `break` in that the rest of the statements in the loop are skipped; unlike `break`, the `continue` command sends the computer back to the beginning of the loop. The fool!

- Both `break` and `continue` are C language keywords and statements unto themselves. They each must end with a semicolon.
- Both `break` and `continue` work inside any C loop.
- Both `break` and `continue` cause horrid errors outside a loop.

Please continue. . . .

The following program is BORC.C, which isn't named after the Muppet's Swedish Chef. Instead, it's an acronym for *b*reak *or* *c*ontinue, the two keywords this program fiddles with:

```
#include <stdio.h>

int main()
{
    int x=0;

    for(;;)
    {
        x++;
        if(x<=5)
        {
            printf("%d, ",x);
            continue;
        }
        printf("%d is greater than 5!\n",x);
        break;
    }
    return(0);
}
```

Type the source code for BORC.C into your editor. Save it to disk as BORC.C, which stands for *b*reak *or* *c*ontinue. (If you keep thinking of Bork-Bork-Bork, you save it to disk as BORK.C, which isn't what I'm after.)

Compile and run the program.

Here's how it goes:

```
1, 2, 3, 4, 5, 6 is greater than 5!
```

The BORC.C program contains an endless `for` loop. Furthermore, the loop is cut short by the `continue` statement. After the value of `x` grows to be more than 5, the `continue` is skipped and, finally, a `break` statement stops the endless loop.

- The `for(;;)` part indicates an endless loop. I read it as "for ever."
- Notice the space after the `%d` and comma in the `printf()` statement.
- The `continue` statement causes the rest of the loop — the `printf()` and `break` — to be skipped, and then the loop is repeated. The increasing value of `x` proves that the loop continues to spin.
- An `else` condition doesn't have to be present to complement the `if` in Line 10. That's because `continue` halts the program right then and there! If no `continue` were present, the `break` in Line 16 would ensure that the loop ran through only once.

The `continue` keyword

Like the `break` keyword, the `continue` keyword is used to affect how a loop loops. This time, the job is to immediately repeat the loop, skipping over the remaining statements and starting the loop over with the first line (the `for`, `while`, or `do` or whatever started the loop in the first place):

```
continue;
```

The `continue` keyword is a C language statement unto itself and must end properly with a semicolon.

The `continue` command comes in handy when you have statements in a loop that you don't want to repeat every time; `continue` just skips over them and starts the loop over at the beginning.

- The `continue` command works in any loop, not just in `while` loops.
- Like `break`, `continue` affects only the loop it's in.
- The `continue` keyword forces the computer to instantly repeat a loop. The rest of the statements in the loop are just skipped, and the loop starts all over.
- Note that `continue` repeats only the loop it's in. If you have a nested loop, keep in mind that `continue` affects only one loop at a time. Also, `continue` cannot repeat a `while` loop when the loop's condition becomes false.

- Keep in mind that although `continue` forces another spin of the loop's wheel, it doesn't reinitialize the loop. It tells the compiler to "go again," not to "start over."
- You should keep in mind only two real warnings about the `continue` command: Don't use it outside a loop or expect it to work on nested loops; and be careful where you put it in a `while` loop, lest you skip over the loop's counter and accidentally create an endless loop.
- As a final, consoling point, this command is rarely used. In fact, many C programmers may be a little fuzzy on what it does or may not know precisely how to use it.

Chapter 19

Switch Case, or, From 'C' to Shining 'c'

In This Chapter

- Solving the endless `else-if` puzzle
- Using `switch-case`
- Creating a `switch-case` structure

Honestly, I don't believe that `switch-case` is really a loop. But the word *loop* works so much better than my alternative, *structure thing*. That's because the statements held inside the `switch-case` structure thing aren't really repeated, yet in a way they are. Well, anyway.

This chapter uncovers the final kind-of-loop thing in the C language, which is called `switch-case`. It's not so much a loop as it's a wonderful method of cleaning up a potential problem with multiple `if` statements. As is true with most things in a programming language, it's just better for me to show you an example than to try to explain it. That's what this chapter does.

The Sneaky `switch-case` *Loops*

Let's all go to the lobby,
Let's all go to the lobby,
Let's all go to the lobby,
And get ourselves a treat!

— Author unknown

And, when you get to the lobby, you probably order yourself some goodies from the menu. In fact, management at your local theater has just devised an interesting computer program to help cut down on pesky, hourly-wage employees. The program they have devised is shown right here:

```
/* Theater lobby snack bar program */

#include <stdio.h>

int main()
{
    char c;

    printf("Please make your treat selection:\n");
    printf("1 - Beverage.\n");
    printf("2 - Candy.\n");
    printf("3 - Hot dog.\n");
    printf("4 - Popcorn.\n");
    printf("Your choice:");

/* Figure out what they typed in. */

    c=getchar();
    if(c=='1')
        printf("Beverage\nThat will be $8.00\n");
    else if(c=='2')
        printf("Candy\nThat will be $5.50\n");
    else if(c=='3')
        printf("Hot dog\nThat will be $10.00\n");
    else if(c=='4')
        printf("Popcorn\nThat will be $7.50\n");
    else
    {
        printf("That is not a proper selection.\n");
        printf("I'll assume you're just not hungry.\n");
        printf("Can I help whoever's next?\n");
    }
    return(0);
}
```

Type this source code into your editor. Save it to disk as LOBBY1.C. This should brighten your heart because you know that more LOBBY programs are on the way. . . .

Compile. Fix any errors. You may get a few because it's such a long program. Watch your spelling and remember your semicolons. Recompile after fixing any errors.

Run:

```
Please make your treat selection:
1 - Beverage.
2 - Candy.
3 - Hot dog.
4 - Popcorn.
Your choice:
```

Press **2**, for Candy. Love them Hot Tamales! You see

```
Candy
That will be $5.50
```

Gadzooks! For Hot Tamales? I'm sneaking food in next time. . . .

Run the program again and try a few more options. Then, try an option not on the list. Type **M** for a margarita:

```
That is not a proper selection.
I'll assume you're just not hungry.
Can I help whoever's next?
```

Oh, well.

The `switch-case` Solution to the LOBBY Program

Don't all those `else-if` things in the LOBBY1.C program look funny? Doesn't it appear awkward? Maybe not. But it is rather clumsy. That's because you have a better way to pick one of several choices in C. What you need is a `switch case` loop.

Right away, I need to tell you that `switch-case` isn't really a loop. Instead, it's a *selection statement,* which is the official designation of what an `if` statement is. `switch-case` allows you to select from one of several items, like a long, complex string of `if` statements — the kind that's now pestering the LOBBY1.C program.

Next is the source code for LOBBY2.C, an internal improvement to the LOBBY1.C program. It's internal because you're just messing with the program's guts here — making them more elegant. Externally, the program still works the same:

```
/* Theater lobby snack bar program */

#include <stdio.h>

int main()
{
    char c;

    printf("Please make your treat selection:\n");
    printf("1 - Beverage.\n");
    printf("2 - Candy.\n");
    printf("3 - Hot dog.\n");
    printf("4 - Popcorn.\n");
    printf("Your choice:");

/* Figure out what they typed in. */

    c=getchar();
    switch(c)
    {
        case '1':
            printf("Beverage\nThat will be $8.00\n");
            break;
        case '2':
            printf("Candy\nThat will be $5.50\n");
            break;
        case '3':
            printf("Hot dog\nThat will be $10.00\n");
            break;
        case '4':
            printf("Popcorn\nThat will be $7.50\n");
            break;
        default:
            printf("That is not a proper selection.\n");
            printf("I'll assume you're just not hungry.\n");
            printf("Can I help whoever's next?\n");
    }
    return(0);
}
```

Keep the LOBBY1.C program in your editor. Use this source code for LOBBY2.C as a guide and edit what you see on your screen.

You're changing all the `if` statements into a `switch-case` thing. Be careful what you type. When you're done, double-check Lines 19 through 37 in the source code to make sure that you got it right. (The first few lines of the program don't change.)

Compile. Fix any errors or typos. Note that those are colons — not semicolons — on the `case` lines. The character constants are enclosed in single quotes. The word *default* also ends in a colon.

Run. You should see no difference in the output. Internally, however, you have converted an ugly string of `if-else` statements into an elegant decision-making structure: the `switch-case` loop (or "structure thing").

- Detailed information on what happens in a `switch-case` loop is covered in the next section.
- The `switch` command in Line 19 takes the single character typed at the keyboard (from Line 18) and tells the various `case` statements in its curly braces to find a match.
- Each of the `case` statements (Lines 21, 24, 27, and 30) compares its character constant with the value of variable `c`. If there's a match, the statements belonging to that `case` are executed.
- The `break` in each `case` statement tells the compiler that the `switch-case` thing is done and to skip the rest of the statements.
- If the `break` is missing, execution falls through to the next group of `case` statements, which are then executed, no matter what. Watch out for that! Missing `break`s are the bane of `switch-case` loops.
- The final item in the `switch-case` thing is `default`. It's the option that gets executed if no match occurs.

The Old `switch-case` Trick

This is one booger of a command to try to become comfy with. Although `switch-case` things are important, they contain lots of programming finesse that many beginners stumble over. My advice is to work through the programs in this chapter to get a feel for things and then check mark bullets in this section for review purposes or to figure out what went wrong when things don't work.

The `switch` keyword is used to give your programs an easy way to make multiple-choice guesses. It should replace any long repetition of `if-else` statements you're using to make a series of comparisons.

Using `switch` involves creating a complex structure that includes the `case`, `break`, and `default` keywords. Here's how it may look:

```
switch(choice)
{
      case item1:
                          statement(s);
                          break;
      case item2:
      case item3:
                          statement(s);
                          break;
      default:
                          statement(s);
}
```

choice must be a variable. It can be a key typed at the keyboard, a value returned from the mouse or joystick, or some other interesting number or character the program has to evaluate.

After the `case` keyword come various *items;* `item1`, `item2`, `item3`, and so on are the various items that *choice* can be. Each one is a constant, either a character or a value; *they cannot be variables*. The `case` line ends in a colon, not in a semicolon.

Belonging to each `case item` are one or more *statements*. The program executes these *statements* when `item` matches the *choice* that `switch` is making — like an `if` statement match. The *statements* are *not* enclosed in curly braces. The *statements* are also optional. (More on that in a second.)

The last statement in a group of `case` statements is typically a `break` command. Without the `break` there, the program keeps working its way through the next `case` statement.

The last item in the `switch` structure is `default`. It contains the statements to be executed when no match occurs — like the final `else` in an `if-else` structure. The `default` statements are executed no matter what (unless you `break` out of the structure earlier).

The most important thing to remember about `switch-case` is that the program always walks through the entire thing unless you put a `break` in there when you want it to stop. For example, consider this program snippet:

```
switch(key)
{
    case 'A':
        printf("The A key.\n");
        break;
```

```
    case 'B':
        printf("The B key.\n");
        break;
    case 'C':
    case 'D':
        printf("The C or D keys.\n");
        break;
    default:
        printf("I don't know that key.\n");
}
```

Suppose that `key` is a single-character variable containing a character that was just typed at the keyboard. Here are three examples of how it would work:

Example 1: Suppose that the `key` variable contains the letter *A*. The program works:

```
switch(key)
```

Pick a key! So, `key` equals big `A`. Mosey on down the `case` list:

```
case 'A':
```

Yup, we have a match. The value of `key` equals the constant, big `A`. Execute those statements:

```
printf("The A key.\n");
```

Message printed. Then:

```
break;
```

Bail out of the `switch-case` thing. I'm done.

If you didn't bail out at this point, the rest of the statements in the `switch-case` structure would be executed *no matter what.*

Example 2: Suppose that a user presses the C key. Here's how it works:

```
switch(key)
```

`key` is a C. It's time to check the `case` statements for a match:

```
case 'A':
```

Nope! Skip to the next `case`:

```
case 'B':
```

Nope! Skip to the next `case`:

```
case 'C':
```

Yup! There's a match. The value of `key` equals the character constant `'C'` right here. What's next?

```
case 'D':
```

The computer just goes ho-hum. There's no match, but it's still waiting for instructions because it matched the `case 'C'`. Because the statements after `case 'D'` are the first that it finds, it executes those:

```
printf("The C or D keys.\n");
```

Message printed. Then:

```
break;
```

The rest of the `switch-case` structure is skipped.

Example 3: This time, the character X is entered at the keyboard. Here's how the `switch-case` thing works:

```
switch(key)
```

`key` is an X. The computer wends its way through the `case` statements for a match:

```
case 'A':
```

Nope! Skip to the next `case`:

```
case 'B':
```

Nope! Skip to the next `case`:

```
case 'C':
```

Nope! Skip to the next `case`:

```
case 'D':
```

Nope! All the cases are done. What's left is the *default,* which supposedly handles everything else — including the X:

```
default:
```

and the only statement:

```
printf("I don't know that key.\n");
```

The switch-case structure is done.

- The thing in switch's parentheses (*choice*) must work out to either a character value or an integer value. Most programmers put a character or integer variable there. You can also put a C language statement or function in the parentheses, as long as it works out to a character value or an integer value when it's done.
- The case line ends with a colon, not a semicolon. The statements belonging to case aren't enclosed in curly braces.
- The last statement belonging to a group of case statements is usually break. This statement tells the computer to skip over the rest of the switch structure and keep running the program.
- If you forget the break, the rest of the switch structure keeps running. That may not be what you want.
- The computer matches each item in the case statement with the choice that switch is making. If there's a match, the statements belonging to that case are executed; otherwise, they're skipped.
- It's possible for a case to lack any statements. In that case, a match simply "falls through" to the next case statement.
- The keyword case must be followed by a constant value — either a number or a character. For example:

  ```
  case 56:          /* item 56 chosen */
  ```

  or

  ```
  case 'L':         /* L key pressed */
  ```

  You cannot stick a variable there. It just doesn't work. You may want to. You may even e-mail me, asking whether you can, but you can't. Give up now.
- Most C manuals refer to the command as switch, and case is just another keyword. I use switch-case as a unit because it helps me remember that the second word is case and not something else.
- You don't need a default to end the structure. If you leave it off and none of the case's items matches, nothing happens.

The Special Relationship between `while` and `switch-case`

Most programs have at their core a `while` loop. But, within that `while` loop, they usually have a nice, big `switch-case` structure. That's because you can keep choosing options over and over until you choose the option that closes the program. The over-and-over thing is a loop handled by `while`, and the selection is done by a `switch-case` structure. To drive this point home, I present the final incarnation of the LOBBY.C program:

```
/* Theater lobby snack bar program */

#include <stdio.h>

int main()
{
    char c;
    int done;
    float total=0;

    printf("Please make your treat selections:\n");
    printf("1 - Beverage.\n");
    printf("2 - Candy.\n");
    printf("3 - Hot dog.\n");
    printf("4 - Popcorn.\n");
    printf("= - Done.\n");
    printf("Your choices:\n");

/* Figure out what they typed in. */

    done=0;
    while(!done)
    {
        c=getchar();
        switch(c)
        {
            case '1':
                printf("Beverage\t$8.00\n");
                total+=8;
                break;
            case '2':
                printf("Candy\t\t$5.50\n");
                total+=5.5;
                break;
            case '3':
                printf("Hot dog\t\t$10.00\n");
                total+=10;
                break;
```

```
            case '4':
                printf("Popcorn\t\t$7.50\n");
                total+=7.5;
                break;
            case '=':
                printf("= Total of $%.2f\n",total);
                printf("Please pay the cashier.\n");
                done=1;
                break;
            default:
                printf("Improper selection.\n");
        }   /* end switch */
    }       /* end while */
    return(0);
}
```

Please type the source code for LOBBY3.C into your editor. You can try editing the LOBBY2.C program, if you want, but I have made many subtle changes to the program and wouldn't want you to miss any. Start from scratch, if you're willing.

Save the file to disk as LOBBY3.C.

Compile. Fix any errors that may have crept into the code.

Run:

```
Please make your treat selection:
1 - Beverage.
2 - Candy.
3 - Hot dog.
4 - Popcorn.
= - Done.
Your choice:
```

To properly run the program, type your choices all at once and then press the equal sign (=) key and then Enter. This strategy avoids the buffering problem with the `getchar()` function, which I could address, but it's beyond the scope of this chapter.

For example, if you want a beverage and a hot dog, type **13=** and then press Enter.

```
Beverage        $8.00
Hot dog         $10.00
Total of $18.00
Please pay the cashier.
```

Run the program again, enter **123412341234xx92431=**, and then press Enter:

```
Beverage          $8.00
Candy             $5.50
Hot dog           $10.00
Popcorn           $7.50
Beverage          $8.00
Candy             $5.50
Hot dog           $10.00
Popcorn           $7.50
Beverage          $8.00
Candy             $5.50
Hot dog           $10.00
Popcorn           $7.50
Improper selection.
Improper selection.
Improper selection.
Candy             $5.50
Popcorn           $7.50
Hot dog           $10.00
Beverage          $8.00
Total of $124.00
Please pay the cashier.
```

This is the last time I'm taking all you guys to the lobby!

- Most programs employ this exact type of loop. The `while(!done)` spins 'round and 'round while a `switch-case` thing handles all the program's input.
- One of the `switch-case` items handles the condition when the loop must stop. In LOBBY3.C, the key is the equal sign. It sets the value of the `done` variable to 1. The `while` loop then stops repeating.
- C views the value `0` as `FALSE`. So, by setting `done` equal to `0`, by using the `!` (not), the `while` loop is executed. The reason for all this is so that the loop `while(!done)` reads "while not done" in English.
- The various `case` structures then examine the keys that were pressed. For each match `1` through `4`, three things happen: The item that is ordered is displayed on the screen; the total is increased by the cost of that item (`total+=3`, for example); and a `break` statement busts out of the `switch-case` thing. At that point, the `while` loop continues to repeat as additional selections are made.
- You may remember the `+=` thing, from Chapter 16. It's a contraction of `total = total + `*`value`*.

Part IV
C Level

The 5th Wave By Rich Tennant

In this part . . .

Your C language journey has been, I hope, a fun one. Sadly, I have lots more ground to cover, but only a scant few more pages in which to cover it. Therefore, I collected what I feel are some important concepts that are touched on earlier in this book and present them in this part of the book in a more formal fashion.

This part of the book answers some questions that may have been nagging you from other parts of this book. For example, why is it `int main()`, and what is the point of the `return(0);` statement? I discuss what exactly `#include <stdio.h>` does as well as provide more information on `printf()` and give you an introduction into arrays, strings, and lots of other fun stuff. So, crack your knuckles and let's get going!

Chapter 20

Writing That First Function

In This Chapter

- Understanding functions
- Creating the `jerk()` function
- Prototyping functions
- Using the upside-down prototype
- Formatting and naming functions

Functions are where you "roll your own" in the C language. They're nifty little *procedures,* or series of commands, that tell the computer to do something. All that's bundled into one package, which your program can then use repeatedly and conveniently. In a way, writing a function is like adding your own commands to the C language.

If you're familiar with computer programming languages, you should recognize functions as similar to subroutines or procedures. If you're not familiar with computer programming (and *bless you*), think of a function as a shortcut. It's a black box that does something wonderful or mysterious. After you construct the function, the rest of your program can use it — just like any other C language function or keyword. This chapter definitely puts the *fun* into function.

(This chapter is the first one in this book to lack a clever use of the letter *C* in the title. Yeah, I was getting sick of it too C sick, in fact.)

Meet Mr. Function

Are functions necessary? Absolutely! Every program must have at least one function, the `main()` function. That's required. Beyond that, you don't need to create your own functions. But, without them, often your code would contain a great deal of duplicate instructions.

A silly example you don't have to type

Suppose that you write a program that plays "Alexander's Rag Time Band" every time a user does something pleasing. Because the programming required to play the song is odd and unique, you decide to write a function to conduct the PC's orchestra. For giggles, suppose that it looks like this:

```
playAlex()
{
        play(466,125);
        play(494,375);
        play(466,125);
        play(494,1000);
        /* and there would be more... */
}
```

Assume that the `play()` function is used to make the computer's speaker squawk at a specific pitch for a certain duration. A gaggle of `play()` functions put together makes the computer whistle a tune.

With all that neatly tucked into a function, your program can then "call" the function every time it wants to play the song. Rather than repeat a vast chorus line of commands, you merely stick the following line into your code:

```
playAlex();
```

That's a C language "command" that says "Go off yonder to said `playAlex()` function, do what you must while you're there, and then return to this here very spot to continue a-workin'." Lo, the function has made writing the program easier.

- You create a function by writing it in your source code. The function has a name, optional doodads, plus its own C language code that carries out the function's task. More on this later in this chapter.
- To use a function, you *call* it. Yoo-hoo! You do this by typing the function's name in your program, followed by the empty parentheses:

  ```
  playAlex();
  ```

  This command calls the `playAlex()` function, and the computer goes off and does whatever it's instructed to do in that function.
- Yes, that's right. Calling (or using) a function is as easy as sticking its name in your source code, just like any other C language statement.
- Some functions require information in their parentheses. For example, `puts`:

  ```
  puts("Oh, what a great way to start the day.");
  ```

- Some functions *return* a value. That is, they produce something that your program can use, examine, compare, or whatever. The `getchar()` function returns a character typed at the keyboard, which is typically stored in a character variable; `thus`:

```
thus=getchar();
```

- Some functions require parentheses stuff *and* return a value.
- Other functions (such as `playAlex()`) neither require parentheses stuff nor return a value.
- Functions are nothing new. Most C programs are full of them, such as `printf()`, `getchar()`, `atoi()`, and others. Unlike your own functions, these functions are part of the compiler's *library* of functions. Even so, the functions you write work just like those others do.
- Creating a function doesn't really add a new word to the C language. However, you can use the function just like any other function in your programs; `printf()` and `scanf()`, for example.

A potentially redundant program in need of a function

I like to think of functions as removing the redundancy from programs. If anything must be done more than once, shuffle it off into a function. That makes writing the program so much easier. It also breaks up the `main()` function in your source code (which can get tediously long).

The following sample program is BIGJERK1.C, a litany of sorts devoted to someone named Bill, who is a jerk:

```
#include <stdio.h>

int main()
{
    printf("He calls me on the phone with nothing say\n");
    printf("Not once, or twice, but three times a day!\n");
    printf("Bill is a jerk!\n");
    printf("He insulted my wife, my cat, my mother\n");
    printf("He irritates and grates, like no other!\n");
    printf("Bill is a jerk!\n");
    printf("He chuckles it off, his big belly a-heavin'\n");
    printf("But he won't be laughing when I get even!\n");
    printf("Bill is a jerk!\n");
    return(0);
}
```

Type this program into your editor. Double-check all the parentheses and double quotes. They're maddening. Maddening!

Compile and run BIGJERK1.C. It displays the litany on the screen. Ho-hum. Nothing big. Notice that one chunk of the program is repeated three times. Smells like a good opportunity for a function.

- Most of the redundancy a function removes is much more complex than a simple `printf()` statement. Ah, but this is a demo.
- None of the Bills I personally know is a jerk. Feel free to change the name Bill into someone else's name, if you feel the urge.
- In the olden days (and I'm showing my age here), every byte in a program was vital. A message such as `Bill is a jerk` repeated over and over meant that precious bytes of data were being wasted on a silly text string. Ancient programmers, such as myself, honed their skills by removing excess bytes from programs like this one. Shaving a program's size from 4,096 bytes to 3,788 bytes was considered a worthy accomplishment. Of course, with today's mega-/gigacomputers, saving space like that is considered trivial.

The noble `jerk()` function

It's time to add your first new word to the C language — the `jerk()` function. Okay, `jerk` isn't a C language word. It's a function. But you use it in a program just as you would use any other C language word or function. The compiler doesn't know the difference — as long as you set everything up properly.

Next, the new, improved "Bill is a jerk" program contains the noble `jerk()` function, right in there living next to the primary `main()` function. This program is a major step in your programming skills — a moment to be savored. Pause to enjoy a beverage after typing it:

```
#include <stdio.h>

int main()
{
    printf("He calls me on the phone with nothing say\n");
    printf("Not once, or twice, but three times a day!\n");
    jerk();
    printf("He insulted my wife, my cat, my mother\n");
    printf("He irritates and grates, like no other!\n");
    jerk();
    printf("He chuckles it off, his big belly a-heavin'\n");
    printf("But he won't be laughing when I get even!\n");
    jerk();
    return(0);
}

/* This is the jerk() function */
```

```
jerk()
{
    printf("Bill is a jerk\n");
}
```

Type the source code for BIGJERK2.C in your editor. Pay special attention to the formatting and such. Save the file to disk as BIGJERK2.C. Compile and run. The output from this program is the same as the first BIGJERK program.

- Depending on your compiler, and how sensitive it has been set up for error reporting, you may see a slew of warning errors when you're compiling BIGJERK2.C: You may see a `no prototype` error; a `Function should return a value` error; a `'jerk' undefined` error; or even a `no return value` error.
- Despite the errors, the program should run. Those are mere "warning" errors — violations of C language protocol — not the more deadly, fatal errors, which means that the program is unable to work properly.
- I show you how to cover — and cure — the errors in a few sections. Hold fast.

How the `jerk()` function works in BIGJERK2.C

A function works like a magic box. It produces something. In the case of the `jerk()` function in BIGJERK2.C, it produces a string of text displayed on the screen. `Bill is a jerk` — like that.

In the BIGJERK2.C program, the computer ambles along, executing C language instructions as normal, from top to bottom. Then, it encounters this line:

```
jerk();
```

That's not a C language keyword, and it's not a function known to the compiler. The computer looks around and finds a `jerk()` function defined in your source code. Contented, it jumps over to that spot and executes those statements in that function. When it reaches the last curly brace in the function, the computer figures that it must be done, so it returns to where it was in the main program. This happens three times in BIGJERK2.C.

Figure 20-1 illustrates what's happening in a graphic sense. Each time the computer sees the `jerk()` function, it executes the commands in that function. This works just as though those statements were right there in the code (as shown in the figure) — which, incidentally, is exactly how the BIGJERK1.C program works.

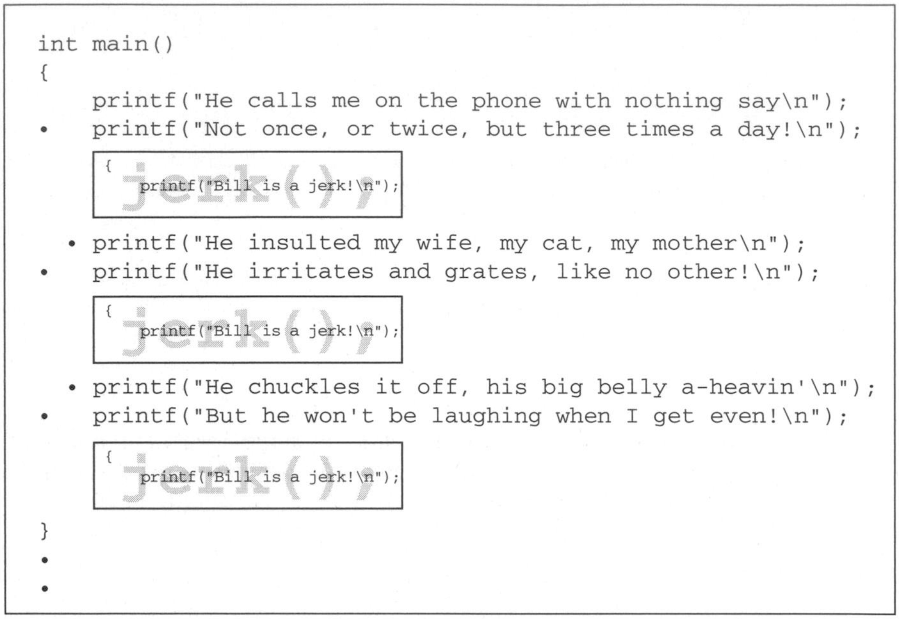
int main()
{
printf("He calls me on the phone with nothing say\n");
printf("Not once, or twice, but three times a day!\n");
{
jerk();
printf("Bill is a jerk!\n");
printf("He insulted my wife, my cat, my mother\n");
printf("He irritates and grates, like no other!\n");
{
jerk();
printf("Bill is a jerk!\n");
printf("He chuckles it off, his big belly a-heavin'\n");
printf("But he won't be laughing when I get even!\n");
{
jerk();
printf("Bill is a jerk!\n");
}

Figure 20-1: How a function works in a program.

- The computer still reads instructions in the source code from the top down in the `main` function. However, when the computer sees another function, such as `jerk()`, it temporarily sidesteps to run the instructions in that function. Then, it returns back to where it was.
- Keep in mind that not all functions are as simplistic as `jerk()`. Most of them contain many lines of code — stuff that would be too complex and redundant to use all over the place in a program.

Prototyping Your Functions

Prototyping refers to the art of telling the compiler what's demanded of a function. It may seem like a silly thing to do, but it is in fact a good way to ensure that functions are used properly — plus it helps you keep track of your code. I know, it sounds a little like the compiler doesn't trust you. But you probably don't trust it much either, so the respect is mutual.

- *Proto* comes from the Greek word for *first.*
- *Typing* comes from the Latin word for "what you do on a keyboard."

Prototypical prototyping problems

You have to do two things to appease the prototyping gods. First, you have to properly configure the `jerk` function itself. Change Line 19 in the BIGJERK2.C source code to read:

```
void jerk()
```

This line tells the compiler that the `jerk()` function returns no values. That takes care of any `function should return a value` type of errors. (I cover functions that return values in Chapter 22; functions that don't return a value are `void`. So there.)

Second, you have to tell the compiler about the `jerk()` function way early in the program. Essentially, that's what prototyping is all about: You tell the compiler, "Hello? There's a `jerk()` function later in this program, and here's what you should expect to see." You do this by sticking a line up top that looks like the start of the `jerk` function — but ends with a semicolon:

```
void jerk(void);
```

Stick this line between the `#include <stdio.h>` and the `int main()` that starts the `main()` function. The first part of your program looks like this:

```
#include <stdio.h>

void jerk(void);

int main()
```

The `void jerk(void);` line is the prototype. It tells the compiler to expect a `jerk()` function later on in the source code. It also says that the function will be of the `void` type, and won't return any values. Furthermore, the `jerk()` function doesn't require any values, which is why a `void` is in its parentheses. It's heavy-duty `void` material. Just follow along if you don't understand it.

Make the editing changes per the preceding instructions. A final rendition of the BIGJERK2.C program is shown here:

```
#include <stdio.h>

void jerk(void);

int main()
{
    printf("He calls me on the phone with nothing say\n");
```

```
    printf("Not once, or twice, but three times a day!\n");
    jerk();
    printf("He insulted my wife, my cat, my mother\n");
    printf("He irritates and grates, like no other!\n");
    jerk();
    printf("He chuckles it off, his big belly a-heavin'\n");
    printf("But he won't be laughing when I get even!\n");
    jerk();
    return(0);
}

/* This is the jerk() function */

void jerk()
{
    printf("Bill is a jerk\n");
}
```

When you're done, resave BIGJERK2.C to disk. Recompile, and you shan't be bothered by the various warning errors again.

- The prototype is basically a rehash of a function that appears later in the program.
- The prototype must shout out what type of function the program is and describe what kind of stuff should be between the parentheses.
- The prototype must also end with a semicolon. This is *muy importanto.*
- I usually copy the first line of the function to the top of the program, paste it in there, and then add a semicolon. For example, in BIGJERK2.C, I copied Line 21 (the start of the `jerk` function) to the top of the source code and pasted it in, adding the necessary `void`s and semicolon.
- No, the `main()` function doesn't have to be prototyped. The compiler is expecting it and knows all about it. (Well, almost. . . .)
- Required prototyping is something they added to the C language after it was first introduced. You may encounter older C source code files that seem to lack any prototyping. Back in the days when such programs were written (before about 1990), this was a common way of doing things.

A sneaky way to avoid prototyping problems

Only the coolest of the C language gurus do this trick — so don't tell anyone that you found out about it in a *For Dummies* book! Shhhh!

Face it: Prototyping is a mess. Why repeat a function's definition at the top of the program when it's so obviously presented when the function is written? Seems redundant, eh? Many others think so, which is why they code their programs *upside down*. To wit, here's another rendition of the BIGJERK program:

```
#include <stdio.h>

/* the jerk() function */

void jerk(void)
{
    printf("Bill is a jerk\n");
}

/* Program starts here */

int main()
{
    printf("He calls me on the phone with nothing say\n");
    printf("Not once, or twice, but three times a day!\n");
    jerk();
    printf("He insulted my wife, my cat, my mother\n");
    printf("He irritates and grates, like no other!\n");
    jerk();
    printf("He chuckles it off, his big belly a-heavin'\n");
    printf("But he won't be laughing when I get even!\n");
    jerk();
    return(0);
}
```

Edit the source code for BIGJERK2.C and make the changes in the preceding program. Basically, you're removing the prototype for `jerk()` and replacing it with the `jerk()` function itself. Note that the `jerk()` function is defined as `void jerk(void)`, just like a prototype, but it's the function itself.

Save the changed source code to disk as BIGJERK3.C. Compile and run. The output is the same, but by turning the function upside down, you have utterly removed the possibility of prototyping errors.

- The program still starts at the `main()` function despite stacking any other functions before it. Yes, the compiler is that smart.
- You don't have to code your programs this way. Rarely do programmers know in advance which functions they need, so most programmers start out coding functions the way it was done earlier in this chapter. Only after the function is written do they cut and paste it to the top of the file.
- Don't add the semicolon to the function's declaration when you list your functions first! If you do, you get one of those nasty parse errors.

- If your source code has more than one function, the order in which they're listed is important; you cannot use a function inside your source code unless it has first been declared or prototyped. If you have multiple functions in your source code, order them so that if one function calls another, that second function is listed first. Otherwise, you're again saddled with prototyping errors.

The Tao of Functions

The C language allows you to put as many functions as you want in your source code. There really is no limit, though most programmers like to keep their source-code text files to a manageable size.

- What is "manageable size"? It depends.
- The larger the source code file, the longer it takes to compile.
- Often times, it pays to break off functions into their own, separate source code files. It not only aids in debugging, but also makes recompiling larger files easier.
- This book's companion volume, *C All-in-One Desk Reference For Dummies* (Wiley), contains information on creating and managing multimodule source code files.

The function format

Here's the format of a typical function:

```
type name(stuff)
```

The `type` tells the compiler whether the function returns a value. If the type is `void`, the function doesn't return any value. (It merely *functs.*) Otherwise, the type describes which type of value the function returns: `char`, `int`, `float`, or any of the standard C language variable declarations.

The *`name`* is the function's name. It must be a unique name, not any keywords or names of other C language library functions, such as `printf()` or `atoi()`. (For more on names, see the next section.)

Parentheses after the function's name are required, as they are on all C language functions. The `stuff` inside the parentheses, if needed, defines whatever value (or values) are sent off to the function for evaluation, manipulation, or mutilation. I cover this subject in Chapter 22. When there's no *stuff,* the parentheses can be left empty.

The statements belonging to the function require curly braces to hug them close. Those statements are the instructions that carry out what the function is supposed to do. Therefore, the full format for the function is shown here:

```
type name(stuff)
{
    statement(s);
    /* more statements */
}
```

The function must be prototyped before it can be used. You do that by either listing the full function earlier than it's first used in your source code or restating the function's declaration at the start of your source code. For example:

```
type name(stuff);
```

This line, with a semicolon, is required in order to prototype the function used later on in the program. It's just a copy-and-paste job, but the semicolon is required for the prototype. (If you forget, your compiler may ever so gently remind you with a barrage of error messages.)

- Call it *defining* a function. Call it *declaring* a function. Call it *doing* a function. (The official term is *defining* a function.)
- Naming rules for functions are covered in the next section.
- Your C language library reference lists functions by using the preceding format. For example:

  ```
  int atoi(const char *s);
  ```

  This format explains the requirements and product of the `atoi()` function. Its *type* is an `int`, and its *stuff* is a character string, which is how you translate `const char *s` into English. (Also noted in the format is that the `#include <stdlib.h>` thing is required at the beginning of your source code when you use the `atoi()` function.)

How to name your functions

Functions are like your children, so, for heaven's sake, don't give them a dorky name! You're free to give your functions just about any name, but keep in mind these notes:

- Functions are named by using letters of the alphabet and numbers. Your C compiler may have specific rules regarding the names and what is and isn't allowed. But you should be safe for now by limiting function names to letters and numbers.

- Don't use spaces in your function names. Instead, use underlines. For example, this isn't a function name:

  ```
  get the time()
  ```

  But this is:

  ```
  get_the_time()
  ```

- You can use upper- or lowercase when you're naming your functions. A common tactic is to capitalize key letters in the function's name:

  ```
  getTheTime()
  ```

- Most compilers are case sensitive, so if you use mixed case, be sure to remember how you type it. For example, if the function is named `getTheTime` and you type `GetTheTime`, you may get a linker error (the function was not found).
- Keep your function names short and descriptive. A function named `f()` is permissible yet ambiguous — it's like saying "Nothing" when someone asks you what you're thinking.
- Avoid naming your functions the same as other C language functions or keywords. Be unique!
- The function name `main()` is reserved for your program's first function.

Chapter 21

Contending with Variables in Functions

In This Chapter

- Naming variables within functions
- Understanding local variables
- Sharing one variable throughout a program
- Using global variables

Each function you create can use its own, private set of variables. It's a must. Just like the `main()` function, other functions require integer or character variables that help the function do its job. A few quirks are involved with this arrangement, of course — a few head-scratchers that must be properly mulled over so that you can understand the enter function/variable gestalt.

This chapter introduces you to the strange concept of variables inside functions. They're different. They're unique. Please avoid the desire to kill them.

Bombs Away with the BOMBER Program!

The `dropBomb()` function in the BOMBER.C program uses its own, private variable *x* in a `for` loop to simulate a bomb dropping. It could be an exciting element of a computer game you may yearn to write, though you probably want to use sophisticated graphics rather than the sloppy console screen used here:

```
#include <stdio.h>

void dropBomb(void);                /* prototype */

int main()
```

```
{
    printf("Press Enter to drop the bomb:");
    getchar();
    dropBomb();
    printf("Yikes!\n");
    return(0);
}

void dropBomb()
{
    int x;

    for(x=20;x>1;x--)
    {
        puts("          *");
    }
    puts("        BOOM!");
}
```

Type the source code as listed here. In the `puts()` function in Line 20 are 10 spaces before the asterisk.) In Line 22 are 8 spaces before `BOOM!`.

Save the file to disk as BOMBER.C. Compile and run.

```
Press Enter to drop the bomb:
          *
          *
          *
```

And so on. . . .

```
          *
          *
        BOOM!
Yikes!
```

Yeah, it happens a little too fast to build up the nerve-tingling anticipation of a true video game, but the point here is not dropping bombs; rather, the variable *x* is used in the `dropBomb()` function. It works just fine. Nothing quirky. Nothing new. That's how variables are used in functions.

- See how the `dropBomb()` function declares the variable *x:*

  ```
  int x;
  ```

  It works just like it does in the `main()` function: Declare the variables right up front. Refer to Chapter 8 for more information about declaring variables.

- The `dropBomb()` function is a void because it doesn't return any values. It has nothing to do with any values used *inside* the function.

Will the dual variable BOMBER.C program bomb?

Modify the source code for BOMBER.C in your editor. Change the `main()` function so that it reads:

```
int main()
{
    char x;

    printf("Press Enter to drop the bomb:");
    x=getchar();
    dropBomb();
    printf("Key code %d used to drop bomb.\n",x);
    return(0);
}
```

What you're doing is creating another *x* variable for use in the `main()` function. This variable operates independently of the *x* variable in the `dropBomb()` function. To prove it, save your changes to disk and then compile and run the program.

The output is roughly the same for this modified version of the program; the key code displayed for the Enter key "character" is either `10` or `13`, depending on your computer.

- See how the two *x* variables don't confuse the computer? Each one works off by itself.
- Variables in different functions can share the same name.
- For example, you could have a dozen different functions in your program and have each one use the same variable names. No biggie. They're all independent of each other because they're nestled tightly in their own functions.
- Variable *x* not only is used in two different functions — independently of each other — but also represents two different types of variable: a character and an integer. Weird.

Adding some important tension

Face it: You're going nowhere fast as a game programmer with BOMBER.C. What you need is some *tension* to heighten the excitement as the bomb drops. Why not concoct your own `delay()` function to make it happen? Here's your updated source code:

```
#include <stdio.h>

#define COUNT 20000000           /* 20,000,000 */

void dropBomb(void);             /* prototype */
void delay(void);

int main()
{
    char x;

    printf("Press Enter to drop the bomb:");
    x=getchar();
    dropBomb();
    printf("Key code %d used to drop bomb.\n",x);
    return(0);
}

void dropBomb()
{
    int x;

    for(x=20;x>1;x--)
    {
        puts("          *");
        delay();
    }
    puts("       BOOM!");
}

void delay()
{
    long int x;

    for(x=0;x<COUNT;x++)
        ;
}
```

Mind the changes! Here they are:

```
#define COUNT 20000000           /* 20,000,000 */
```

A constant named `COUNT` is declared, equal to 20 million. It's the `delay` value. (If the delay is too long, make the value smaller; if the delay is too short, make the value bigger.)

Next, the delay() function must be prototyped:

```
void delay(void);
```

The delay() function is added into the dropBomb() function, right after puts() displays the "bomb:"

```
delay();
```

Finally, the delay() function is written. A long integer named x — a different x from any other used in any other function — is used in a for loop to create the delay.

Double-check your source code. Save to disk. Compile. Run. This time, the anticipation builds as the bomb slowly falls toward the ground and then — *BOOM!*

REMEMBER

- The line used to create a constant (starting with #define) does *not* end with a semicolon! Go to Chapter 8 if you don't know about this.
- You can adjust the delay by changing the constant COUNT. Note how much easier it is than fishing through the program to find the exact delay loop and value — one of the chief advantages of using a constant variable.
- Variables with the same names in different functions are different.
- What's the point again? I think it's that you don't have to keep on thinking of new variable names in each of your functions. If you're fond of using the variable i in your for loops, for example, you can use i in all your functions. Just declare it and don't worry about it.

How We Can All Share and Love with Global Variables

Sometimes, you do have to share a variable between two or more functions. Most games, for example, store the score in a variable that's accessible to a number of functions: the function that displays the score on the screen; the function that increases the score's value; the function that decreases the value; and functions that store the score on disk, for example. All those functions have to access that one variable. That's done by creating a global variable.

A *global variable* is one that any function in the program can use. The main() function can use it — any function. They can change, examine, modify, or do whatever to the variable. No problem.

The opposite of a global variable is a *local variable*. It's what you have seen used elsewhere in this book. A local variable exists inside only one function — like the variable *x* in the BOMBER.C program. The *x* is a local variable, unique to the functions in which it's created and ignored by other functions in the program.

- A global variable is available to all functions in your program.
- A local variable is available only to the function in which it's created.
- Global variables can be used in any function without having to redeclare them. If you have a global integer variable `score`, for example, you don't have to stick an `int score;` declaration in each function which uses that variable. The variable has already been declared and is ready for use in any function.

- Because global variables exist all over the place, naming them is important. After you declare *x* as a global variable, for example, no other function can declare *x* as anything else without ticking off the compiler.

Making a global variable

Global variables differ from local variables in two ways. First, because they're global variables, any function in the program can use them. Second, they're declared *outside* of any function. Out there. In the emptiness. Midst the chaos. Strange, but true.

For example:

```
#include <stdio.h>

int score;

int main()
{
```

Etc. . . .

Think of this source code as the beginning of some massive program, the details of which aren't important right now. Notice how the variable `score` is declared. It's done outside of any function, traditionally just before the `main()` function and after the pound-sign dealies (and any prototyping nonsense). That's how global variables are made.

If more global variables are required, they're created in the same spot, right there before the `main()` function. Declaring them works as it normally does; the only difference is that it's done outside of any function.

- Global variables are declared outside of any function. It's typically done right before the `main()` function.
- Everything you know about creating a variable, other than being declared outside a function, applies to creating global variables: You must specify the type of variable (`int`, `char`, and `float`, for example), the variable's name, and the semicolon.
- You can also declare a group of global variables at one time:

  ```
  int score,tanks,ammo;
  ```

- And, you can preassign values to global variables, if you want:

  ```
  char prompt[]="What?";
  ```

An example of a global variable in a real, live program

For your pleasure, please refer *again* to the BOMBER.C source code. This final modification adds code that keeps a running total of the number of people you kill with the bombs. That total is kept in the global variable `deaths`, defined right up front. Here's the final source code, with specific changes noted just afterward:

```
#include <stdio.h>

#define COUNT 20000000                /* 20,000,000 */

void dropBomb(void);                  /* prototype */
void delay(void);

int deaths;                           /* global variable */

int main()
{
    char x;

    deaths=0;
    for(;;)
    {
        printf("Press ~ then Enter to quit\n");
        printf("Press Enter to drop the bomb:");
        x=getchar();
        fflush(stdin);                /* clear input buffer */
        if(x=='~')
        {
            break;
        }
```

```
        dropBomb();
        printf("%d people killed!\n",deaths);
    }
    return(0);
}

void dropBomb()
{
    int x;

    for(x=20;x>1;x--)
    {
        puts("              *");
        delay();
    }
    puts("          BOOM!");
    deaths+=1500;
}

void delay()
{
    long int x;

    for(x=0;x<COUNT;x++)
        ;
}
```

Bring up the source code for BOMBER.C in your editor. Make the necessary changes so that your code matches what's shown here. Here are the details:

First, the global variable `deaths` is declared right before the `main()` function:

```
int deaths;                          /* global variable */
```

Second, the `main()` function is rewritten to contain an endless loop (refer to the preceding code block). The loop allows you to drop bombs over and over; pressing the ~ (tilde) key ends the loop.

Third, the global variable `deaths` is incremented inside the `dropBomb()` function by a simple addition to that function:

```
deaths+=1500;
```

Double-check your source code! Then, save BOMBER.C to disk one more time (though you don't quite finish it until you read Chapter 22).

Compile and run the program.

The program effectively keeps a running tally of the dead by using the global `deaths` variable. The variable is manipulated (incremented) in the `dropBomb()` function and is displayed in the `main()` function. Both functions share that global variable.

- See how the global variable is declared right up front? The `#include`s usually come first, and then the prototyping stuff, and then the global variables.
- No, this game doesn't challenge you.
- For more information about the endless `for` loop, see Chapter 25.
- In Unix-like operating systems, be sure to use `fpurge(stdin)` in Line 20 rather than `fflush(stdin)`. Refer to Chapter 13.

Chapter 22

Functions That Actually Funct

In This Chapter

- Sending a value to a function
- Sending multiple values to a function
- Using the `return` keyword
- Understanding the `main()` function
- Writing tighter code

A function is like a machine. Although the do-nothing void functions that you probably have read about in earlier chapters are still valid functions, the real value in a function is having it do something. I mean, functions must chew on something and spit it out. Real meat-grinder stuff. Functions that funct.

This chapter explains how functions can be used to manipulate or produce information. It's done by sending a value to a function or by having a function return a value. This chapter explains how all that kooky stuff works.

Marching a Value Off to a Function

Generally speaking, you can write four types of functions:

- **Functions that work all by themselves, not requiring any extra input:** These functions are described in previous chapters. Each one is a ho-hum function, but often necessary and every bit a function as a function can be.
- **Functions that take input and use it somehow:** These functions are passed values, as either constants or variables, which they chew on and then do something useful based on the value received.
- **Functions that take input and produce output:** These functions receive something and give you something back in kind (known as *generating a value*). For example, a function that computed your weight based on your shoe size would swallow your shoe size and cough up your weight. So to speak. Input and output.

- **Functions that produce only output:** These functions generate a value or string, returning it to the program — for example, a function that may tell you where the *Enterprise* is in the Klingon Empire. You call the `whereEnt()` function, and it returns some galactic coordinates.

Any function can fall into any category. It all depends on what you want the function to do. After you know that, you build the function accordingly.

How to send a value to a function

Sending a value to a function is as easy as heaving Grandma through a plate glass window. Just follow these steps:

1. **Know what kind of value you're going to send to the function.**

   It can be a constant value, a number or string, or it can be a C language variable. Either way, you must declare that value as the proper type so that the function knows exactly what type of value it's receiving: int, char, or float, for example.

2. **Declare the value as a variable in the function's parentheses.**

   Suppose that your function eats an integer value. If so, you need to declare that value as a variable that the function will use. It works like declaring any variable in the C language, though the declaration is made inside the function's parentheses following the function's name:

   ```
   void jerk(int repeat)
   ```

   Don't follow the variable declaration with a semicolon! In the preceding example, the integer variable `repeat` is declared, which means that the `jerk()` function requires an integer value. Internally, the function refers to the value by using the `repeat` variable.

3. **Somehow use the value in your function.**

   The compiler doesn't like it when you declare a variable and then that variable isn't used. (It's a waste of memory.) The error message reads something like `jerk is passed a value that is not used` or `Parameter 'repeat' is never used in function jerk`. It's a warning error — and, heck, it may not even show up — but it's a good point to make: Use your variables!

4. **Properly prototype the function.**

   You must do this or else you get a host of warning errors. My advice: Select the line that starts your function; mark it as a block. Then, copy it to up above the `main()` function. After pasting it in, add a semicolon:

   ```
   void jerk(int repeat);
   ```

   No sweat.

5. **Remember to send the proper values when you're calling the function.**

   Because the function is required to eat values, you must send them along. No more empty parentheses! You must fill them, and fill them with the proper type of value: integer, character, floater — whatever. Only by doing that can the function properly do its thing.

- The parameter is referred to as an *argument.* This term gives you a tiny taste of C's combative nature.
- The name you give the function's parameter (its passed-along variable, argument, or whatever) is used when you're defining and prototyping the function, and inside the function.
- You can treat the function's parameter as a local variable. Yeah, it's defined in the prototype. Yeah, it appears on the first line. But, inside the function, it's just a local variable.
- By the way, the variable name used inside the function must match the variable name defined inside the function's parentheses. More on this later.
- Information on passing strings to functions is provided in my book *C All-in-One Desk Reference For Dummies* (Wiley).
- Sending a value to a function or getting a value back isn't the same as using a global variable. Although you can use global variables with a function, the values the function produces or generates don't have to be global variables. (Refer to Chapter 21 for more information about global variables.)

An example (and it's about time!)

Blindly type the following program, a modification of the BIGJERK.C cycle of programs you work with in Chapter 20:

```
#include <stdio.h>

void jerk(int repeat);

int main()
{
    printf("He calls me on the phone with nothing say\n");
    printf("Not once, or twice, but three times a day!\n");
    jerk(1);
    printf("He insulted my wife, my cat, my mother\n");
    printf("He irritates and grates, like no other!\n");
    jerk(2);
    printf("He chuckles it off, his big belly a-heavin'\n");
    printf("But he won't be laughing when I get even!\n");
    jerk(3);
```

```
    return(0);
}

/* The jerk() function repeats the refrain for the
value of the repeat variable */

void jerk(int repeat)
{
    int i;

    for(i=0;i<repeat;i++)
        printf("Bill is a jerk\n");
}
```

You can edit this source code from the BIGJERK2.C file, but save this file to disk as BIGJERK4.C. It has some changes, mostly with the `jerk()` function and the statements that call that function. Don't miss anything, or else you get some nasty error messages.

Compile and run.

The program's output now looks something like this:

```
He calls me on the phone with nothing say
Not once, or twice, but three times a day!
Bill is a jerk
He insulted my wife, my cat, my mother
He irritates and grates, like no other!
Bill is a jerk
Bill is a jerk
He chuckles it off, his big belly a-heavin'
But he won't be laughing when I get even!
Bill is a jerk
Bill is a jerk
Bill is a jerk
```

The `jerk()` function has done been modified! It can now display the litany's refrain any old number of times. Amazing. And look what it can do for your poetry.

The details of how this program worked are hammered out in the rest of this chapter. The following check marks may clear up a few key issues.

- Notice how the `jerk()` function has been redefined in the prototype:

  ```
  void jerk(int repeat);
  ```

  This line tells the compiler that the `jerk()` function is hungry for an integer value, which it calls `repeat`.

- The new `jerk()` function repeats the phrase `Bill is a jerk` for whatever number you specify. For example:

```
jerk(500);
```

This statement calls the `jerk()` function, which then repeats the message 500 times.

- The C-geek vernacular for sending a value of a variable to a function is "passed." So you *pass* the value 3 to the `jerk()` function with this statement:

```
jerk(3);
```

- The value you send along to a function is called a *parameter.* It can be said, in a nerdly way, that the `jerk()` function has one parameter, an integer variable (which is a number).
- If you forget to put a value in the `jerk()` function, you see a `Too few parameters` type of error. That's one of the reasons that you prototype functions. If you don't, and you use `jerk()` to call the function, your program invariably screws up.
- The variable `repeat` is not a global variable. Instead, it's a value that's *passed* to the `jerk` function, which that function then uses to do something wonderful.
- Note that `jerk()` also retains its own variable, `i`. Nothing new there.

Avoiding variable confusion (must reading)

You don't have to call a function by using the same variable name the function uses. Don't bother reading that sentence twice. It's a confusing concept, but work with me here.

Suppose that you're in the `main()` function where a variable named `count` is used. You want to pass along its value to the `jerk()` function. You do so this way:

```
jerk(count);
```

This line tells the compiler to call the `jerk()` function, sending it along the value of the `count` variable. Because `count` is an integer variable, this strategy works just fine. But, keep in mind that it's the variable's *value* that is passed along. The name `count`? It's just a name in some function. Who cares! Only the value is important.

In the `jerk()` function, the value is referred to by using the variable name `repeat`. That's how the `jerk()` function was set up:

```
void jerk(int repeat)
```

Whatever value is sent, however it was sent, is always referred to as `repeat` inside the function.

- I bring this concept up because it's confusing. You can call any function with any variable name. Only inside that function is the function's own variable name used.
- This topic is confusing because of the variable names used by the function. You can find this subject in your C manual as well. You see some function listed like this:

  ```
  int putchar(int c);
  ```

  This line indicates that the `putchar()` function requires an integer value, which it refers to as `c`. However, you can call this function by using any variable name or a constant value. It makes no difference. What's important, however, is that it must be an integer variable.

Sending More than One Value to a Function

The tray you use to pass values along to functions is quite large. It can hold more than one item — several, in fact. All you have to do is declare the items inside the function's parentheses. It's like announcing them at some fancy diplomatic function; each item has a type and a name and is followed by a lovely comma dressed in red taffeta with an appropriate hat. No semicolon appears at the end because it's a formal occasion.

For example:

```
void bloat(int calories, int weight, int fat)
```

This function is defined as requiring three integer values: `calories`, `weight`, and `fat`. But, they don't all have to be the same type of variable:

```
void jerk(int repeat, char c)
```

Here you see a modification of the `jerk()` function, which now requires two values: an integer and a character. These values are referred to as `repeat` and `c` inside the `jerk()` function. In fact, the following source code uses said function:

```
#include <stdio.h>

void jerk(int repeat, char c);

int main()
```

```
{
        printf("He calls me on the phone with nothing say\n");
        printf("Not once, or twice, but three times a day!\n");
        jerk(1,'?');
        printf("He insulted my wife, my cat, my mother\n");
        printf("He irritates and grates, like no other!\n");
        jerk(2,'?');
        printf("He chuckles it off, his big belly a-
             heavin'\n");
        printf("But he won't be laughing when I get even!\n");
        jerk(3,'!');
        return(0);
}

/* The jerk() function repeats the refrain for the
value of the repeat variable*/

void jerk(int repeat, char c)
{
        int i;

        for(i=0;i<repeat;i++)
                     printf("Bill is a jerk%c\n",c);
}
```

Type the preceding source code. You can start with the BIGJERK4.C source code as a base. You have to edit Line 3 to modify the `jerk()` function prototype; edit Lines 9, 12, and 15 to modify the way the `jerk()` function is called (remember to use single quotes); then, redefine the `jerk()` function itself; and change the `printf()` statement inside the function so that it displays the character variable `c`.

Save the file to disk as BIGJERK5.C.

Compile and run the program. The output looks almost the same, but you see the effects of passing the single-character variable to the `jerk()` function in the way the question marks and exclamation points appear:

```
He calls me on the phone with nothing say
Not once, or twice, but three times a day!
Bill is a jerk?
He insulted my wife, my cat, my mother
He irritates and grates, like no other!
Bill is a jerk?
Bill is a jerk?
He chuckles it off, his big belly a-heavin'
But he won't be laughing when I get even!
Bill is a jerk!
Bill is a jerk!
Bill is a jerk!
```

Functions That Return Stuff

For some functions to properly funct, they must return a value. You pass along your birthday, and the function magically tells you how old you are (and then the computer giggles at you). This process is known as returning a value, and a heck of a lot of functions do that.

Something for your troubles

WARNING!

To return a value, a function must obey these two rules:

Warning! Rules approaching.

- The function has to be *defined* as a certain type (`int`, `char`, or `float`, for example — just like a variable). Use something other than `void`.
- The function has to return a value.

The function type tells you what type of value it returns. For example:

```
int birthday(int date);
```

The function `birthday()` is defined on this line. It's an integer function and returns an integer value. (It also requires an integer parameter, `date`, which it uses as input.)

The following function, `nationalDebt()`, returns the national debt of the United States as a `double` value:

```
double nationalDebt(void)
```

The `void` in parentheses means that the function doesn't require any input. Likewise, when a function doesn't produce any output, it's defined as a `void`:

```
void USGovernment(float tax_dollars)
```

The `USGovernment()` function requires very large numbers as input, but produces nothing. Therefore, it's a function of type `void`. It's easy to remember.

- Any value produced by a function is returned by using the `return` keyword. Details appear later in this chapter.
- Notice that C language functions, like `atoi()` or `getchar()` — functions that return values — are listed in your C language library reference by using the same format as described here:

```
int atoi(char *s)
char getchar(void)
```

  This means that the `atoi()` function returns an integer value and that `getchar()` returns a single-character value.
- Another reason functions should be prototyped: The compiler double-checks to confirm that the function is returning the proper value and that other parts of the program use that `int`, `float`, or `char` value as defined.
- You need a `double`-size variable to handle the national debt. The `float` variable, although it's capable of handling a number in the trillions, is accurate to only 7 digits. The `double` is accurate to 15 digits. If the debt were calculated as a `float`, it would lose accuracy around the $100,000 mark (like they care about values that small!).
- Although you can define a function as a type of `void`, you cannot declare a `void` variable. It just doesn't work that way.
- `void` functions don't return values.
- Functions can return only a single value. Unlike sending a value to a function, in which the function can receive any number of values, they can cough up only one thing in return. I know — it sounds like a gyp.
- The preceding check mark is untrue. Functions can return several values. They do it through the miracle of pointers and structures, two advanced subjects touched on in this book's companion, *C All-in-One Desk Reference For Dummies* (Wiley).

Finally, the computer tells you how smart it thinks you are

The following program calculates your IQ. Supposedly. What's more important is that it uses a function that has real meaning. If you have read the past few chapters, you have used the following set of C language statements to get input from the keyboard:

```
input=gets();
x=atoi(input);
```

The `gets()` function reads in text that's typed at the keyboard, and `atoi()` translates it into an integer value. Well, ho-ho, the `getval()` function in the IQ.C program does that for you, returning the value happily to the `main()` function:

```
#include <stdio.h>
#include <stdlib.h>

int getval(void);

int main()
{
    int age,weight,area;
    float iq;

    printf("Program to calculate your IQ.\n");
    printf("Enter your age:");
    age=getval();
    printf("Enter your weight:");
    weight=getval();
    printf("Enter the your area code:");
    area=getval();

    iq=(age*weight)/area;
    printf("This computer estimates your IQ to be %f.\n",iq);
    return(0);
}

int getval(void)
{
    char input[20];
    int x;

    gets(input);
    x=atoi(input);
    return(x);
}
```

Type the source code for IQ.C into your editor. The new deal here is the `getval()` function, which returns a value by using the `return` keyword. (Does that look familiar? I tell you more in a second!)

Save the source code file to disk as IQ.C.

Compile. Run.

Here's what the sample output may look like, using fictitious figures for myself:

```
Enter your age:33
Enter your weight:175
Enter your area code:208
The computer estimates your IQ to be 27.000000.
```

Of course. I knew my IQ was that high. I'm not boasting or anything. It's only an estimate, after all.

- By using this formula, only old, fat people living in low-numbered area codes can get into Mensa.
- This program has some problems. For example, the IQ value that's calculated should be a floating point number, and it's not (unless your age, weight, and area code are very special). This problem is fixed in the nearby sidebar, "Fixing IQ.C by using the old type-casting trick."
- Note how `getval()` is defined as an integer function. Inside `getval()`, an integer value is produced by the `atoi()` function. It's saved in the *x* variable, which is then returned to the main function by using the `return(x);` statement. Everything is an integer, so the function is of that type as well.
- In the `main()` function, `getval()` is used three times. The values it produces (what it functs) is saved in the `age`, `weight`, and `height` integer variables, respectively.
- Yeah, you probably lied too when you entered your weight. Don't! The more tumid you are, the smarter the program makes you.

Return to sender with the `return` keyword

Functions that return values need some type of mechanism to send those values back. Information just can't fall off the edge, with the compiler assuming that the last curly brace means "Hey, I must return the variable, uh, *x*. Yeah. That's it. Send *x* back. Now I get it."

Fixing IQ.C by using the old type-casting trick

In the IQ.C source code, the computer estimates your IQ based on this formula:

```
iq=(age*weight)/area;
```

That is, your IQ is equal to your age multiplied by your weight, with that total divided by your area code. All those variables are integers, and, incidentally, it's the exact formula used by my kids' school district.

Alarm! Whenever you divide any two values, the result is probably a `float`. No, count on it being a `float`. That's just the way math works. Decimals and fractions — it's messy stuff.

To make this function work, the variable `iq` is declared as a `float` — right up at the beginning of the source code, just as it should. But there's a problem: The value calculated by the equation is still stuffed into an integer. (Eh?) Even though the calculated result probably has a decimal part, all those variables are integers, and the result is an integer. (Hey, the compiler doesn't assume anything, remember?)

To fix the problem, you must do something known as *type casting,* where you tell the compiler to temporarily forget what type of variable is there and instead assume that it's something else.

Edit Line 19 in the IQ.C source code to read:

```
iq=(float)(age*weight)/area;
```

Insert the word `float` in parentheses right after the equal sign. Save the file back to disk. Compile and run. Notice that your IQ changes to a more floaty number in the output:

```
The computer estimates your IQ
   to be 27.764423.
```

Now the number is a true `float`.

No. To properly return a value, you need the proper `return` keyword.

The `return` keyword is used to send a value back from a function, to return a value from the function. Here's the format:

```
return(something);
```

The *`something`* is a value that the function must return. What kind of value? It depends on the type of function. It must be an integer for `int` functions, a character for a `char` function, a string (which is tricky), a floater for a `float` function, and so on. And, you can specify either a variable name or a constant value.

```
return(total);
```

The value of the variable `total` is returned from the function.

```
return(0);
```

The function returns a value of zero.

By the way, the `something` is optional. For the `void` type of functions, you can use the `return();` statement by itself to cause the program to return, for example, in the middle of something (see BONUS.C, later in this chapter, for an example).

- Technically speaking, all functions can end with a single `return;` as their last statement. When `return` isn't there, the compiler automatically returns when it sees the function's last curly brace. (Execution falls off the edge. Ahhh!)
- Functions defined as an `int`, `char`, or whatever must return that type of value.

WARNING!

- `void` functions can use `return`, but it must not return anything! Just use `return();` or `return;` by itself in a `void` function. Otherwise, the compiler waggles its warning error finger at you.
- If your function is supposed to return something but has nothing to return, use the `return(0);` statement.

TIP

- The `return` keyword doesn't necessarily have to come at the end of a function. Sometimes, you have to use it in the middle of a function, such as in BONUS.C, shown next.

Now you can understand the `main()` function

In all your programs, and in all the programs shown to this point in the book, you have seen the `main()` function declared as an `int` and always ending the `return(0);`. These are basic requirements of the C language, as defined by the ANSI standard; `main()` must be an `int`, and it must return a value.

The value returned by `main()` is made available to the operating system. For most programs, it's not used, so any value is okay to return. But, for some programs, a `return` value is the way the program communicates with the operating system.

For example, some command-line utilities may return 0 if the program completed its task. Any value other than 0 may indicate some error condition.

- In DOS/Windows, you can write a batch file to examine the value returned by a program's `main()` function. The `ERRORLEVEL` variable in the batch programming language stores the value.
- In Unix operating systems, you can use the shell scripting language to examine the return code from any program.

- Before the ANSI standard, the `main()` function was commonly declared as a `void`:

  ```
  void main()
  ```

  You may see this line in some older programming books or source code examples. Note that *nothing* is wrong with it; it doesn't cause the computer to error, crash, or explode. (Nor has there ever been a documented case of declaring `void main()` ever being a problem on any computer.) Even so, it's the standard now to declare `main()` as an `int`. If you don't, zillions of upset university sophomores will rise from the Internet to point fingers at you. Not that it means anything, but they will point at you.

Give that human a bonus!

The following program, BONUS.C, contains a function that has three — count 'em, three — `return` statements. This program proves that you can stick a `return` plum-dab in the middle of a function and no one will snicker at you — not even university sophomores:

```
#include <stdio.h>

float bonus(char x);

int main()
{
    char name[20];
    char level;
    float b;

    printf("Enter employee name:");
    gets(name);
    printf("Enter bonus level (0, 1 or 2):");
    level=getchar();
    b=bonus(level);
    b*=100;
    printf("The bonus for %s will be $%.2f.\n",name,b);
    return(0);
}

/* Calculate the bonus */

float bonus(char x)
{
    if(x=='0') return(0.33);          /* Bottom-level bonus */
    if(x=='1') return(1.50);          /* Second-level bonus */
    return(3.10);                     /* Best bonus */
}
```

Type this source code into your editor. Save it to disk as BONUS.C. Notice that the `bonus()` function contains three `return` statements, each of which returns a different value to the `main()` function. Also, the function is a `float` type, which you haven't yet seen in this book if you have been reading the chapters in order.

Compile and run.

Here's a sample of the output:

```
Enter employee name:Bill
Enter bonus level (0, 1, or 2):0
The bonus for Bill will be $33.00
```

Run the program a few more times with some new names and values. Try not to be impressed by its flexibility.

- Poor Bill.
- You may be tempted to type-cast the value 100 in Line 15: `b*=100;`. Don't! The assignment operator, = , carries out the conversion between `int` and `float` for you.

```
b*=(float)rate;
```

- Notice how the floating-point value `0.33` is written out. Values should always begin with a number, not a decimal point. If the value `.33` is specified, the compiler may choke. Always begin values with a number, 0 through 9.
- You may think of the statements in the `bonus()` function as being rather brief. Ha! What do you know. . . .

Actually, they are. They're scrunched up really tight, but that doesn't mean that you have to write your programs like that. In the following section," you can see several alternative formats that get the same job done. It's something you should try with your C programs constantly: See whether you can write your programs with brevity and legibility.

No Need to Bother with This C Language Trivia If You're in a Hurry

C is a flexible language that offers many ways to format a solution to a particular problem. Take the `bonus()` function in the BONUS.C program. Here are four different ways that function can be written and still carry out the same task.

The long, boring way:

```
float bonus(char x)
{
    int v;

    if(x=='0')
    {
        v=0.33;
    }
    else if(x=='1')
    {
        v=1.50;
    }
    else
    {
        v=3.10;
    }
    return(v);
}
```

The long, boring way minus all the darn curly braces:

```
float bonus(char x)
{
    int v;

    if(x=='0')
        v=0.33;
    else if(x=='1')
        v=1.50;
    else
        v=3.10;
    return(v);
}
```

And, without the integer variable *v:*

```
float bonus(char x)
{
    if(x=='0')
        return(0.33);
    else if(x=='1')
        return(1.50);
    else
        return(3.10);
}
```

Same line, anyone?

```
float bonus(char x)
{
    if(x=='0') return(0.33);
    else if(x=='1') return(1.50);
    else return(3.10);
}
```

Finally, without the `else`:

```
float bonus(char x)
{
      if(x=='0') return(0.33);
      if(x=='1') return(1.50);
      return(3.10);
}
```

You can substitute any of the preceding `bonus()` functions in your BONUS.C source code. Everything works just fine.

Chapter 23

The Stuff That Comes First

In This Chapter

- Discovering how the `#include` thing works
- Creating your own header files
- Understanding how libraries work
- Using `#define` directives
- Ignoring macros

In case you haven't noticed, there seems to be lots of detritus piling up at the head of your C programs. There are `#include` things. There can be `#define` things. Then you have the occasional function prototype. Perhaps a global variable is sitting up there in the yon. Maybe some comments. All that stuff seems to pile up at the head of your source code, right before you get into the meat of the matter with the `main()` function.

Is it normal?

Is it useful?

Is it even necessary?

Welcome to the chapter that describes the Stuff That Comes First. Now that you have most likely read all the other chapters and been roundly exposed to the C language, a summary and description of those items is in order. Specifically, this chapter covers the `#include` things.

- An introduction to the `#define` thingy is in Chapter 8.
- Prototyping functions is covered in Chapter 20.
- Global variables are mulled over in Chapter 21.
- Other items that may appear at the beginning of your C code include external and public variable declarations. You use them when you write several source code modules, which is an advanced topic, fully covered in *C All-in-One Desk Reference For Dummies* (Wiley).

Please Don't Leave Me Out!

What exactly does the following line mean?

```
#include <stdio.h>
```

It's an instruction for the compiler to do something, to *include* a special file on disk, one named STDIO.H, in with your source code.

Figure 23-1 illustrates the concept for the #include <stdio.h> instruction. The contents of the STDIO.H file are read from disk and included (inserted) into your source code file when it's compiled.

Figure 23-2 shows how several lines of #includes work. Each file is read from disk and inserted into your source code, one after the other, as the source code is compiled.

Say! Aren't you the #include construction?

The #include construction is used to tell the compiler to copy lines from a *header file* into your source code. This instruction is required by the compiler for using many of the C language functions. The header file contains information about how the functions are used (yes, *prototypes*), as well as other information that helps the compiler understand your program.

Here's the format for using #include:

```
#include <filename>
```

The #include directive is followed by a *filename* held in angle brackets. The *filename* must be in lowercase and typically (though it's not a rule) ends with a period and a little *h*. Like all #-sign things at the start of your source code, don't end this line with a semicolon!

Sometimes, the filename is a partial path, in which case the partial path needs to be included, as in

```
#include <sys/socket.h>
```

The path is sys/, followed by the header filename, socket.h.

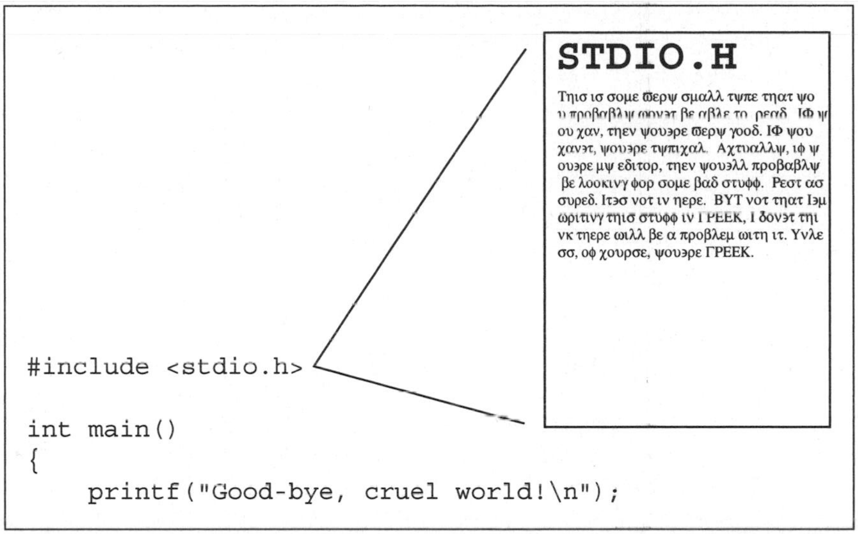

Figure 23-1: How an `#include` thingy affects a program.

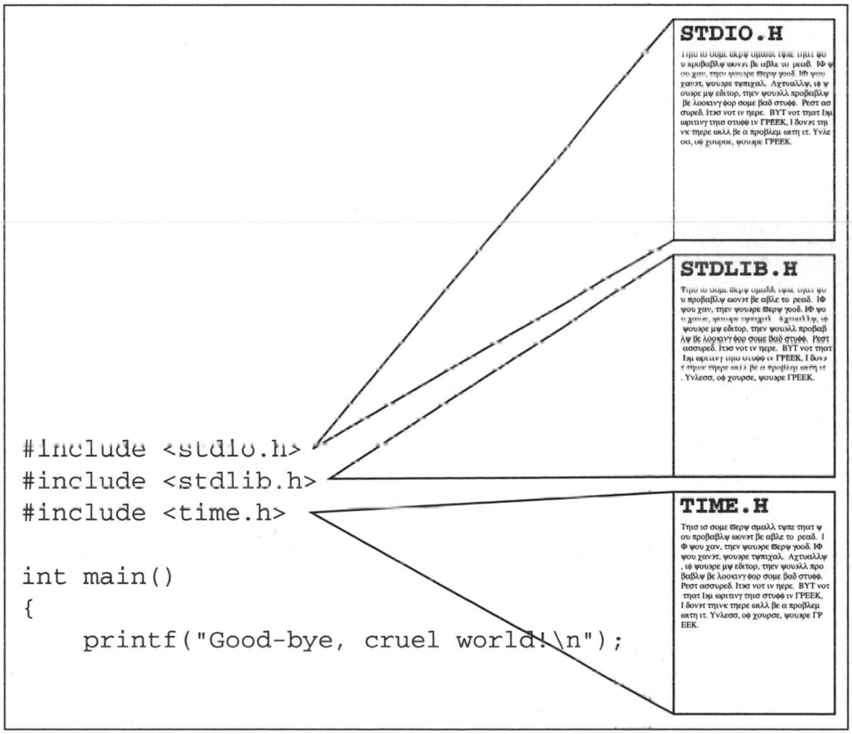

Figure 23-2: Multiple `#include` thingies in a program.

A second format is used whenever you want to include a header file that you make yourself or whenever you're using a header file not found in the compiler's INCLUDE directory:

```
#include "filename"
```

The format is essentially the same except that the *filename* is enclosed in double quotes rather than in angle brackets. The compiler looks for that header file in the same directory as your source code file.

- Header files are necessary to help the compiler properly create your programs. Remember that the C language contains only some 32 keywords (see Table 3-1, in Chapter 3). Everything else — `printf` and `getchar`, for example — is a function. Those functions are prototyped in the various header files you include at the beginning of your programs. Without the header files, the compiler doesn't recognize the functions and may display oodles of error messages.
- The .H part of the filename means *header.*
- You know when to use a certain header file by looking up a function in your C language library reference. The header file is listed along with the format for the function that needs it.
- Always use lowercase when you're writing out an `include` directive. Remember that it doesn't end in a semicolon and that the angle brackets are required around the header filename.
- You need to specify a header file only once, even if two different functions require it.
- You probably have seen the effects of including a header file with some compilers. For example, the compiler may report "435 lines compiled" when your source code is only 20 or 30 lines long. Those extra lines come from the `#include` file (or files).
- A complete path to the header file isn't necessary. That's because the compiler knows where to find them. Header files are located in a special subdirectory installed on your hard disk with your C compiler. The subdirectory is named INCLUDE, and it contains all the *.H files that came with your compiler. They're all text files, and you can look at them by using a file viewer or your editor. (Please don't change them!)
- In Windows, the INCLUDE folder is found beneath the folder where your compiler was installed.
- In Unix-like operating systems, the INCLUDE folder is found in the `/usr` directory: `/usr/include`.

Long, tedious information that you want to miss

You may remember that I tell you how a text file becomes a program. Remember the section "The compiler"? Probably not. Anyway, I lied in there. I omitted a step that was kinda superfluous at the time. Before your compiler compiles, it takes a quick look at your source code and runs it through a gizmo called the *preprocessor.*

The preprocessor doesn't compile anything. Instead, it scopes out your source code for any line beginning with a pound sign (#). Those lines are secretive instructions to the preprocessor, telling it to do something or to make something happen.

The compiler recognizes several preprocessor directives. The most common directives are `#include` and `#define`. Others are used for something called °which tell the compiler whether to compile certain parts of your source code — sort of like "If such-and-such is true, ignore the following several lines." This is stuff you can freely ignore, unless you get really geeky with the C language.

What's up with STDIO.H?

The common `#include <stdio.h>` thing forces the compiler to look on disk for a file named STDIO.H and copy every line from that file into your source code. No, you don't see it done; it happens as your source code is converted to object code. (See the nearby sidebar, "Long, tedious information that you want to miss.")

The STDIO.H is the *st*andar*d* *i*nput/*o*utput header file, which is where they pull `stdio` from. (It's not pronounced "studio-h," though many people say that.) STDIO.H defines all the prototypes for the standard I/O commands: `printf()` and `puts()`, for example. Plus, it contains definitions for common things in C, options for the compiler, and other junk.

You can view this file and its contents, as you can view any header file. Simply log on to the INCLUDE folder on your computer's hard drive and use the proper command to view the file.

In Windows, use this command:

```
type stdio.h | more
```

In the Unix operating systems, do this:

```
less stdio.h
```

Search through the file for some old friends, such as `printf()`, to see how it's defined and prototyped inside the header file.

Writing your own dot-H file

You have absolutely no need to write your own header file. Not now, not ever. Of course, if you dive deeply into C, you may one day write some multimodule monster and need your own custom header, one that you can proudly show your fellow C Masters and one that they will ponder and say, jealously and guardedly, "I wish I could do that."

To get a feel for it, and because this chapter would be unduly short otherwise, create the following header file, HEAD.H, in your editor. Type the lines exactly as written, matching lowercase for lowercase and uppercase for uppercase:

```
/* This is my wee li'l header file */

#define HAPPY 0x01
#define BLECH printf
#define SPIT {
#define SPOT }
```

Save the file to disk as HEAD.H. You have to type the dot-H, lest your editor save it to disk with a C, TXT, or DOC extension.

You don't compile or "run" a header file. Instead, you use it by `#include`-ing it in your source code. This type of program is listed next. Granted, it may not look at all like a C program. In fact, you may just shake your head in disgust and toss this book down right now. Please, I beg, give me a few moments before you run off all huffy to Mr. Software and buy a Visual Basic book:

```
#include <stdio.h>
#include "head.h"

int main()
SPIT
    BELCH("This guy is happy: %c\n",HAPPY);
    return(0);
SPOT
```

Start over on a new slate in your editor. Type the preceding source code exactly. The second `#include` brings in your header file; note how it has `head.h` in double quotes. That's how the compiler finds your header file instead of looking for it with the other, traditional headers. Also, don't let the `SPIT`, `BELCH`, `SPOT` stuff toss you. It's explained later.

Save the file to disk and name it HTEST.C. Compile and run. Don't be stunned if you find no errors. Believe it or not, everything should work out just fine. Here's a peek at what the output should look like:

```
This guy is happy: ☺
```

Mr. HAPPY is happy. You may be happy too, after understanding what went on. Here's the blow-by-blow:

The second `#include` (Line 2) brings into your source code the HEAD.H file you may have created earlier in this chapter. All the instructions in that file are magically included with your source code when HTEST1.C is compiled (as are the instructions from the standard I/O header file, STDIO.H).

If you recall, inside the HEAD.H header file are a few of those `#define` directives, which tell the compiler to substitute certain characters or C language words with happy euphemisms. (Refer to your HEAD.H file, if you need to.) For example, the word `SPIT` was defined as equal to the left curly brace. So, `SPIT` is used in the program rather than the first curly brace in Line 5:

```
SPIT
```

The word `BELCH` was defined to be equal to the word `printf`, so it serves as a substitute for that function as well in Line 6, and in Line 8 you see the word `SPOT` used rather than the final curly brace.

Just about anything in a C program can wend its way into your own, personal header files. `#define` statements are the most popular. Also allowed are comments, variable definitions, advanced things called *structures*, and even source code (though that's rare). Remember that because it's eventually copied into your source code, anything that normally would go there can also go into a header file.

- Mostly, any header file you write yourself contains a lot of `#defines`. A doozy I wrote for one program, for example, listed all the `#defines` for strange key combinations on the keyboard. For example:

  ```
  #define F1 0x3B00
  ```

  This line allows me to use the characters `F1` rather than have to remember (or constantly look up) the ugly value the computer understands as the F1 key.

- Can't remember the code for the happy face? Just `#define` it in your own header file and use it instead, which is what is done here.

- There's no reason to redefine C language words and functions (unless you want to goof someone up). However, the first `#define` in HEAD.H sets the word `HAPPY` equal to the value of the PC's happy-face character, `0x01`.

A final warning about header files

The typical header file used in C contains lots of information. What it doesn't contain, however, is *programming code*. By that, I mean that although the `printf()` function may be defined, prototyped, massaged, and oriented inside the STDIO.H file, the programming code that carries out `printf()`'s task isn't in the header file.

I mention this because occasionally a reader writes to me and says something along the lines of "Dan! I need the DOS.H header file in order to compile an older DOS program. Can you find it for me?" My answer is that even if I could find it, the header file alone *does not help*. You also need the *library* file in order to do the job.

Library files are like object code: They contain instructions for the microprocessor, telling it how to go about doing certain tasks. The instructions for `printf()` to do its thing are contained in a standard C language library file, *not* in the header file.

Figure 23-3 illustrates the process. First, you take your source code, named HOLLOW.C in the figure. STDIO.H is `#include`d, so it's combined with the source code by the compiler. The result is an object file named HOLLOW.O (or HOLLOW.OBJ).

To turn the object file into a program file, a library is added. The library contains the instructions for the C language functions. These are carefully *linked* into your source code so that a final program, HOLLOW (or HOLLOW.EXE) is produced.

It's the library that contains the code, not the header file! If you want to compile an older DOS program, you need an older DOS library to link into your source code. Without it, the header file really means nothing.

- Library files live in the LIB folder, which is usually found right next to the INCLUDE folder. For example, in Unix, the `/usr/lib` folder dwells right next-door to the `/usr/include` folder.
- More information on using library files is in *C All-in-One Desk Reference For Dummies* (Wiley).

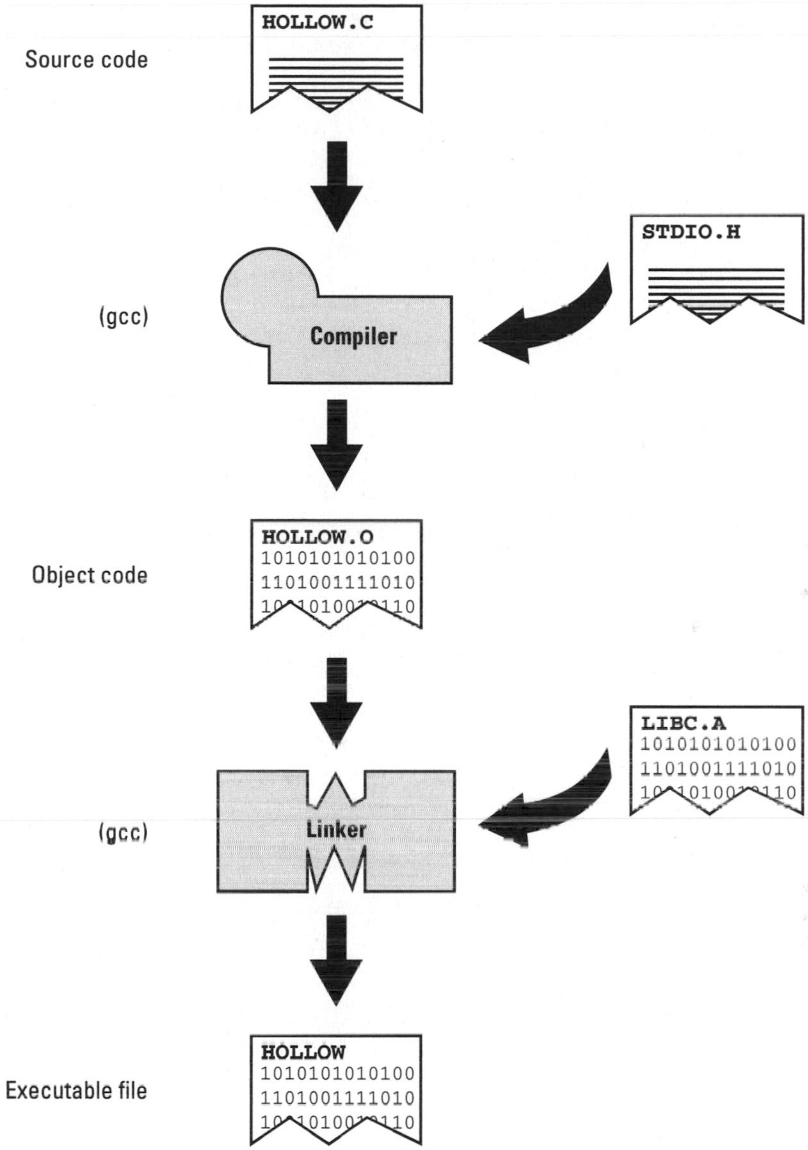

Figure 23-3: How library files fit into the big picture.

What the #defines Are Up To

The #define directive is another one of those things the compiler eats before it works on your source code. Using #define, you can set up some handy, clever, and memorable word equivalents to big numbers, constant values, or just about anything that appears in your C source code.

The full scope of the #define "construction" is offered in Chapter 8. Because I'm on an anti-redundancy campaign, I don't repeat it here. Let me add, however, that #define is the most popular item placed into a header file. Edit your HEAD.H file, in fact, and add these two lines:

```
#define TRUE 1
#define FALSE (!TRUE)
```

Save HEAD.H back to disk with these modifications.

What you have done is to create a shortcut word, TRUE, that you can use as a "true" condition.

The FALSE shortcut word is defined as being "not" true. The exclamation point in C means not. The value of FALSE is obviously !TRUE. (It works out to be 0; no big deal.)

To make immediate use of the two new shortcut words, modify the source code for HTEST.C:

```
#include <stdio.h>
#include "head.h"

int main()
SPIT
    if(TRUE)
        BLECH("Must be true!\n");
    if(FALSE)
        BLECH("Never see this message.\n");
    return(0);
SPOT
```

Carefully type this source code into your editor. Save it to disk. Compile. Run.

The output looks something like this:

```
Must be true!
```

- The best time for using the `TRUE` or `FALSE` shortcut words is when you create a `while` loop. Refer to Chapters 17 and 18.
- In the C language, the value `1` is taken to be TRUE, and `0` is FALSE.
- Some C programmers prefer to define `TRUE` and `FALSE` this way:

  ```
  #define FALSE 0
  #define TRUE(!FALSE)
  ```

  Whatever. This book defines `TRUE` as 1 and `FALSE` as "not true," which works out to 0. If you see the preceding `#define`s in a program, everything still works as advertised. Just don't let it throw you.
- Some compilers may issue a warning message when no comparison is in the `if` statement's parentheses. That's just the compiler being smart again; it recognizes the certainty of the `if` keyword's "comparison" and tells you whether it is always TRUE or is always FALSE.
- Some compilers may also point out that the second `if` statements are never executed because the `if` condition is always false. Big deal. Run the program anyway.

Avoiding the Topic of Macros

Another # thing used in the C language is the *macro*. Like `#include` and `#define`, macros are instructions to the compiler that tell it how to handle conditions and whether specific parts of the source code are to be used or skipped. Weird, but handy.

Though there's no reason to describe in detail what macros are and because I'm not crazy enough to waste time with an example, you may see even more pound-sign goobers playing the macro game in someone else's C source code. Pick any from this list:

- `#if`
- `#else`
- `#endif`
- `#ifdef`
- `#ifndef`

These are also instructions to the C compiler, designed primarily to indicate whether a group of statements should be compiled or included with the final program.

For example:

```
#if GRAPHICS
      //do graphical wonders here
#else
      //do boring text stuff here
#endif
```

Suppose that `GRAPHICS` is something defined earlier in the program or in a header file — `#define GRAPHICS 1`, for example. If so, the compiler compiles the statements only between the `#if GRAPHICS` and `#else` lines. Otherwise, the statements between `#else` and `#endif` are compiled. The result? Potentially two different programs using one source code.

Crazy! Why bother?

I have used this trick only once: I wrote a program that had two versions — one that ran on old color PC systems and a second that ran on monochrome systems. On the color PCs, I had statements that displayed text in color, which didn't work on the old monochrome monitors. Therefore, I used the `#if` goober so that I needed to write only one source code file to create both versions of the program.

- There's really no need to bother with this stuff. I'm mentioning it here because it fits in the section heading and because some C poohbah somewhere would chastise me for ignoring it.
- The `#if` thing is followed by a shortcut word defined elsewhere in the program with the `#define` construction. If it's value isn't 0, the `#if` condition is true and the statements between `#if` and `#endif` are compiled. Oh, and there's an `#else` in there too, which serves the same purpose as the C language `else` word.
- You may see some of the `#ifdef` or `#ifndef` things in various header files. I have no idea what they're doing in there, but they look darn impressive.
- Another #-goober is `#line`. It's rarely used. Supposedly, what it does is force the compiler to report a unique line number just in case an error occurs. (Don't worry — I don't get it either.)

Chapter 24

The printf() Chapter

In This Chapter

- Using printf() to display text
- Displaying forbidden characters with escape sequences
- Displaying the values of variables
- Understanding conversion characters

Perhaps one of the most familiar fellows you have met on your C programming journey is the printf() function. Though you may have been using it, and despite my various and sundry hints about some of its power, I don't feel that you have really been formally introduced. Now, after all that time, this chapter is your formal introduction to the full power of printf().

A Quick Review of printf()

You should know three printf() tricks:

- printf() displays the text you put inside the double quotes.
- printf() requires the backslash character — an escape sequence — to display some special characters.
- printf() can display variables by using the % conversion character.
- The % conversion characters can also be used to format the output of the information that's printed.

The Old Displaying-Text-with-printf() Routine

Printf()'s main purpose in life is to display text on the screen. Here is its most basic format:

```
printf("text");
```

text is the text you want to see on the screen. It's enclosed in double quotes. The double quotes are enclosed in parentheses, and the entire statement must end with a semicolon.

- Special characters — such as a double quote, tab, backspace, and Enter (a new line) — can be included in the text that printf() displays. These characters require the printf() escape sequences, as described in the next section.
- printf() can display two or more lines of text by using the \n (newline) escape sequence.
- To specify a double quote in your text string, use the \" escape sequence.

The printf() Escape Sequences

Table 24-1 lists many of the printf() escape sequences. Most of these you know from using them. Others are very specific, and you may never ever use them in your entire programming life.

Table 24-1 printf() Escape Sequences

Sequence	*Shortcut for or Equivalent to*
\a	Beeps the speaker
\b	Backspace (moves the cursor back, no erase)
\f	Form feed (ejects printer page; may clear the screen on some computers)
\n	Newline, like pressing the Enter key
\r	Carriage return (moves the cursor to the beginning of the line)

Sequence	Shortcut for or Equivalent to
\t	Tab
\v	Vertical tab (moves the cursor down a line)
\\	The backslash character
\'	The apostrophe
\"	The double-quote character
\?	The question mark
\0	The "null" byte (that's 0, not the letter *O*)
\0*nn*	A character value in octal (base 8)
\x*nnn*	A character value in hexadecimal (base 16)

The final two items in Table 24-1 are the most flexible. They allow you to insert any character into any text after you know that character's octal or hexadecimal code value.

Suppose that you need to display the Escape character in your text. A quick look into Appendix B shows that the hexadecimal code for Escape is `1b`. As an escape sequence — an Escape escape sequence — that would be written as

```
\x1b
```

Here's how it would look in `printf()`:

```
printf("On some consoles, this clears the screen \x1b[2J");
```

TIP: You may want to flag this page with a sticky note or dog-ear the corner. The page has stuff no one remembers, so you wind up referring to Table 24-1 often.

The printf() escape-sequence testing program deluxe

To see how some of these characters work, create the PRINTFUN.C program, listed next. You modify the `printf()` statement at the core of the program to demonstrate how the various escape sequences affect text:

```
/*
printf() escape sequence demonstration program
*/

#include <stdio.h>

int main()
{
    printf("Here is the \\a sequence: \a");
    getchar();
    return(0);
}
```

Enter this program into your text editor. Save it to disk as PRINTFUN.C.

Compile and run PRINTFUN.C. Its purpose is to see how the `\a` sequence "appears" in the text that's displayed. Here's a sample of the program's output:

```
Here is the \a sequence: BEEP!
```

The speaker beeps. How ghastly! Pray that you're not testing this program in the early afternoon, or else you may wake up your cellmates.

- When the program runs, `getchar()` waits for you to press a key at the keyboard. This pause allows you to examine the output before the program quits.
- The text string in `printf()` contains two escape sequences. The first is `\\`, a double backslash that displays the backslash character. In this example, `\\a` displays `\a` — the escape sequence being tested. The second escape sequence is at the end of the string, `\a`.
- Notice that the string in `printf` doesn't end in `\n`. The newline character would goof up the display for some of the fancier escape sequences (`\r`, `\t`, and `\b`).

Putting PRINTFUN to the test

The true test of the PRINTFUN program is to reedit it and replace the `\\a` and `\a` with another escape sequence. This way, you can test all the sequences to get a feel for what each of them does.

Begin by replacing Line 9 in the program with this one:

```
printf("Here is the \\b backspace sequence:\b\b\b\b");
```

This line tests the \b, backspace, escape sequence. Save the changes to the program, compile it, and run it.

You see the cursor sitting below the *n* in sequence when the program runs. That's because \b backs up the cursor but *does not erase*.

There are four instances of \b, which back up the cursor four places from the end of the line. (If the cursor isn't right there, you have a rogue space in the program or you specified more or fewer instances of \b.)

The \n character you're familiar with, but what does \r do? How is a carriage return different from a new line? Edit Line 9 in PRINTFUN.C to look like this and find out:

```
printf("Here is the \\r sequence:\r");
```

Save the change to disk, compile, and run.

In the output, you see the cursor flashing under the H at the beginning of the line. The carriage return resembles the carriage return on a typewriter: It moves you to the beginning of the line. It was only by whacking the line-feed bar on a typewriter that the page was advanced.

The \t character produces a tab, like pressing the Tab key. The cursor moves a predefined number of characters to the right. This is good for producing a table in which text has to be lined up. Edit Line 9 in the program to read:

```
    printf("Able\tBaker\tCharlie\n");
```

Then, insert the following lines immediately after the preceding printf() statement:

```
    printf("1\t2\t3\n");
    printf("Alpha\tBeta\tGamma\n");
```

No spaces are in this printf text string. The words Able, Baker, and Charlie are separated by \t (tab) escape sequences. The line ends with \n, the newline. The same holds true for the two new lines: instances of \t separate the numbers and words.

Double-check your source code! Ensure that you have \t twice in each printf() statement and that \n ends each quoted string of text. Beware of rogue backslashes, which you have a tendency to type as you enter each line. When everything looks okay, save the PRINTFUN.C source code file to disk. Compile it. Run it. Here's some sample output:

```
Able    Baker   Charlie
1       2       3
Alpha   Beta    Gamma
```

Though the `\t`s in the `printf` statements look sloppy, the output is definitely organized. Tabular, dude!

- The "tab stops" are preset to every eighth column in C's output. Using a `\t` inserts a given number of space characters in the output, lining up the next bit of text at the next tab stop. I mention this because some people assume that the tab always moves over eight (or however many) characters. That is not the case.
- The `\f` and `\v` characters display special symbols at the Windows command prompt. Rather than a form feed, `\f` displays the ankh character. Rather than a vertical tab, `\v` displays the male symbol.
- REMEMBER: As long as you know a character's hexadecimal code value, you can always get it displayed by using the `\x` escape sequence. Just plug in the hexadecimal code and there you go!

The Complex printf() *Format*

The `printf()` function can also be used to display the contents of variables, which you have been seeing throughout this book with integer variables and the `%d` placeholder, character variables and `%c`, and so on. To make it happen, `printf()` uses this format:

```
printf("format_string"[,var[,...]]);
```

Text still appears in double quotes, but after it's used to display the values in variables, it becomes a *format string.* (It's still the same text in double quotes.) The format string is followed by one or more variables, *var.*

Those *var* variables are plugged in to appropriate spots in the `format_string` according to special percent-sign placeholders. Those percent-sign placeholders are called *conversion characters.* For example:

```
printf("Yeah, I think %s is a jerk, too.\n",jerk);
```

The format string is text that `printf()` displays on the screen: `Yeah, I think _____ is a jerk, too.` The `%s` is a conversion character — a blank — that must be filled by a string of text. (I call them placeholders, but the lords of C claim that they're conversion characters.)

After the format string is a comma and then `jerk`. The `jerk` is a string variable whose contents replace the `%s` in `printf()`'s output.

- You can specify any number of conversion characters in `printf()`'s format string. Each conversion character, however, must have a corresponding variable; three `%s` characters would require three string variables.
- Yeah, this works like fill-in-the-blanks; the `%` conversion characters are the blanks.
- You can specify both strings of text and numbers by using the proper conversion characters, as described in the next section.
- Refer to Figure 4-2, in Chapter 4, for an illustration of how the conversion characters work with variables in a `printf()` statement.

The `printf()` *Conversion Characters*

Table 24-2 lists all the `printf()` conversion characters in the known universe — even those you haven't seen before and some you may never see again.

Table 24-2 The `printf()` Conversion Characters

Conversion Character	*Displays Argument (Variable's Contents) As*
%c	Single character
%d	Signed decimal integer (int)
%e	Signed floating-point value in E notation
%f	Signed floating-point value (float)
%g	Signed value in %e or %f format, whichever is shorter
%i	Signed decimal integer (int)
%o	Unsigned octal (base 8) integer (int)
%s	String of text
%u	Unsigned decimal integer (int)
%x	Unsigned hexadecimal (base 16) integer (int)

Additional formatting stuff

Your C compiler's documentation should contain a list of additional `printf()` formatting information, bonus characters that can be used in conjunction with the conversion characters to additionally format `printf()`'s output. That information is too complex and detailed to list here for every compiler. Instead, look up `printf` in your online reference manual and note these formatting sections:

- Flags
- Width specifiers
- Precision specifiers
- Input-size modifiers

You don't need this information now for understanding the C programming language. However, it comes in handy as you begin working with numbers or require a little fancier output than what you have done with `printf()` in this chapter.

In addition to the conversion characters in Table 24-2, three other characters exist: `%p`, `%n` and `%%`. The `%p` and `%n` are advanced conversion characters, beyond the scope of this book. The `%%` merely prints a `%` on the screen.

- As with the escape sequences, the conversion characters are something you use often but never remember. I advise tacking a sticky note to this page for future reference.
- The `%x`, `%e`, and `%g` conversion characters also have uppercase equivalents: `%X`, `%E` and `%G`. By using capital letters rather than lowercase, you ensure that any letters in the output are all listed as uppercase. For example, `%x` would display a hexadecimal value as `1ba2`, but `%X` would display `1BA2`. Otherwise, the conversion character's behavior is the same.
- `%p` is used to print a value as a pointer. Pointers are covered in this book's companion, *C All-in-One Desk Reference For Dummies* (Wiley).

Chapter 25

Math Madness!

In This Chapter

- Using more complex math functions
- Understanding the `pow()` and `sqrt()` functions
- Linking in the math library for Unix
- Doing the post-/pre-increment/-decrement thing

Most people think that computer programming is all math. Boy, are they wrong. It involves math, to be sure, but the hard part — figuring out the answer — is done by the computer. So, what's the beef? Why run screaming and hiding from this innocent, kind little chapter that merely discusses the various C language details, spells, and dance steps for juggling numbers?

More on Math

The basic four computer math symbols should be familiar to you by now:

- Addition symbol: +
- Subtraction symbol: –
- Multiplication symbol: *
- Division symbol: /

These doojabbies are common throughout computerdom. If you use a spreadsheet, they're the symbols you use to do math. All these symbols are clustered about your keyboard's numeric keypad. The most cryptic one is the asterisk (*), for multiplication.

Other than the symbols, the only thing worth keeping in mind about math in C is that the calculation always goes on the *right* side of the equal sign. Therefore:

```
meals=breakfast+lunch+dinner;
```

This equation, assuming that everything is a numeric variable, is correct. The following statement, however, is a boo-boo:

```
breakfast+lunch+dinner=meals;
```

The math goes on the right side of the equal sign. Always.

- Goofing up a math equation is where you get those horrid `Lvalue` errors.
- You can always remember the cryptic mathematical symbols in the C language by looking at your keyboard's numeric keypad; each of the symbols is right there.
- Math problems in C work from left to right, the way you read. Some operations, however, have priority over others. If you forget, remember My Dear Aunt Sally, from Chapter 11.
- Another mathematical symbol is the `%`, which means *modulus.* This dreadful topic is covered in Chapter 26, where it's appropriate uses are apparent.
- It can be said that a C language operator exists for every odd symbol, shape, jot, and tittle on your keyboard. This statement is *almost* true. Pray that you never have to memorize them all.

Taking your math problems to a higher power

Two mathematical operations that seem to be lacking in C's granola of symbols are the power-of symbol and the square root symbol. Of course, I'm assuming that you give a hoot about either of them, but you never know when they may crop up.

The power-of thing deals with problems that contain the words *squared* and *cubed* in addition to *power of.* For example:

"Four squared" means 4×4, or 4^2. The latter reads "Four to the second power."

"Four cubed" means $4 \times 4 \times 4$, or 4^3. This one reads "Four to the third power."

Beyond cubed, or to the third power, you just say the power number; So, $4 \times 4 \times 4 \times 4 \times 4$ is 4^5, or "four to the fifth power." (Don't even bother trying to figure out the answer; the computer does it for you!)

Alas, there just isn't any handy way to express 4^5 in C. There's no cool symbol. For example, you cannot write

```
answer=4♠5;
```

This line just doesn't work, even considering that ♠ isn't a symbol anywhere on the keyboard (even in Las Vegas). It would be nice, but it just isn't so.

You need to draw on the C language's vast library of supplemental math functions. A few dozen functions compute such things as power-of, square root, terrifying trigonometric functions, and so on (see Table 25-1, later in this chapter). To take a number to a higher power, you use the `pow()` function.

The `pow()` function is used to calculate one value taken to a certain power, such as 4 taken to the second power (4^2). Here's the format:

```
value = pow(n,p)
```

In this line, `value`, `n`, and `p` all must be double-precision variables (defined using the `double` declaration). The `pow()` function calculates `n` to the `p` power. The answer is stored in the `value` variable.

To prevent your compiler from going mad, you must include the MATH.H header file at the beginning of your source code. Stick the following line up there somewhere:

```
#include <math.h>
```

This line is required for the `pow` function as well as for other math functions you may dare to use.

Putting `pow()` *into use*

Using the `pow()` function is easy it's just like using any other function. Just declare your variables as doubles, include the MATH.H thing, and you're all set. Why not put it forth in one of those endearing math-sentence problems? To wit:

Suppose that you have tasked Milton — your brilliant, Mensa-club-leader son — with decorating the house for Christmas. Because he's too smart to drive, he directs you to go to the store and pick up 2^8 ("two to the eighth power") twinkly lights. You quickly dash off to your computer and use the C language to decipher what he means:

```
#include <stdio.h>
#include <math.h>

int main()
{
    double lights;

    lights=pow(2,8);        /* figure 2 to the 8th power */
    printf("Milton, we need %0.f lights.\n",lights);
    return(0);
}
```

Type this silly program on a new screen in your editor. Save the contraption to disk as LIGHTS1.C.

Compile and run.

If you get a linker error in your Unix-like operating system, please refer to the following sidebar, "Gotta link in that math library!"

Here's the output:

```
Milton, we need 256 lights.
```

There. Now you both know how many lights are needed. The computer successfully concluded that 2^8 is equal to 256.

- Two to the eighth power is written out longways; thus:

  ```
  2 x 2 x 2 x 2 x 2 x 2 x 2 x 2
  ```

- The `pow` function expects to deal with `double` variables. In fact, many of the MATH.H functions deal with anything except integers.
- Constant values, such as `2` and `8` inside LIGHTS1.C, don't have to be `double`s (or even typecast as `double`s). Thankfully, the compiler is pretty smart about that stuff.
- The `printf()` placeholder used for printing a floating-point number is `%f`. It works for both `float`s and `double`s. The `0.` part of `%0.f` tells `printf()` to format the floating-point output using only the part of the number on the *left* of the decimal.
- Some languages and spreadsheets use the caret symbol (^) for *power,* as in 2^8 for 2^8. This technique doesn't work in C. (The ^ in C is a bitwise exclusive `OR` logical operation, whatever that means.)

Gotta link in that math library!

If you're using Unix, Linux, or Mac OS X, you need to know that GCC isn't normally configured to do high-level math functions, such as `pow()` and `sqrt()`. The reason is that the standard C library doesn't come with those math functions in it. The advantage is that programs produced with the standard library are small. The disadvantage is that you need to remember to link in the math library when you write programs that use math.

The standard math library in C is named `libm`, but you can link it into your program by modifying the `gcc` command:

```
gcc -lm source.c -o output
```

Follow `gcc` with the `-lm` switch. This switch tells GCC to also link in the `libm` math library along with the standard library. The input file is `source.c`, and the output file is `output`. To properly compile `lights1.c`:

```
gcc -lm lights1.c -o lights1
```

Again, this option is necessary only for programs that use high-level math functions. To confirm, use the `man` command to look up the function:

```
man sqrt
```

It says, right there on top, under the `LIBRARY` heading, that the standard math library must be linked in to make the function work.

Rooting out the root

Another math problem you may have to work out is the square root. For the life of me, I can't cite a practical example because, honestly, I find all math stupid. In any event, no keyboard symbol in C is used to calculate the square root of a number. As with the power-of deal, you use a special function: `sqrt()`.

The `sqrt()` function is used to divine the square root of a number — to find out which number, when multiplied by itself, equals the number you want the square root of. Something like that. In any event, it's not the "squirt" function. Here's the format:

```
value = sqrt(n)
```

The double variable `value` is equal to the square root of the double variable `n`. Yes, everything must be `double` here. You also need the following `include` at the beginning of your source code:

```
#include <math.h>
```

The only limitation on the sqrt() function is that n, the number you're finding the root of, cannot be negative. Even though my Vulcan friends tell me that there is such a thing, I would be leery of attempting it in the C language.

Because you and Milton have this light thing going, you're going to surprise him by telling him the square root of the number of lights you bought for Christmas. To make that process easier, you devise the LIGHTS2.C program.

Type this program into your editor. Be careful when you're typing because that long printf() line was split in order to fit into this book's format; the single backslash is used to show that the line continues on the following line:

```
#include <stdio.h>
#include <math.h>
#define TOOTH 253

int main()
{
    double lights;

    lights=sqrt(256);          /* square root of 256 */
    printf("Milton, I got your %0.f%c lights.\n",\
                    lights,TOOTH);
    return(0);
}
```

Save this puppy to disk as LIGHTS2.C:

Compile and run. (Unix users, refer to the preceding sidebar, "Gotta link in that math library!" for more details.)

```
Milton, I got your 16² lights.
```

The sqrt() function boasts that the square root of 256 is 16. Or, to put it another way, 16^2 (or 16×16) is equal to 256. Milton would be pleased.

- The square root of 256 is 16, and 16 squared (162) is 256. Is math great or what?
- Character code 253 is equal to the tiny ^{2} — the squared number.
- Character code 251 is equal to the traditional square root symbol. Even if you can manage to get that symbol into your text editor, you still need the sqrt() function to wrangle up a square root.
- In some cases, codes 253 and 251 may not display the same symbol as described in the two preceding notes. Oh, well.
- The %c in the printf() formatting string is used to bring in the special character, 253, defined as TOOTH earlier in the source code.

- No, `sqrt()` isn't what the Roman legions paraded on their standards. (That was SPQR, which stands for *Senatus Populus Que Romanus,* the Senate, and People of Rome.)
- A reader once wrote me e-mail asking whether the C language had some equivalent of the mathematical *i* dingus, used to represent the *imaginary number* √-1, or the square root of "negative one." Because I don't know everything, I had to say that I don't know. Some mathematical C language library somewhere may deal with *i*. But, as far as any other workaround is concerned, I have no idea — though I believe it can be worked into the C++ programming language. (But I don't do C++, so I can't confirm it.)

Strange Math? You Got It!

Most C language libraries are just bursting with math functions. Lots of them. I have listed some of the more common ones in Table 25-1, along with their formats. Pretty much all of them want a `double` or `float` value, which makes sense when you figure that if math had no decimals, more of us would enjoy it.

Table 25-1 Weirdo Math Functions You Never Use

Function	*What It Computes*	*Format*	*Include*	*Library*
`abs`	Absolute value	a=abs(b)	STDLIB.H	standard
`acos`	Arc cosine	x=acos(y)	MATH.H	libm
`asin`	Arc sine	x=asin(y)	MATH.H	libm
`atan`	Arc tangent	x=atan(y)	MATH.H	libm
`cos`	Cosine	x=cos(y)	MATH.H	libm
`exp`	Exponential	x=exp(y)	MATH.H	libm
`log`	Natural logarithm	x=log(y)	MATH.H	libm
`log10`	Base 10 logarithm	x=log10(y)	MATH.H	libm
`sin`	Sine	x=sin(y)	MATH.H	libm
`tan`	Tangent	x=tan(y)	MATH.H	libm

- In Table 25-1, variables *a, b,* and *c* denote integer values. Variables *x, y,* and *z* are doubles.
- The `libm` library is needed only for compiling programs under a Unix-like operating system. Refer to the earlier sidebar "Gotta link in that math library!"

- The absolute value of a number is its value without the minus sign.
- Even more complex functions than this one exist. Wise men truly run from them.
- TIP The best source for discovering what these commands do and how they work is to look in the C language library reference that came with your compiler. If you're lucky, it's in a book; otherwise, it's in your compiler's online help feature.
- Most of the time, you can replace the variables in a math function's parentheses with constant values. For example:

  ```
  x=sqrt(1024);
  ```

Something Really Odd to End Your Day

It's your old pal ++ again, and his sister, -- — the increment and decrement operators from days gone by. They're favorites, to be sure, but they're kind of puzzling in a way. For example, consider the following snippet of code that you may find lurking in someone else's program:

```
b=a++;
```

The variable `b` equals the contents of variable `a` plus `1`. Or does it?

Remember that `a++` can be a statement by itself. As such, doesn't it work out first? If so, does `b` equal `a+1`, or does `b` equal `a` and then `a` is incremented after it all? And will Cody realize that Miranda is cheating on him so that he'll be free to marry Jessica? Hmmm. . . .

It's a puzzle that has an answer — an important answer that you have to know if you don't want your programs getting all goofy on you.

The perils of using a++

Here's the rule about using ++ to increment a variable so that you know what happens before running the sample program:

> The variable is incremented last when ++ appears after it.

So:

```
b=a++;
```

The compiler instantly slides the value of variable `a` into variable `b` when it sees this statement. Then, the value of `a` is incremented. To drive this point home, test out the INCODD.C program.

Type this program into your editor. Save it to disk as INCODD.C:

```
#include <stdio.h>

int main()
{
    int a,b;

    a=10;
    b=0;
    printf("A=%d and B=%d before incrementing.\n",a,b);
    b=a++;
    printf("A=%d and B=%d after incrementing.\n",a,b);
    return(0);
}
```

Compile and run! Here's what the output looks like:

```
A=10 and B=0 before incrementing.
A=11 and B=10 after incrementing.
```

The first line makes sense: The `a` and `b` variables were given those values right up front. The second line proves the ++ conundrum. First, `b` is assigned the value of `a`, which is `10`; then `a` is incremented to `11`.

- Whenever you see a variable followed by ++ in a C statement, know that the variable's value is incremented *last,* after any other math or assignments (equal-sign things) elsewhere on that line.
- A good way to remember this rule is that the ++ comes after the variable. It's as though C sees the variable first, raids its contents, and then — oh, by the way — it increments its value.
- This rule screws you up if you ever combine the ++ with something else inside an `if` comparison:

  ```
  if(a==b++)
  ```

  This technique is common — sticking the `b++` inside the comparison rather than on a line before or afterward. You have to keep in mind, however, that `b` is incremented after the `if` command compares them. If the comparison is true, `b` is still incremented. Remember that when you notice that your program is acting funny.

Oh, and the same thing applies to a `--`

The decrementing operator, `--`, also affects a variable's value after any other math or equal-sign stuff is done in the program. To witness this effect, here's the DECODD.C program:

```
#include <stdio.h>

int main()
{
    int a,b;

    a=10;
    b=0;
    printf("A=%d and B=%d before decrementing.\n",a,b);
    b=a--;
    printf("A=%d and B=%d after decrementing.\n",a,b);
    return(0);
}
```

Save the file to disk as DECODD.C. Compile and run. Here's the output, proving that decrementing happens after any math or assignments:

```
A=10 and B=0 before decrementing.
A=9 and B=10 after decrementing.
```

The value of `b` is equal to `10`, which means that the `a` variable was decremented last.

All this makes sense, and you should understand it by now — or at least be aware of what's happening. If you can't remember the rule, just keep your incrementing or decrementing on a line by itself, as shown in this example:

```
a++;
b=a;
```

Reflections on the strange `++a` phenomenon

Load the program INCODD.C back into your editor. Change Line 10 to read

```
b=++a;
```

This line looks stranger than it is. You can type it like this to avoid thinking that =++ is some weird C command:

```
b = ++a;
```

The ++ is still the incrementing operator. It still increases the value of the a variable. Because it comes before the variable, however, the incrementing happens first. It reads "Increase me first, and then do whatever else comes next."

Save the source code for INCODD.C to disk. Compile and run it. Here's what you see:

```
A=10 and B=0 before incrementing.
A=11 and B=11 after incrementing.
```

It worked! The ++a operation came first.

Again, this is just something strange you should know about. Rarely have I seen the ++ operator appear before a variable, but it can be done. It may help iron out some screwy things if you notice trouble when you're putting ++ after a variable name.

- You can use ++ before or after a variable when it appears on a line by itself. There's no difference between this:

  ```
  a++;
  ```

  and this:

  ```
  ++a;
  ```

- a++ is known as *post-incrementing*. ++a is known as *pre incrementing.*
- Yes, this process also works with decrementing. You can change Line 10 in DECODD.C to this:

  ```
  b=--a;
  ```

  Save, compile, and run the program. Variable a is decremented first, and then its new value is given to variable b.
- Most people use the word *anxious* when they really mean *eager.*

- Don't even bother with this:

  ```
  ++a++;
  ```

  Your logical mind may ponder that this statement first increments the a variable and then increments it again. Wrong! The compiler thinks that you forgot something when you try to compile this type of statement; you get one of the dreadful Lvalue required errors. That message means that the compiler was expecting another variable or number in there somewhere. Sorry, but the "fortress effect" of the incrementing or decrementing operators just doesn't work.

Chapter 26

The Old Random-Number Function

In This Chapter

- Introducing the `rand()` function
- Seeding the `rand()` function
- Performing mod (%) calculations
- Producing random numbers in a given range

The original plans for this book had it run about 1,600 pages. That's because I never wanted to break the slow, easy pace with which the C language was taught. The problem is that you cannot fit 1,600 pages into a roughly 400-page book without cutting something out. What to cut out?

You may think that it's odd that I chose to cut what I did, yet kept this chapter on the random-number function. I did that because, believe it or not, random numbers are a big deal when it comes to programming a computer. They come in handy, for example, with computer games. No computer game would ever be possible without a random number here or there. Without them, the game would be predictable: "Oh, I'm passing by the planet Bothar again, and here is where the Omnivorous Space Slug tries to taunt me into a gavotte."

On Being Random

What's random? The next card drawn from a well-shuffled deck. The roll of a dice. The spin of a roulette wheel. Whether Cindy will overlook your huge beer gut as you attempt your first date after the divorce. These are all random, maybe-this-or-that events. If you want to include this random aspect in your programs, you need a special function that produces random numbers. After that's done, no one can predict when the *Enterprise* will be attacked or when the tornado will whip through your village or whether Door Number 2 leads to the treasure this time or to certain peril.

- The phone company is rumored to have a random-number program that it routinely uses to foul up your bill.
- Random-number routines are the root of the most evil program ever devised for a budding programmer: The Guess the Number program. I spare you that torture in this book. (Well, maybe not.)
- In the C language, random numbers are produced by using the `rand()` function. I formally introduce it next.
- Random numbers must be *seeded* in order for them to be more unpredictable. I cover this subject also, later in this chapter.
- Random numbers generated by a computer aren't truly random. See the nearby sidebar, "You too can waste a few seconds reading this information about random numbers," for more information.

Using the `rand()` function

Random numbers are generated in C by using the `rand()` function. It spits back a random number depending on the whims of your PC's microprocessor carefully combined with the birthdate of the guy who wrote your C compiler plus his girlfriend's weight in drams. Or something like that.

Here's the format for the `rand()` function:

```
int rand();
```

You too can waste a few seconds reading this information about random numbers

Are they random numbers? Only if they can't be predicted. Unfortunately, with computers, the numbers can be predicted. They're still more or less jumbled, like street numbers in Seattle. But, overall, the random numbers a computer generates aren't truly random. Instead, they're *pseudorandom.*

A pseudo- ("SOO-doh") random number is random enough for most purposes. But because the number is based on a computer algorithm, or set routine, its outcome isn't truly random. Even if you base the random number on the time of day — or *seed* the random number by using another, potentially random value — the results still aren't random enough to appease the mathematical purists. So you live with it.

The `rand()` function returns an integer value, somewhere in the range of 0 through 32,767. If you want to save the random number into the `r` variable, you use the following statement:

```
r=rand();
```

Cinchy stuff.

To make the compiler understand the `rand()` function, you must add this line at the beginning of your source code:

```
#include <stdlib.h>
```

This line tells the compiler all about the `rand()` function and makes everyone happy.

The following program shows the `rand()` function in action. RANDOM1.C produces 100 random numbers, which it displays neatly on the screen. The random numbers are produced by the `rand` function inside this program's `rnd()` function. The reason that this was done, as you may be fearing, is that you modify the `rnd()` function to new levels of spiffiness as this chapter progresses.

```
#include <stdio.h>
#include <stdlib.h>

int rnd(void);

int main()
{
    int x;

    puts("Behold! 100 Random Numbers!");
    for(x=0;x<100;x++)
        printf("%d\t",rnd());
    return(0);
}

int rnd(void)
{
    int r;

    r=rand();
    return(r);
}
```

Type the source code for RANDOM1.C into your editor. Double-check everything. Save the file to disk as RANDOM1.C.

Compile the program. Fix any errors, which are probably limited to missing semicolons or forgotten parentheses.

Run it!

The output displays ten columns by ten rows of random numbers on the typical console display — no point in repeating that here! But, on your screen, note how the numbers are different — nay, random. I mean, would you have thought of that many that quickly?

- The random numbers are probably in the range of 0 to 32,000-something — as promised. The numbers you see on your screen are probably different from those from the code just shown.
- Some versions of the GCC compiler produce larger random number values than 0 to 32,000-something. That maximum value is set by the value of `RAND_MAX`, as defined in the STDLIB.H header. On my FreeBSD machine, for example, the value of `RAND_MAX` is `0x7FFFFFF` (hexadecimal), which translates to 2,147,483,647.
- To see the value of `RAND_MAX` on your computer, add this line to the program before the `return(0);` in the `main()` function:

```
printf("\nRAND_MAX is equal to %u\n",RAND_MAX);
```

  `%u` is the placeholder for an unsigned long integer.

Planting a random-number seed

Ho! Before you get all happy about the new CASINO program you're about to write and sell for millions to Las Vegas, try rerunning the RANDOM1.C program again. Just choose Run from your compiler's integrated environment or type the RANDOM1 command again at the DOS prompt:

(Output suppressed!)

Yup, on your screen, you see 100 more random numbers. Wait a second. Aren't those the *same* numbers? Identically the same numbers? Did the compiler goof? Did you foul up?

Fortunately, that was no error. The computer generated the set of random numbers because that's all it knows. Sure, they're random, all right, but they're the same numbers because, between then and now, the compiler's `rand()` function remained unchanged.

Don't feel cheated! This situation is a common one. The `rand()` function is only quasirandom. To make it more random (more *pseudo*random), you have to plant a wee, tiny seed. This seed is a value the compiler uses to help make the random numbers more random. To plant the seed, you use the `srand()` function.

The `srand` function is used to help kick off the computer's random-number machine in a more *random* manner. Here's the format:

```
void srand((unsigned)seed)
```

The `seed` value is an unsigned integer value or variable, ranging from 0 up to 65,000-something. It's that value the compiler uses to help *seed* the random-number-generation equipment located in the bowels of your PC.

You must include the following line at the beginning of your source code to make the `srand()` function behave:

```
#include <stdlib.h>
```

Because the `rand()` function already requires this line, you have no need to specify it twice (unless you're just seeding the random-number generator out of some perverse horticultural lust).

- The `(unsigned)` deal is used to ensure that the number `srand()` uses is of the unsigned type (not negative). It's known as *type casting*.
- Using the value 1 (one) to seed the random-number generator causes the compiler to start over, by using the same, uninspirational numbers you witness when `srand()` isn't used. Avoid doing that, if possible.

Randoming up the RANDOM program

Now comes the time for some really random numbers. The following source code is for RANDOM2.C, a mild modification to the original program. This time, a new function is added, `seedrnd()`, which lets you reset the random-number generator and produce more random numbers:

```
#include <stdio.h>
#include <stdlib.h>

int rnd(void);
void seedrnd(void);

int main()
{
     int x;

     seedrnd();
     puts("Behold! 100 Random Numbers!");
```

```
    for(x=0;x<100;x++)
        printf("%d\t",rnd());
    return(0);
}

int rnd(void)
{
    int r;

    r=rand();
    return(r);
}

/* seed the random number */

void seedrnd(void)
{
    int seed;
    char s[6];

    printf("Enter a random number seed (2 - 65000):");
    seed=(unsigned)atoi(gets(s));
    srand(seed);
}
```

Type this program into your editor. You can start by editing the RANDOM1.C source code. Add the prototype for `seedrnd()` up front, and then insert the call to `seedrnd()` in the `main()` function. Finally, tack the `seedrnd()` function itself to the end of the source code. Double-check the whole thing before you save it to make sure that you don't leave anything out.

Use your editor's Save As command to save the file to disk as RANDOM2.C.

Compile and run. You see this line:

```
Enter a random number seed (2-65000):
```

Type a number, from 0 up to 65,000-something. Press Enter and you see a new and more random bunch of numbers displayed.

The true test that it worked is to run the program again. This time, type a different number as the seed. The next batch of random numbers is completely different from the first.

TIP

- You have to seed the randomizer only once, as this program does up in the `main()` function. Some purists insist on calling the `seedrnd()` function (or its equivalent) lots of times. Hey, random is random as random can be with a computer. No sense in wasting time.

- This program combines three C statements into one. The statement appears in Line 34:

```
seed=(unsigned)atoi(gets(s));
```

  This line is a compilation of the following two statements:

```
gets(s);
seed=(unsigned)atoi(s);
```

  First, `gets()` reads in a string variable. Second, that value is converted into an integer variable by the `atoi` function, which is passed over to the `seed` variable in the proper unsigned format.

- There's no need for the `seedrnd()` function to return any values. As I explain in Chapter 22, some functions neither require nor return values. This function is one of them. Yet, calling the function is important because it seeds the randomizer used elsewhere in the program.

Streamlining the randomizer

Nothing annoys me like a klutzy program. I'm talking not about how it's written, but, rather, about how it looks — its presentation. When a program must ask you to seed the randomizer, something is wrong. A computer should be smart enough to do that itself. And it can, as long as it finds a source of ever-changing numbers that it can use to seed the randomizer.

One source is the computer's clock. Most PCs keep time down to the hundredths of seconds: Every 1⁄100th of a second, a new number is available to seed the randomizing gears. Heck, even the current second would be good enough to seed the randomizer. It just needs to be a number that's different from one second to the next, that's all.

The following source code is for the RANDOM3.C program. This program is nearly identical to RANDOM2.C except that the `seedrnd()` function now uses the current time to seed the random-number generator:

```
#include <stdio.h>
#include <stdlib.h>
#include <time.h>

int rnd(void);
void seedrnd(void);

int main()
{
    int x;

    seedrnd();
    puts("Behold! 100 Random Numbers!");
```

```
    for(x=0;x<100;x++)
        printf("%d\t",rnd());
    return(0);
}

int rnd(void)
{
    int r;

    r=rand();
    return(r);
}

/* seed the random number */

void seedrnd(void)
{
      srand((unsigned)time(NULL));
}
```

Create the source code for RANDOM3.C in your editor. You can start with RANDOM2.C. Add the new third line, #include <time.h>, which lets you use the computer's clock to seed the random-number generator. Then, modify the seedrnd() function as shown in this block of code. Save the file to disk as RANDOM3.C by using your editor's Save As command.

Compile and run the program. Notice that the output is similar and randomly different. What you don't notice is the program begging you to seed the randomizer. That's all handled automatically now.

- The time() function in Line 31 returns the time of day from the computer's internal clock. The function is called by using the constant value NULL, which is essentially the value 0. (This constant is defined in the stdio.h header file — the #include <stdio.h> line sets it all up; see Chapter 23 for more information.)
- The value returned by the time() function is some number, which isn't important. What's important is that it's an unsigned integer value, which is what the (unsigned) type cast does.
- TIP: No matter what, know that the following statement in any of your C programs properly and somewhat randomly seeds the random-number-generating apparatus:

```
srand((unsigned)time(NULL));
```

- The `time()` function (and therefore the preceding randomizing seeding statement) requires the following statement at the beginning of your source code:

```
#include <time.h>
```

- And, this one:

```
#include <stdlib.h>
```

The Diabolical Dr. Modulus

You may have noticed that the random numbers produced by the RANDOM series of programs have been wildly random and often unsuitable. For example:

```
Your turn, BOB.
You rolled a 23415 on the dice. This lands you on Boardwalk,
           but you've passed Go 585 times, which nets you a
           gross of $117,000!
```

That gets old after a while.

You need to have a way to round down the numbers — a hacksaw to chop off excess values and just give you numbers in a certain range, for example.

Lo, you have a way. It's the mathematical concept *modulus.*

Ah-ooga! Ah-ooga! Mathematical concept alert! Ah-ooga!

Modulus — bah! This term is better known to you as "the remainder," as in "When you divide 6 into 10, you get a remainder of 4." Well, 6 gazinta 10 is *modulo 4.* It's written in C as

```
4 = 10 % 6;
```

I don't expect you to remember what a modulus is or does, nor do I expect you to know when to use modulus, or the ablative, *modulo.* The format is the same for any of C's mathematical operators. What's important to know is that you can use the modulus doohickey to pare down larger numbers into smaller, more convenient chunks.

```
modulus = big % little;
```

Read it this way: If you take the huge number `big` and divide it by the smaller number `little`, you get a remainder, which is the `modulo` value.

Suppose that big is a big number in this statement:

```
m = big % 5;
```

The values of variable m are in the range of 0 through 4, depending on the remainder of big divided by 5.

The values of variable m for the following statement are either 0 or 1, depending on whether oddoreven is even or odd, respectively:

```
m = oddereven % 2;
```

For example, a die has six sides. Suppose that the computer coughs up the random value 23,415. To pare it to a multiple of 6, you use this line:

```
dice1=23415 % 6;
```

The computer calculates how many times 6 gazinta 23,415. It then places the remainder in the dice1 variable. (The result is the number 3, which is a more realistic roll of a die than 23,415.)

- If the second value is *larger* than the first, as in 5 % 10, the result is always equal to the second value. Therefore, you want the larger value to come first in a modulus operation.
- The modulus operator is %, the percent sign. Pronounce it "mod."
- No math! The modulus is used to help you pare your random numbers. That's all! You can dwell on the mathematical aspects of the % in other C language books.
- *Gazinta* means "goes into." I point it out here because my managing editor loathes it when I use nondictionary words.
- If you want to pare a large random number as a roll of the dice, you need this equation:

  ```
  dice1=(random_value % 6)+1;
  ```

  The *random_value* the computer produces must be pared via % 6 (mod 6). It produces a number in the range of 0 to 5 (0 to 5 as a remainder — you can't have a remainder of 6 when you divide by 6.) After the % calculation, you add 1 to the number and get a value in the range of 1 to 6, which are the true numbers on any given side of a die.
- In the My Dear Aunt Sally theme of things, a modulus operation comes just after division and before addition. See the nearby Technical Stuff sidebar, "Introducing My Dear Mother's Aunt Sally (Ugh!)."
- "Ah, yes, Dr. Modulus. I'm familiar with your work in astrogenetics. Is it true that you got kicked out of the academy for engineering a third gender in mice?" "You read too much, lad."

Introducing My Dear Mother's Aunt Sally (Ugh!)

Did you read about My Dear Aunt Sally in Chapter 11? It's a mnemonic device (a thing that makes you remember something) for multiplication, division, addition, and subtraction, which is the order in which things get done in a long C math statement. Well, add to that the modulus operation, which takes precedence over addition and subtraction. It goes like this:

My Dear Mother's Aunt Sally:

*	*M*ultiplication
/	*D*ivision
%	*M*odulus
+	*A*ddition
–	*S*ubtraction

Therefore, the following statement to get a roll of the dice:

```
dice1=(23415 % 6)+1;
```

does the same thing without the parentheses:

```
dice1=23415 % 6+1;
```

The modulus operation (`23415 % 6`) comes first regardless, and then `1` is added to the result. Of course, putting the parentheses in there for readability's sake is always forgivable.

Rolling the Dice with the Final RANDOM Program

If you have been working through this chapter, you should have a whole pile of random numbers spewing forth from your computer, like New Yorkers fleeing their buildings during an August power outage. One more keen improvement to the `rnd()` function remains. It's time to add an automatic range-finder. The following program, RANDOM4.C (the last in the suite), has a `rnd()` function that coughs up random values only in the range of `0` to whatever number you specify. This program should bring some order to your random numbers:

```
#include <stdio.h>
#include <stdlib.h>
#include <time.h>

int rnd(int range);
void seedrnd(void);

int main()
{
    int x;

    seedrnd();
    for(x=0;x<100;x++)
        printf("%i\t",rnd(10));
```

```
    return(0);
}

int rnd(int range)
{
      int r;

      r=rand()%range;
      return(r);
}

void seedrnd(void)
{
      srand((unsigned)time(NULL));
}
```

Create the source code for RANDOM4.C. Start with your RANDOM3.C program, and make modifications per the source code just shown. Save the file to disk by using the name RANDOM4.C.

Compile and run the program. Here's a sample of the output you may see:

```
4     1     3     0     6     6     1     0     8     9
2     9     5     9     8     7     6     8     0     9
5     6     2     0     5     8     5     5     9     0
9     9     2     6     1     2     0     2     0     7
8     4     4     7     1     6     0     0     5     1
3     7     1     2     1     2     5     0     8     5
9     2     0     7     9     8     4     5     6     0
8     8     7     6     0     8     3     9     3     4
0     4     0     5     5     6     3     0     4     3
7     6     1     2     2     7     6     7     4     8
```

Everything is in the range of `0` through `9`, which is what the `rnd(10)` call does in Line 14.

- The `rnd()` and `seedrnd()` functions become handy as you write your own C programs — specifically, games. Feel free to copy and paste these functions to other programs you may write. Remember that both require the `#include <stdlib>` directive, with `seedrnd()` also requiring `#include <time.h>`.
- To generate a roll of the dice, you stick the `rnd()` function in your program and use this statement:

```
dice=rnd(6)+1;                /* Roll dem bones! */
```

- Using the ever-collapsing C language function ability, you can rewrite the `rnd()` function to only one statement:

```
return(rand()%range);
```

- You're now only moments from writing your own Monopoly game. . . .

Part V
The Part of Tens

The 5th Wave

By Rich Tennant

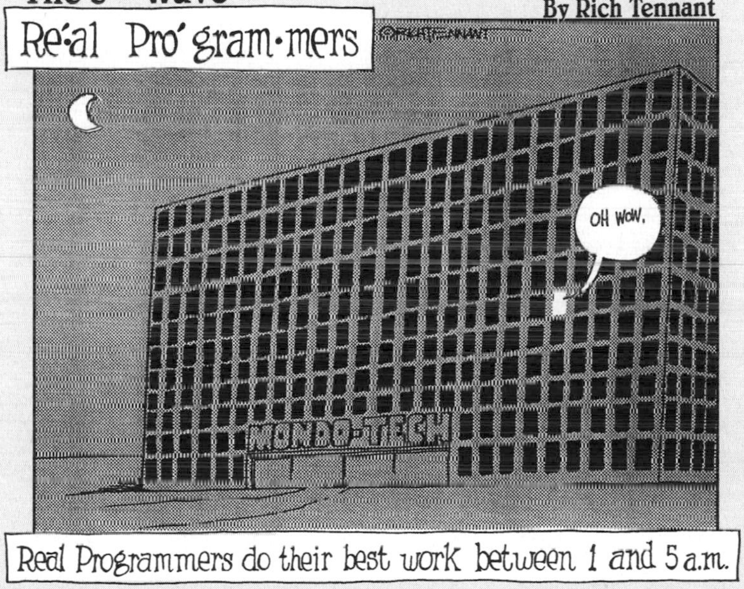

Real Programmers do their best work between 1 and 5 a.m.

In this part . . .

```
for(item=1;item<11;item++)
{
    printf("This part of the book contains\n");
    printf("various lists; ten items to a\n");
    printf("chapter. It's the traditional\n");
    printf("last part of a For Dummies
           book.\n");
    printf("In the chapters that follow,
           you'll\n");
    printf("find numerous lists, each with
           ten\n");
    printf("items that offer tips, tricks,
           and\n");
    printf("bonus information to help
           conclude\n");
    printf("your first voyage into the\n");
    printf("C programming language.\n");
}
```

Chapter 27

Ten More Things You Need to Know about the C Language

In This Chapter

- Using arrays
- Understanding strings
- Dealing with structures
- Growing frustrated over pointers
- Messing with linked lists
- Manipulating bits
- Interacting with the command line
- Doing disk access
- Interacting with the operating system
- Building big programs

Your C language journey is far from over. C has so much more ground to be covered that it just couldn't all possibly fit into this one book, at least not at the same easygoing pace.

To give you a hint of things to come, here are ten more important aspects of the C language — and programming in general — that you may want to consider pursuing. (Note that these topics are all covered in this book's companion volume, *C All-in-One Desk Reference For Dummies,* also published by Wiley.)

Arrays

An *array* is a multivariable. It allows you to store many different integers, floating-point values, characters, strings, or any variable type in a single unit. Suppose that the combination to the Big Safe at Fort Knox is

32, 17, 96

Those three numbers are integers, of course. But the three of them stored together form an array.

- Arrays are declared just like other variables, though the variable name ends with a set of square brackets:

  ```
  int combination[3];
  ```

  In this example, the `combination` array is declared. It can hold three items, which is what the `3` in square brackets specifies.

- Arrays can also be declared and assigned at the same time, as in

  ```
  float temps[] = { 97.0, 98.2,  98.6, 99.1 };
  ```

  This array is named `temps` and contains four floating-point values.

- Each item inside the array can be referred to individually. The items are known as *elements*.

- The first element in an array is numbered *zero*. This is important to remember. So element zero in the `temps[]` array is `97.0`.

- Values are assigned to arrays just as they are to regular variables. For example:

  ```
  combination[0] = 32;
  combination[1] = 17;
  combination[2] = 96;
  ```

  These three statements assign the values 32, 17, and 96 to the three elements in the `combination[]` array. (Note that the first element is zero.)

- WARNING! The only bummer about arrays in the C language is that their size is fixed. After you set, or *dimension,* an array to hold a specific number of elements, that number is fixed and cannot be changed, which will cause you endless frustration in the future. For now, consider yourself forewarned.

Strings

A *string* is nothing more than an array of characters. For example:

```
char myname[] = "Dan";
```

This declaration creates a string variable named `myname`. The contents of that variable are `Dan`, or the letters `D`, `a`, and `n`. You can also write it in a more traditional array style:

```
char myname[] = { 'D', 'a', 'n' };
```

Strings in the C language always and with the null character, ASCII code 0 or character code `\0` (backslash zero). Here's the long way to create the string `myname`:

```
myname[0] = 'D';
myname[1] = 'a';
myname[2] = 'n';
myname[3] = '\0';
```

That final null character tells the compiler where the string ends. Remember that strings can contain characters, such as Enter and Tab. The C language uses character code 0, or null, to mark the end of text.

- A *string* is nothing more than a character array.
- All strings end with the null character.
- This book shows you how to use `scanf()` and `gets()` to read in strings. And, you can use the `%s` placeholder in the `printf()` function to display string values.
- Many, many functions in the C language manipulate strings.
- One C language string function is `strcmp()`, which is used to compare strings. Remember that you cannot use `==` in an `if` statement to compare strings, but you can use the `strcmp()` or similar functions.

Structures

The C language lets you combine variables into a single package called a structure. It's similar to a record in a database in that the structure variable can be used to describe a number of different things all at once. It's roughly the equivalent of a 3-by-5 card.

Structures are declared by using the `struct` keyword. It's followed by the name of the structure and its contents.

```
struct sample
{
     int a;
     char b;
}
```

This structure is named *sample*. It contains two variables: an integer named `a` and a character named `b`. Note that this command merely creates the structure — it doesn't declare any variables. To do that, you need another line.

The following line declares a structure variable named `s1`. The structure it uses is of the type defined as `sample`:

```
struct sample s1;
```

Suppose that you're writing a game and need some way to track the characters inside the game. Consider the following structure:

```
struct character
{
    char name[10];
    long score;
    int strength;
    int x_pos;
    int y_pos;
}
```

This structure is named `character`. It contains variables that describe variable attributes of a character in the game: the character's name, score, strength, and location on the game grid.

To define four characters used in the game, the following declarations are needed:

```
struct character g1;
struct character g2;
struct character g3;
struct character g4;
```

Or:

```
struct character g1, g2, g3, g4;
```

Items within the structure are referred to by using *dot notation*. Here's how the name for character `g1` are displayed:

```
printf("Character 1 is %s\n",g1.name);
```

Suppose that character `g2` is decimated by a sword thrust:

```
g2.strength -= 10;
```

This statement subtracts 10 from the value of `g2.strength`, the `strength` integer in character `g2`'s structure.

- Yes, structures are one way to do database work in the C language.
- Obviously, there is quite a bit to this structure thing — much more than can be included in one section.

Pointers

Over in Chapter 1, I explain how the C programming language is a mid-level language, containing both high-level and low-level programming attributes. Well, welcome to the lowest of the low. Pointers are used in C to directly manipulate the computer's memory — specifically, variables stored inside memory.

At first, this idea seems utterly useless. I mean, why do you need a pointer when you can change a variable's value by using a function or an equal sign? Yet, pointers give the C language a certain muscle power unlike any other programming language.

The problem with pointers is that it takes about four or five times to understand them, and then about six or seven programs showing how they can be used before you *really* get into the good "Oh, I get it now!" moments.

- Pointers are declared by using the asterisk, which is confusing because the asterisk also means multiplication.
- The following line declares an integer pointer, `s`:

  ```
  int *s;
  ```

- The ampersand is also used in Pointer Land, but its implementation is so bizarre that I dare not mention anything further.
- The number-one foul-up when it comes to pointers: not assigning them before they're used. All pointers must be declared, assigned, and then used. I mean, *duh!*

Linked Lists

Want to terrify any university sophomore? Mention *linked lists* and they will blanche with horror. Linked lists are the bane of the C language, almost as horrid as pointers. But they're really nothing devious — just a strange concept because in order to know about linked lists, you must know about pointers. That can be tough.

In the C language, linked lists combine the concept of an array with structures and pointers. In a way, a linked list is really like an array of structures. But, unlike with an array of structures, you can add and remove structures from the linked list easily.

And that's all I really want to say about that!

Binary Operators

Along with the pointer, another low-level aspect of C is the binary operator. Binary operators work to manipulate the bits inside any C language variable except for a `float` or `double`. Table 27-1 lists the lot of them.

Table 27-1 Bitwise Operators

Operator	*Function*
&	AND
^	Exclusive OR (EOR or XOR)
|	Inclusive OR
~	One's complement
<<	Shift bits left
>>	Shift bits right

The only place I have seen these types of operators used are when programs interact with the operating system or PC hardware. For example, if some port on the PC has its low bit set, you can use one or more of these operators to determine whether that's true.

A special feature of the `>>` and `<<` operators is that they perform superfast binary division and multiplication. For example:

```
x = y >> 1;
```

This function divides the value of `y` by 2, which is what happens when you shift the bits in the value of `y` one step to the left. It's much faster than using this statement:

```
x = y/2;
```

To divide `y` by 4, you can use this function:

```
x = y >> 2;
```

Now, you have to *think* in binary to make this work, but it's possible. Likewise, you can double a value by using the `<<` operator. But save that one for another day.

Interacting with the Command Line

In Chapter 22, you may have read briefly about how the `main()` function returns a value to the operating system when the program quits. That's one way that a program can communicate with the operating system. The other way is to read in options directly from the command line. For example:

```
grep pirntf *.c
```

This shell command searches for misspellings in your C language source code. The command has two command-line arguments: `pirntf` and `*.c`. These two strings of text are passed to the `main()` function as arguments as well, which the program can then evaluate and act on, just as arguments passed to any function.

The problem with introducing such a thing in this book is that you need to understand more about arrays and pointers to be able to deal with the information passed to the `main()` function. That too will have to wait for another day.

Disk Access

One of the reasons you have a computer is to store information and work on it later. The C language is equipped with a wide variety of functions to read and write information from and to the disk drives. You can save data to disk using C just as you can with any program that has a File⇨Save command — though in C, it is *you* who writes the File⇨Save command.

Interacting with the Operating System

The C language also lets you perform operating system functions. You can change directories, make new directories, delete files, rename files, and do a host of other handy tasks.

You can also have your programs run other programs — sometimes two at once! Or, your program can run operating system commands and examine the results.

Finally, you can have your program interact with the environment and examine the state of your computer. You can even run services or prowl out on the network. Just about anything the computer can do, you can add into your program and do it yourself.

Building Big Programs

There's nothing wrong with having a 50,000-line source code file. True, it takes longer to compile, and searching for mistakes takes time. But I wouldn't recommend it.

The best approach to writing large programs is to break things up into smaller modules. For example, one module may contain disk routines; another, initialization; and another, routines to display things on the screen. This strategy not only makes debugging things easier, but —here's a secret — if you make the modules well enough, you can also reuse them on other programming projects. That definitely saves time over the long haul.

In C, each source code file is compiled to produce an object code file. The object files are then linked with various libraries to produce the final executable file. It works quite well. In fact, you can share variables across different source code modules, call functions in other modules, and do lots of other cool stuff.

This book lacks the room to show an example, so I put it in the companion volume, *C All-in-One Desk Reference For Dummies* (Wiley). There, you can find an example of such a program, one that I hope will inspire you to go on to bigger and better programming projects in the C language.

Chapter 28

Ten Tips for the Budding Programmer

In This Chapter

- Using the command history
- Keeping your editor open in another window
- Enjoying a color-coded editor
- Knowing your editor's line number commands
- Keeping a command-prompt window open
- Understanding a few commands
- Naming your variables
- Solving incrementing and decrementing riddles
- Breaking out of a loop

Here are some of my top-notch suggestions for programmers just starting out. Man, I wish I had had this list back in the steam-powered computer days, when I first started learning how to program.

Use the Command-Line History

Going back and forth between your editor and compiler at the command prompt gets tedious. Fortunately, most of the command-line shells out there (in both Unix and Windows) have a command-repeat button. Use it!

For example, if you press the up-arrow key, you can recall the preceding command line. Pressing the up-arrow key again recalls the command before that. If you find that you're reediting a lot, use the up-arrow key to recall the command to start your editor, and ditto for the commands to recompile.

Keep Your Editor Open in Another Window

The preceding tip can be null and void if you use your operating system's graphical environment. Keep a command prompt open in one window, and keep your text editor open in another window (see Figure 28-1). As long as you can remember to *save* your source code, it's perfectly fine to open a separate window for your editor and use it to edit your source code file. Then, in the other window, run a command prompt so that you can compile the source code as well as run the result.

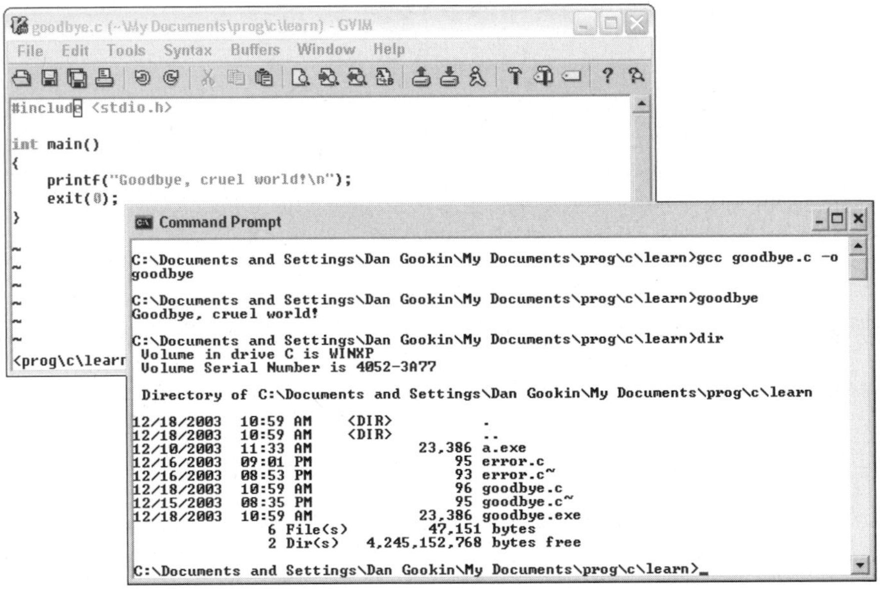

Figure 28-1: Switching between editor and command-prompt windows.

Switch between windows by clicking the mouse in one or the other. Or, use the Alt+Tab key to switch windows, which seems to work in most graphical environments.

REMEMBER

The key is to remember to *save* the document in one window before compiling in another window.

Use a Context-Colored Text Editor

This is why I recommend the Vim editor: As long as you put that `.c` on the end of the source code filename, Vim recognizes your C language code and uses different colors to present it to you on the screen. This feature is so useful that if you ever go back to a monochrome editor, you notice that it slows you down!

- To activate the colors in Vim, type a colon, **:**, and then **syntax enable**, and press Enter.
- When you're running Vim in a Windows window, choose Syntax➪Automatic so that C language keywords are highlighted.
- In Unix, to keep `syntax enable` activated, edit or create a file named `.vimrc` in your home directory. Into that file, add or include the following command:

  ```
  :syntax enable
  ```

  Then save the `.vimrc` file back to disk.
- Another bonus to highlighted text is that you can easily spot missing quotes; text between quotes is color-coded, so if a quote is missing, the source code looks like blech.
- Turn on auto-indenting if your editor has such a feature. Vim turns on auto-indenting when you use the syntax-enable command, or choose Syntax➪Automatic from the menu.

Know the Line-Number Commands in Your Editor

The C language compiler reports errors in your source code and lists the lines on which the errors occur. If your text editor displays line numbers, you can easily locate the specific line containing the error and then fix the error.

- In Windows Notepad, you can display the line and column number on the status bar. To do so, first ensure that Word Wrap is off (choose Format➪Word Wrap if necessary), and then choose View➪Status Bar. (Note that the Status Bar command may not be available in earlier versions of Notepad.)
- Vim displays the cursor's position on the bottom of the window, toward the right side. (The line number is followed by a comma and the column number, shown as `1,1` in Figure A-1 in Appendix A.)
- In Vim, the command to go to a specific line is G. For example, if the compiler reports an error in Line 64, type **64G** and VIM instantly jumps to Line 64. Think "Line number, Goto" to remember this trick.

Keep a Command Prompt Window Open If You're Using the IDE

In Windows, most compilers come with an Integrated Development Environment (IDE). It's a window that contains the editor, plus other gizmos for making Windows programs. It can be quite complex, but also very handy; like Vim, for example, the Dev-C++ IDE color-codes your C commands.

One thing most IDEs don't do is show you the output of the console programs created in this book. Because of that, if you use an IDE, be sure to keep a console window handy, open, and logged to the `prog\c\learn` folder in Windows. That way, you can type the names of the programs you create and see their output in that window. Otherwise, the output isn't visible from the IDE.

Know a Few Handy Command-Prompt Commands

I strongly advise that you become familiar with using a command prompt. While there are hundreds of command prompt commands to type, with a bazillion options and more ways to make typos than typing with welder's gloves on, pay heed to the few commands listed in Table 28-1.

Table 28-1 Command-Prompt Commands

Windows/DOS	*Unix*	*What It Does*
`dir`	`ls`	Lists all files in the current directory or folder. In Unix, the `-l` switch after `ls` is used to display more details about the files in the directory.
`dir *.c`	`ls *.c`	Lists only the C language source-code files in a folder or directory.
`cls`	`clear`	Clears the screen.
`ren`	`mv`	Renames a file; `ren` or `mv` is followed by the file's original name and then the new name, such as `ren goodbye.c bye.c` or `mv goodbye.c bye.c`, which renames the file `goodbye.c` to `bye.c`.

Windows/DOS	Unix	What It Does
cd	pwd	Displays the name of the current directory or folder. Use this command to ensure that you're in the prog/c/learn directory.
type	cat	Displays a text file's contents on the screen; follow type or cat with the name of the file you want displayed: type source.c cat source.c
del	rm	Deletes a file; follow del or rm with the name of the file to delete, as in del bye.c or rm bye.c.
exit	exit	Closes the command-prompt window and closes the terminal.

Refer to a good book or reference about the command prompt for more details on these and other handy commands you can use while you program.

Carefully Name Your Variables

Though I use a lot of single letter variable names in this book, be a better, wiser person when it comes to naming variables in your own programs. For example, x is an okay variable name, but counter is much better.

This may seem like a silly thing for a tiny program, but when your programs get larger, you may find that that a quick x or a variable you declared is being used by some other part of the program. Bad news!

Know Your Post- and Pre-Incrementing and Decrementing Riddles

The ++ and -- operators can certainly come in handy for incrementing or decrementing a variable's value. But keep all your C language statements on a single line, and remember that ++ or -- before the variable name does its job *before* the variable's value is used. If you put the ++ or -- after the variable name, the operation takes place afterward.

Refer to Chapter 25 to find out about this concept.

Breaking Out of a Loop

All your loops need an exit point. Whether that point is defined in the loop's controlling statement or set inside the loop by using a `break` command, be sure that it's there!

I recall many a time sitting at the computer and waiting for the program to "wake up," only to realize that it was stuck in a loop I had programmed with no escape clause. This is especially easy to do when you work on larger programs with "tall" loops; after the source code for the loop extends past the height of your text editor, it's easy to lose track of things.

Chapter 29

Ten Ways to Solve Your Own Programming Problems

In This Chapter

- Work on one thing at a time
- Break up your code
- Simplify your job
- Talk through problems
- Set breakpoints
- Monitor variables
- Document
- Use debugging tools
- Use an optimizer
- Read more books!

Welcome to the world of debugging. In my travels, I've met only *one* programmer who could sit and code a whole project from scratch and have it compile *and* run the first time. As it turns out, he was able to do it only once — and it was a project he was well familiar with. Although he's one of the world's best programmers, the dream of writing, compiling, and running, all in that order, remains a dream for most programmers.

Yes, your programs error. You have typos that the compiler shouts out at you. But your programs also have bugs. That is, they compile and link just fine, but when they run, they do unexpected things. Well, all programs obey their orders. It just happens that the programmer may forget something now and then. It's those times when you need to turn to this chapter and review my ten ways of solving your own programming problems. Do this before you phone, e-mail, or post your problem to the public. The public will thank you!

Work on One Thing at a Time

Address your bugs one at a time. Even if you're aware that the program has several things wrong with it, fix them methodically.

For example: You notice that the title is too far to the right, random characters are at the bottom of the screen, and the scrolling technique doesn't move the top row. Avoid the temptation to address all three issues in the same editing job. Instead, fix one problem. Compile and run to see how that works. Then fix the next problem.

The problem you run into when you try to fix too much at once is that you may introduce *new* errors. Catching those is easier if you remember that you were working on, for example, only Lines 173 and 174 of your source code.

Break Up Your Code

As your source code gets larger, consider breaking off portions into separate modules. I know that this topic isn't covered in this book — and it probably isn't a problem you will encounter soon — but separate modules can really make tracking bugs easy.

Even if you don't use modules, consider using comments to help visually break up your code into separate sections. Even consider announcing the purpose of each section, such as

```
/********************************************
Verification function
---------------------
This function takes the filename passed to it
and confirms that it's a valid filename and
that a file with that name doesn't already
exist.

Returns TRUE/FALSE as defined in the header.
********************************************/
```

I also put a break between functions, just to keep them visually separated:

```
/********************************************/
```

Simplify

Avoid the temptation to gang up several commands on one line until you're certain that that part of your code works well. Do this for many reasons, but most importantly because it makes your code more readable. The more readable your code is, the easier it is for folks (including you) to find an error.

For example, rather than write this line:

```
while(toupper(getch())!=ZED)
```

write this one:

```
while( ch != ZED)
{
     ch = getch();
     ch = toupper(ch);
     /* and so on */
```

Yeah, it may take a few more lines, but if you get an error in one of those lines, you know *exactly* where to look. Before then, you could have had several potential trouble spots.

Also, the second example is more readable to other programmers.

Finally, when you're certain that your code works, you can compact things on one line — if you want to. Remember that the object is to get the program to work, not to try to impress other programmers with your source code.

Talk through the Program

One of the best ways to find bugs almost instantly is to show your code to another programmer. But that other programmer isn't familiar with what you're doing. What you do is start "talking through" the logic of your code. You explain what does what and why you made the choices you did.

Suddenly, as you're explaining what you did, you discover that one spot in your code that doesn't match your intentions. You say, "A-ha!" The other programmer nods in agreement, and you're on with your work.

This technique of talking through your program works whether or not another programmer is present.

Set Breakpoints

You know that the bug is in the `windshield()` function, but you don't know where. Does the bug lurk at the beginning of your code? In the initialization routines? Just before the big math functions? Near the end? Where? Where? Where?

One way to find out is to put breakpoints into your program. At a certain spot, stick in a `return()` or `exit()` function, which immediately stops the program. That way, you can narrow down the pesky code. If the program stops per the breakpoint, the fault lies beyond that point in the program. If the program doesn't stop with the breakpoint, the fault lies before it.

Monitor Your Variables

Sometimes, a program runs amok because the values that you suspected were in your variables just aren't there. To confirm that the variables aren't carrying something outrageous, occasionally toss in a `printf()` statement to display their values to the screen. Never mind if this technique screws up the display; the purpose is debugging.

For example, I had a program with a nasty endless loop in it. I couldn't figure out for the life of me why it repeated and repeated. Talking through the source code did nothing. But after I stuck in a `printf()` statement that displayed the looping variable's value, I noticed that it merrily skipped over the end-of-loop value and kept incrementing itself to infinity and beyond. I added a simple `if` statement to fix the problem, and the program ran just fine afterward.

Document Your Work

At university, they're on you like gum on a theater floor about *comments*. Comment this! Comment that! I remember seeing classmates turn in projects that were three pages of greenbar paper in length, and half of that consisted of the dumb comments at the "top" of the program. Such nonsense impresses no one.

True, document your work. But documentation merely consists of notes to a future version of yourself. It's a reminder to say "This is what I was thinking" or "Here is where my train of thought is going."

You don't have to document every little stupid part of the program. This comment is useless:

```
i++;                    /* add one to the value of i */
```

Here's a better comment:

```
/* Remember that zero is the first item, so increment
variable i here to account for that and not confuse
the user. */

i++;
```

Comments can also tell a future version of yourself where to start working on the program if you come back to it later:

```
/* This is the payoff routine. In the future, it would
be cool to add a sound effect here, say, coins in a
hopper a la a slot machine. */
```

Comments can also be notes on what to fix, to remind you of what went wrong before and to give you tips on how to approach the problem:

```
/* I can't get the dumb address to resolve here. The
routine is supposed to work, but it keeps returning
a null value. Appendix C of the Davis book contains
the original routine. */
```

Use Debugging Tools

If your compiler features a debugger, use it! Debuggers let you surgically view your program as it runs, monitoring variables and examining how the computer literally steps through the code.

The problem with debuggers is that you usually need to compile a special version of the program, after it contains the debugging code. This makes the program huge and sluggish. If you use a debugger, remember to *not* use the debugger code when you compile your final program.

Use a C Optimizer

Many fun tools out there examine your code and make suggestions for optimization. One common tool is `lint`. Other tools exist as well; any C programming Web site lists the variety — and many of them are open source (thank you, open source community).

- Just as a spell checker doesn't make you a better writer, optimizers don't make you a better programmer. But they can help hone your code so that it runs better.
- Other programming tools are available as well. In fact, the whole Unix operating system is designed around programming. If you have time, consider looking into these tools: `touch`, `make`, and `grep`.

Read More Books!

One question I often get from programming acolytes via e-mail is "What book should I read next?" Well, obviously, the companion to this book, *C All-in-One Desk Reference For Dummies,* (Wiley) is an excellent choice. But the real answer is "Where do you want to go with your programming?"

If you want to program games, get books on game programming. You can find books for programming networks, programming the operating system, programming graphics, and on and on. Some, you may have to find in university bookstores, but they exist.

- As far as other programming languages are concerned, after reading through this book, you will know about 95 percent of the C++ programming language. That would be a natural extension to this book. But also consider finding out how to use Perl, Java, Python, or any combination of those languages.
- The PHP Web page creation language is also a good choice if you happen to be into the Web.
- Above all, *program*. Practice. Devise new projects and work on ideas. Programming, to many folks, is like solving an enjoyable puzzle. Immerse yourself in it. Have fun!

Appendix A

The Stuff You Need to Know before You Read All the Other Stuff in This Book

In This Appendix

- Configuring your computer as a programming workstation
- Selecting a compiler
- Choosing an editor
- Creating programs

You need a few things before C programming is possible on your computer. The purpose of this appendix is to outline what you need and how to use it in order to work with the sample programs in this book. It's not that hard, but it may be something you're not used to, so pay attention!

Setting Things Up

You need two things to program in C on your computer:

- A compiler
- A place to put your programs

For Linux, Unix, and the Mac OS X operating system, your C language compiler is already included; it comes with the operating system. For Windows and older Mac systems, you must obtain a compiler. That's not as difficult as it sounds.

The C language compiler

Thanks to the C language's popularity, many compilers are available for you to use with this book. I do, however, recommend the following:

Windows: If you're using Windows, I recommend that you get a GCC-compatible C compiler. A list of compilers is provided on this book's Web page, at `www.c-for-dummies.com`.

For this book, I used the MinGW compiler, which comes with the Dev-C++ IDE (Integrated Development Environment). It's free and available from `www.bloodshed.net`.

Whichever compiler you use, note its location on your PC's hard drive. You have to use this location to create a batch file or modify your system's path so that you can access the compiler from any folder in your disk system. More on that later.

- Other compilers are out there, including the best-selling Microsoft Visual C++ (MSVC). If you have MSVC, fine; you should be okay with running the programs in this book. Note, however, that I'm not familiar with the current version of MSVC and don't refer to it in this book, nor can I answer questions about it via e-mail. If you don't have MSVC, you have no reason to buy it.
- Plenty of free, shareware, and open-source C compilers are available on the Internet.
- If you have other books on the C language, check in the back of the book for a free compiler.
- Any GCC- or GNU-compatible C compiler works best with this book.

Linux, FreeBSD, or Mac OS X: If you're using any of these variations of Unix, you should already have the GCC compiler installed and ready to use. To confirm, open a terminal window and type the following line at the command prompt:

```
gcc -v
```

The version number of GCC and other information is displayed on the screen. If you get a `Command not found` error, GCC isn't installed; you have to update your operating system to include GCC as well as all the C programming libraries and other materials. (You can generally do that through your operating system's setup or configuration program; it doesn't typically require that the entire operating system be reinstalled.)

Unix: If you have a "real" version of Unix, the command is `cc` and not `gcc`. In fact, you may notice that `cc` even works on other Unix-like operating systems, where the `cc` command is often linked to the GCC compiler, for compatibility's sake.

Mac (before OS X): Older versions of the Mac lack a built-in C language compiler. I recommend the Code Warrior compiler, though you should also check the Apple Web site to see whether any other (free) compilers are available: `http://developer.apple.com/`.

The place to put your stuff

When you learn to program, you create scads of files. These files include the original-text source code files, the final program files, and perhaps even object code files, depending on the compiler. Obviously, you want to keep those files organized and separate from your regular junk.

For this book, I recommend creating a `prog` folder or directory. Create this folder off your main folder — the `$HOME` folder in Unix or the My Documents folder in Windows. The `prog` folder is designed to hold all your programming projects.

Beneath `prog`, you should put the `c` folder, for all your C language programming projects.

Finally, create a `learn` folder, in which you put all the projects for this book. The rest of this appendix provides specific examples.

Windows. To create a folder for your C language projects, follow these steps:

1. **Open the My Documents icon on the desktop.**
2. **Choose File⇨New⇨Folder to create a new folder and then name the folder `prog`.**
3. **Open the `prog` folder.**
4. **Choose File⇨New⇨Folder to create a new folder, and then name it `c`.**
5. **Open the `c` folder.**
6. **Create a folder inside the `c` folder, and name that folder `learn`.**
7. **Close the `c` folder window.**

The `learn` folder is where you place all the files created in this book.

Linux, FreeBSD, Mac OS X, or Unix: To create a folder for your C programming projects, obey these steps:

1. **If you're using a graphical shell, open a terminal window. You need to get at the command prompt.**

   The terminal window should open into your account's home directory. If you aren't in your home directory, type the **cd** command to return there.

   Ensure that you're not logged in as the root account; creating programs as the root user is a security risk.

2. **Create the prog/c/learn directory branch:**

   ```
   mkdir -p prog/c/learn
   ```

   The `-p` switch directs `mkdir` to create all the subdirectories that are specified; it's the same as issuing three separate `mkdir` commands at once. With one command, you have created the `prog` directory, the `c` subdirectory, and, finally, the `learn` subdirectory. Ta-da.

You use the `learn` folder for storing all the source code and program files created in this book.

Mac (before OS X). Alas, the old Mac operating system lacked a "home folder" for all your stuff. If you have such a folder, use it as a base to create the subfolders in the following steps. Otherwise, you can create these folders right on the desktop for handy access:

1. **Press +N to create a new folder.**
2. **Name that folder** `prog`**, for "programming."**
3. **Open the** `prog` **folder.**
4. **Press +N to create a subfolder inside the** `prog` **folder.**
5. **Name that folder** `c`**.**
6. **Open the** `c` **folder.**
7. **Press +N to create a subfolder inside the** `c` **folder.**
8. **Name that subfolder** `learn`**.**
9. **Close all the open windows you just created.**

When using your compiler, remember to save all your files in the `learn` folder.

Making Programs

To build programs, you need two tools: an editor and a compiler. You use the editor to create or edit the source code — which is merely a text file. Then, you use the compiler to magically transform that text into the language the computer understands, stuffing it all into a program file.

This book illustrates programming techniques by using small programs targeted to showcase specific examples of the C language. Because of that, you can use the command prompt for compiling programs more easily than the IDE that may have come with your compiler. I recommend that you become familiar with the command prompt.

The following steps don't apply to programming on the Macintosh before OS X. If you're using an older Mac, refer to your compiler's documentation to find out how to edit and compile programs. Remember to use the `learn` folder you created to save all your stuff.

Finding your `learn` directory or folder

The first step to programming is to navigate your way to the `learn` directory (or folder) by using the command prompt. Follow these steps:

1. **Start a terminal or command-prompt window.**

   In Windows, run the CMD.EXE program, also known as the MS-DOS prompt.

   This program is on the Accessories or, often, main Programs menu, off the Start button. Or, you can type **CMD** in the Run dialog box to start the command-prompt window.

   In Linux, OS X, FreeBSD, and other Unix-like operating systems, open a terminal window if you're using a graphical shell. Otherwise, any terminal works.

2. **Change to your home directory.**

   In Windows XP, type this command:

   ```
   cd "my documents"
   ```

   In other versions of Windows, type this command:

   ```
   cd "\My Documents"
   ```

The command prompt should now reflect that you're using the My Documents folder, similar to:

```
C:\Documents and Settings\Dan\My Documents>
```

or:

```
C:\My Documents>
```

(The last part of the prompt reads "My Documents.")

In Linux, FreeBSD, or Mac OS X, type the **cd** command to change to your home directory. That single command does the job.

3. **Change to the `learn` directory.**

   Everyone, type:

```
cd prog/c/learn
```

   except for older versions of Windows, where it's

```
cd prog\c\learn
```

   (Note the backslashes, not forward slashes.)

4. **Confirm that you're in the proper directory.**

   You do this in Windows by typing the **cd** command; in Unix, type **pwd**. The current directory is displayed, which should look like one of these:

```
C:\Documents and Settings\name\My Documents\prog\c\learn
C:\My Documents\prog\c\learn
/home/user/prog/c/learn
/Users/user/prog/c/learn
```

   Note that the common part is the last part, `prog/c/learn`. If you see that (or `prog\c\learn`), you're ready to start work.

The `learn` directory is where you're working while you use this book. That's where you edit, create, compile, and manage files.

Running an editor

To concoct your C language source code, you need to use a text editor. In Windows, you can use the `EDIT` command to summon the MS-DOS Editor. It's rather simple to understand and use, it works with the mouse, and it's free and available.

For the various Unix operating systems, you have multiple editor choices. The simplest text editor is Easy Editor, activated with the `ee` command. Otherwise, you can use any of the Unix editors — and quite a few of them are available.

My favorite editor for working with C is vim, a variant on the infamous vi editor in Unix (see Figure A-1). Unlike vi, vim uses colors to code text. When you edit your source code in vim, you see keywords, values, and other parts of the C language highlighted in color.

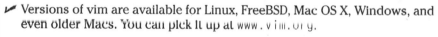

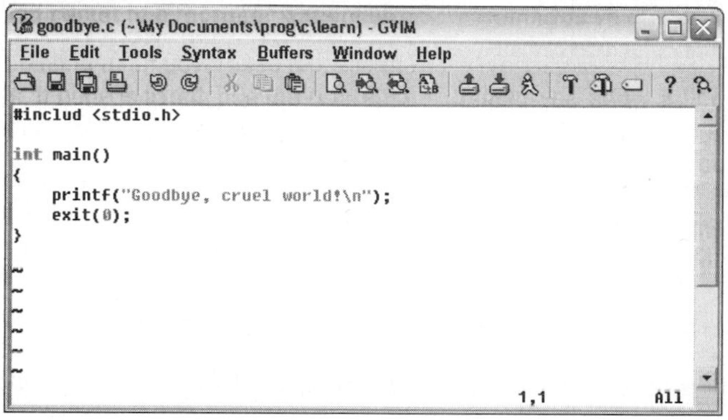

Figure A-1: The vim editor.

- Versions of vim are available for Linux, FreeBSD, Mac OS X, Windows, and even older Macs. You can pick it up at `www.vim.org`.
- Windows XP may not like the `EDIT` command. As an alternative, you can use Notepad to edit your source code. For example, to edit the `GOODBYE.C` text file, you type this command at the prompt:

```
NOTEPAD GOODBYE.C
```

  Notepad opens in another window, where you can edit the text file. Simply close the window when you're done.

Compiling and linking

After the source-code text file is created, your next step is to compile and link. This step transforms the meek and mild text file into a robust and useable program on your computer.

Read the proper subsection for compiling and linking specifics for your operating system. For Macs before OS X, see the reference material that came with your compiler.

Making GCC work in Windows

Heck, for all the advances made with Windows, you may as well be using DOS when it comes to compiling programs at the command prompt. Anyway. . . .

Windows compilers aren't designed to be friendly for command-line compiling. Because of that, it's up to you to make the compiler work at every command prompt and in every folder in your computer system. One way to make that happen is to create a batch file that runs the GCC (or whatever) command that runs the compiler. It isn't the easiest thing to do, but, fortunately, it needs to be done only once.

These steps assume that you have installed the Dev-C++ environment on your PC. Furthermore, they assume that you have installed Dev-C++ into the `C:\Dev-C++` folder.

(If you installed Dev-C++ in another folder, you need to make a note of that folder's path. For example, if you installed it in the `Program Files` folder, the path is `C:\Program Files\Dev-C++`. You *must* remember the path!)

Take a deep breath.

1. **Start a command prompt or MS-DOS window.**

   TIP: You know what? Making a shortcut to the MS-DOS window and putting it on the desktop may be a good idea — especially for the duration of time that you use this book. See your favorite book on Windows for detailed instructions.

2. **Change to the `Windows` folder:**

   ```
   cd \windows
   ```

   (I'm assuming that `Windows` is the name of your Windows folder. If not — it's `WINNT` or something — substitute the folder's name for `windows` in the `cd \windows` command.)

   Inside the `Windows` folder, you create a batch file program — a shortcut to the GCC command used by Dev-C++. You can then use the GCC command at any command prompt in Windows.

3. **Carefully type** copy con gcc.bat **and press the Enter key.**

4. **Carefully type this line:**

   ```
   @c:\Dev-C++\bin\gcc %1 %2 %3 %4 %5 %6
   ```

   The line starts with an at sign, @. That's followed by the full pathname to Dev-C++'s GCC compiler, either `c:\Dev-C++\bin\gcc`. (If you have installed GCC into another folder, put its path there instead; remember to enclose the path in double quotes if it contains spaces!)

   After `gcc` comes a space, and then `%1`, a space, `%2`, space, and so on. This is important!

If you make a mistake, use the Backspace key to back up and correct.

If all this seems strange to you, get someone else who better understands Windows (or DOS) to help you.

5. **Review the line.**

   Double-check everything. Only when it looks like the example in this book do you do the next step.

6. **Press the Enter key.**

7. **Press the F6 key.**

   A `^Z` appears on the screen.

8. **Press the Enter key.**

   You see `1 file(s) copied` and the `GCC.BAT` file has been created.

Now you need to test the GCC.BAT file, to ensure that it's working. Follow the steps listed earlier in this appendix so that you're in the `learn` folder. (It may be easier to close the current Command Prompt window and open a new one). When you're in the `learn` folder, type this command at the prompt:

```
gcc -v
```

If you see a whole lotta blech appear on the screen, congratulations! You got it to work!

If it doesn't work, review the preceding steps. You probably didn't copy the text properly in Step 4, or you could have created the file in the wrong folder. Repeat the steps, and press Y after Step 3 to overwrite the current GCC.BAT file with a new one.

Windows: Compiling, linking, and running

After setting up the GCC.BAT file, you're ready to start creating programs. Eventually, you repeat the following steps often enough that you no longer need to refer to this appendix for help.

1. **Ensure that you're in the proper folder.**

   Refer to the section "Finding your `learn` directory or folder," earlier in this appendix.

2. **Use your text editor to create your source code file.**

   Refer to Chapter 1 for the listing of the GOODBYE.C program. Type that text into your editor per the instructions in Chapter 1.

3. **Compile and link the source code.**

You do this step with the GCC command — both steps at once. Here's the command to type:

```
gcc goodbye.c -o goodbye
```

You type these four things:

- `gcc`, the command to compile and link the source code
- `goodbye.c`, the name of the source code file
- `-o`, the output switch
- `goodbye`, the name of the final program

If you leave off the `-o` switch and its option, GCC creates the program file named A.EXE in Windows. I don't recommend it. Instead, remember the `-o` option and specify a name for the output program. The name can be the same as the source code file. (C language source code files end in `.C` and program files end in `.EXE`.)

4. **Run the program.**

   Type the program file's name at the prompt. For this example, type **goodbye** and press Enter. This step executes that program's code and displays something on the screen or does something interesting, depending on what the program is supposed to do.

Those are the basic steps you take (all in the `learn` folder) to create the program examples in this book. As I have said, eventually it become second nature to you.

- If you get an error message, such as the compiler cannot find its files or some installation problem has occurred, please refer to the compiler's documentation or Web site for help. I cannot help you with problems related to the compiler or its installation.
- For each program you create, there are two files: the source code file (a text file) and the program file. That's generally how things go in this book.

- Some C language compilers are 2-stage, requiring compiling first and then linking as a separate step. The extra stage involves the creation of a third file on disk — the `OBJ`, or object file. GCC combines compiling and linking and deletes the object file after linking successfully.
- I recommend keeping the programs around for future reference; don't delete them until you have been programming a while and really no longer need them.

Linux, FreeBSD, and Mac OS X: Compiling, linking and running

The main thrust of programming the individual examples in this book involves the following three steps. You eventually repeat these steps often enough that you don't have to return to see what's next:

1. **Ensure that you're in the `learn` folder.**

   Heed the steps in the section "Finding your `learn` directory or folder," earlier in this appendix.

2. **Use your text editor to create your source code file.**

   Use vi, ee, or whatever your favorite text editor is to create and save the source code file. For an example, you can refer to the listing of the GOODBYE.C source in Chapter 1; type that text into your editor.

3. **Compile and link the source code.**

   Compiling and linking are both handled by the GCC command. As an example, here's what you need to type to compile and link the GOODBYE.C source code created in Step 1:

   ```
   gcc goodbye.c -o goodbye
   ```

   The code has four items:

   - `gcc`, the command to compile and link the source code
   - `goodbye.c`, the name of the source code file
   - `-o`, the output switch
   - `goodbye`, the name of the final program

   If you leave off the `-o` switch and its option, GCC creates the program file named `a.out`. I don't recommend this. Instead, remember the `-o` option and specify a name for the output program. The name can be the same as the source code file, but without the `.c` extension.

4. **Run the program.**

   Alas, your operating system doesn't run your program if you type its name at the prompt. That's because Unix runs only programs found on the path, and I don't recommend putting your `learn` directory on the path. (If you create your own programs that you want to run, copy them to a `bin` directory beneath your home directory, and put *that* directory on the path.)

   To get the operating system to notice your program, you have to be specific about where the program lives (in the current folder, for example). You do that by prefixing `./` to the program's name. To run the `goodbye` program, type the following at the prompt:

   ```
   ./goodbye
   ```

   And the program runs.

Those steps are the basic ones you take (all in the `learn` folder) to create the program examples in this book. As I have said, it eventually becomes second nature to you.

TIP

- Filename extensions are optional in Unix, but I do recommend that you use `.c` to suffix all your C language source code files. That helps you keep them straight. As a bonus, the vim editor, GCC, and other programs recognize the `.c` and treat the file accordingly.
- For each program you create, there are two files on disk: the source code file (a text file) and the program file. That's generally how things go in this book.
- The GCC compiler automatically sets the permission bits on the resulting program file, allowing it to be run. Usually, it's `-rwxr-xr-x`, or the equivalent of a `chmod 755` command.
- I recommend keeping the programs around for future reference; don't delete them until you have been programming a while and really no longer need them.

Appendix B
ASCII Table

Code	*Character*	*Hex*	*Binary*	*Notes*
0	^@	00	0000 0000	Null character, \0
1	^A	01	0000 0001	
2	^B	02	0000 0010	
3	^C	03	0000 0011	
4	^D	04	0000 0100	Exit key (Unix)
5	^E	05	0000 0101	
6	^F	06	0000 0110	
7	^G	07	0000 0111	Bell, \a
8	^H	08	0000 1000	Backspace, \b
9	^I	09	0000 1001	Tab, \t
10	^J	0A	0000 1010	Vertical tab, \v
11	^K	0B	0000 1011	
12	^L	0C	0000 1100	Form feed, \f
13	^M	0D	0000 1101	Enter key, \n (or \r)
14	^N	0E	0000 1110	
15	^O	0F	0000 1111	
16	^P	10	0001 0000	
17	^Q	11	0001 0001	
18	^R	12	0001 0010	
19	^S	13	0001 0011	

(continued)

Code	Character	Hex	Binary	Notes
20	^T	14	0001 0100	
21	^U	15	0001 0101	
22	^V	16	0001 0110	
23	^W	17	0001 0111	
24	^X	18	0001 1000	
25	^Y	19	0001 1001	
26	^Z	1A	0001 1010	End of file (DOS)
27	^[	1B	0001 1011	Escape
28	^\	1C	0001 1100	
29	^]	1D	0001 1101	
30	^^	1E	0001 1110	
31	^_	1F	0001 1111	
32		20	0010 0000	Space
33	!	21	0010 0001	
34	"	22	0010 0010	
35	#	23	0010 0011	
36	$	24	0010 0100	
37	%	25	0010 0101	
38	&	26	0010 0110	
39	'	27	0010 0111	
40	(	28	0010 1000	
41	)	29	0010 1001	
42	*	2A	0010 1010	
43	+	2B	0010 1011	
44	,	2C	0010 1100	
45	-	2D	0010 1101	
46	.	2E	0010 1110	

Code	*Character*	*Hex*	*Binary*	*Notes*
47	/	2F	0010 1111	
48	0	30	0011 0000	(Numbers)
49	1	31	0011 0001	
50	2	32	0011 0010	
51	3	33	0011 0011	
52	4	34	0011 0100	
53	5	35	0011 0101	
54	6	36	0011 0110	
55	7	37	0011 0111	
56	8	38	0011 1000	
57	9	39	0011 1001	
58	:	3A	0011 1010	
59	;	3B	0011 1011	
60	<	3C	0011 1100	
61	=	3D	0011 1101	
62	>	3E	0011 1110	
63	?	3F	0011 1111	
64	@	40	0100 0000	
65	A	41	0100 0001	(Uppercase alphabet)
66	B	42	0100 0010	
67	C	43	0100 0011	
68	D	44	0100 0100	
69	E	45	0100 0101	
70	F	46	0100 0110	
71	G	47	0100 0111	
72	H	48	0100 1000	
73	I	49	0100 1001	

(continued)

Code	Character	Hex	Binary	Notes
74	J	4A	0100 1010	
75	K	4B	0100 1011	
76	L	4C	0100 1100	
77	M	4D	0100 1101	
78	N	4E	0100 1110	
79	O	4F	0100 1111	
80	P	50	0101 0000	
81	Q	51	0101 0001	
82	R	52	0101 0010	
83	S	53	0101 0011	
84	T	54	0101 0100	
85	U	55	0101 0101	
86	V	56	0101 0110	
87	W	57	0101 0111	
88	X	58	0101 1000	
89	Y	59	0101 1001	
90	Z	5A	0101 1010	
91	[	5B	0101 1011	
92	\	5C	0101 1100	
93	]	5D	0101 1101	
94	^	5E	0101 1110	
95	_	5F	0101 1111	
96	`	60	0110 0000	
97	a	61	0110 0001	(Lowercase alphabet)
98	b	62	0110 0010	
99	c	63	0110 0011	
100	d	64	0110 0100	

Code	Character	Hex	Binary	Notes
101	e	65	0110 0101	
102	f	66	0110 0110	
103	g	67	0110 0111	
104	h	68	0110 1000	
105	i	69	0110 1001	
106	j	6A	0110 1010	
107	k	6B	0110 1011	
108	l	6C	0110 1100	
109	m	6D	0110 1101	
110	n	6E	0110 1110	
111	o	6F	0110 1111	
112	p	70	0111 0000	
113	q	71	0111 0001	
114	r	72	0111 0010	
115	s	73	0111 0011	
116	t	74	0111 0100	
117	u	75	0111 0101	
118	v	76	0111 0110	
119	w	77	0111 0111	
120	x	78	0111 1000	
121	y	79	0111 1001	
122	z	7A	0111 1010	
123	{	7B	0111 1011	
124	|	7C	0111 1100	
125	}	7D	0111 1101	
126	~	7E	0111 1110	
127		7F	0111 1111	Delete (or "rubout")

Index

• Numbers & Symbols •

0*nn*, printf() escape sequence, 307
100.C, 192–193
& (ampersand), do-while loops, 227
& (AND) bitwise operator, 344
&& logical operator, 180
<> (angle brackets), 13
* (asterisk)
  comments and, 56
  as multiplication sign, 88, 134, 313
\ (backslash)
  \' (apostrophe), printf() escape sequence, 307
  \" (double-quote), printf() escape sequence, 307
  \0 (null), printf() escape sequence, 307
  \? (question mark), printf() escape sequence, 307
  escape sequences, 45
  printf() escape sequence, 307
  RULES.C, 37–38
  text strings, 31
[] (brackets), single-character variables, 123
^ (caret) symbol, 316
^ (EOR/XOR) bitwise operator, 344
% conversion character, printf() function, 305
{} (curly braces)
  comparisons and, 153
  else keyword, 159
  functions and, 31
  introduction, 13
= (equal sign)
  location, 314
  numeric variables and, 80
== (equal to) comparison operator, if statement, 151, 160
- (hyphen)
  one's complement, bitwise operator, 344
  subtraction symbol, 87, 134, 313
-- (decrementation) operator, 207–208, 322
> (greater than) comparison operator, if statement, 152, 160
>= (greater than or equal to) comparison operator, if statement, 152, 160
| (inclusive OR) bitwise operator, 344
|| logical operator, 178, 180
< (less than) comparison operator, if statement, 151, 160
<= (less than or equal to) comparison operator, if statement, 152, 160
% (modulus)
  introduction, 333
  math operator, 314
!= (not equal) comparison operator, if statement, 152, 160
+ (plus symbol)
  mathematical operator, 134
  symbol, 87, 313
++ (incrementation) operator
  introduction, 202–203
  LARDO.C, 203–204
  location, 322–323
  variables, 320–321
#define directive, 104–105, 302–303
#else, 303
#endif, 303
#if, 303
#ifdef, 303
#ifndef, 303
#include
  construction, 294–297
  description, 30
<< (shift bits left) bitwise operator, 344
>> (shift bits right) bitwise operator, 344
/ (slash)
  with asterisk (/*), 56
  division symbol, 87, 134, 313
  double (//), 60, 63
// (double slash)
  C++ comments, 60
  nested comments and, 63

• A •

\a, printf() escape sequence, 306
abs() function, 319
absolute value of numbers, 320
acos() function, 319
addition symbol (+), 87

alphabet trivia, 172
ampersand (&)
  do-while loops, 227
  pointers, 343
AND (&) bitwise operator, 344
AND logical operator
  code example, 183
  introduction, 180
angle brackets (< >), 13
arguments, 277, 282
arrays, 339–340, 341
ASCII characters
  character variables, 129
  extended codes, 129
  table, 371–375
  typing in, 122
ASCII.C, 193–194
asin() function, 319
ASSESSED.C, 140–141
assigning pointers, 343
assignment operators, 212
asterisk (*), comments and, 56
atan() function, 319
atoi() function
  HEIGHT.C, 136
  introduction, 81–82
  returning values, 283

• B •

\b, printf() escape sequence, 306
B programming language, 10
backslash (\)
  escape sequences, 45
  printf(), 305
  RULES.C, 37–38
  text strings, 31
backward counting loops, 205
BASIC programming language, 10
BCPL (Basic Combined Programming Language), 10
BIGJERK1.C, 255–256
BIGJERK2.C, 256–260
BIGJERK3.C, 261–262
BIGJERK4.C, 277–278
binary numbers, integers and, 112
binary operators, 344
bitwise operators, 182, 344
blank lines in code, 14
BLOWUP1.C
  if command, 173–174
  logic, 176
BOMBER.C
  dual variables, 267
  global variable, 271–272
  variables, 265–267
bonus() function, 288–289
BONUS.C, 288–289
books for further reading, 358
BORC.C, 236
bounds checking, do-while loops, 229–230
brackets ([ ]), single-character variables, 123
break command, 244, 352
break keyword, 198–199
  for(;;) loops, 237
  case statements, 243
  do-while loops, 228
  nested loops, 235–237
break statements, while loops, 221
breaking loops, 197–198
breakpoints, 356
bugs, 27
bulletproofing, 229
bytes, 128

• C •

%c conversion character, printf() function, 311
calling functions, 254, 279–280
caret (^) symbol, 316
case keyword, 244, 247
case sensitivity
  else keyword, 159
  function naming, 264
  include directives, 296
  keywords, 33
  printf(), 42
  source code, 13
case statement, 243, 244, 247
cat command, 351
cd command, 351
char keyword
  introduction, 50
  numeric data types, 108
  single-character variables, 122–123
  string variable declaration, 57
  unsigned char keyword, 109
  variable declaration, 40, 123–124
character data types, 108
character variables
  char keyword, 121
  characters in, 124

as integer, 111
quotes, 123
value assignment, 124
as values, 128–129
characters
comparing, 166
conversion, 46
clear command, 350
cls command, 350
code. *See* source code
code blocks, 151
code size, 346
COLOR.C, 51–52
command line, 345, 347
command prompt
commands, 350–351
IDE and, 350
commands
cat, 351
cd, 351
clear, 351
cls, 351
command prompt, 350–351
del, 351
dir, 351
exit, 351
if, 147–148
line numbers, text editor, 349
ls, 351
mv, 351
pwd, 351
ren, 351
return, 31
rm, 351
switch, 243
type, 351
comments
/* (slash with asterisk), 56
C++, 60
compiler and, 55
disabling statements, 61
introduction, 55
MADLIB1.C, 56–57
nested, 62–63
reasons for, 58
single-line, 59
styles, 58–60
tips, 356–357
variables, 95
comparisons
{} (curly braces) and, 153
characters, 166
else keyword and, 159
GREATER.C, 167–168
if keyword, 150–151
operators, 151–152
strings, if keyword and, 174
compiler
comments and, 55
errors, 27
FreeBSD, 360
GCC compiler, 15, 360, 365–367
GOODBYE.C, 15–16
header files and, 296
introduction, 14–15
Linux, 360
Mac, 361
Mac OS X, 360
MiniGW compiler, 360
MSVC (Microsoft Visual C++), 360
setup, 359
Unix, 361
Windows, 360
compiling
FreeBSD, 368–370
linking and, 17
Linux, 368–370
Mac OS X, 368–370
recompiling, 21–22
variable declaration and, 95
WHORU.C, 40–41
conditions
do-while loops, 227
infinite loops, 196
const keyword, 106
constants
defining, 101–102
definition, 91
numeric, 101
numeric, shortcut, 102–104
semicolons, 269
string constants, 53, 101
symbolic, 103
variables and, 101
contents of variables, 76
context-colored text editors, 348–349
continue keyword
loops, 237–238
nested loops, 235–236
conversion characters
formatting strings, 46
printf() function, 311–312
converting, string numbers to integer value, 81–82

cos() function, 319
COUNTDOWN.C
  do-while loops, 226–227
  error, 228–229
critical errors, 25
curly braces ({ })
  case keyword statements, 244
  comparisons and, 153
  else keyword, 159
  functions and, 31
  introduction, 13

• D •

%d conversion character, printf() function, 311
data types, numeric, 108
DBLQUOTE.C, 43
dead_horse variable, 223
debugging
  order, 354
  tools, 357
declaring arrays, 340
declaring functions, 263
declaring pointers, 343
declaring variables
  float, 113
  global, 270–271
  integer variables, 110–111
  introduction, 40
  location in program, 95
  multiple, 100–101
  reasons for, 94–95
  values as, 276
DECODD.C, 322
decrementation. *See also* incrementation
  -- operator, 207–208, 322
  assignment operators, 212
  for loops, 206–207
  introduction, 204–205
  operator shortcuts, 212
  skipping values, 210
default statements, switch structure, 244
defining functions, 263
del command, 351
delay() function, prototyping, 269
delay loops, 233
development cycle, 11
dir command, 350
disabling statements, comments and, 61
disk access, 345
displaying text, printf() and, 306
division symbol (/), 87
do keyword, 227
dot notation, structures, 342
do_this statement, for loop, 189
double keyword, numeric data types, 109
double quotes. *See also* quotes
  DBLQUOTE.C, 42–43
  formatting strings, 46
  strings, 42–43
double slash (//), 60
double variables
  double precision numbers, 118
  pow() function, 316
double-precision data types, 109, 118
do-while loops
  & (ampersand), 227
  bounds checking, 229–230
  break keyword, 228
  conditions, 227
  execution, 227
  input bounds, 229–230
  introduction, 186
  number checking, 229–231
  semicolons, 227
  statements, 227
dropBomb() function, 265–266
dual variables, BOMBER.C, 267

• E •

%e conversion character, printf() function, 311
E notation, 116–117
editing, source code, 19–21, 24–25
elements in arrays, 340
else keyword
  {} (curly braces), 159
  case sensitivity, 159
  if statements and, 158
  semicolon, 159
else statement, 157–158
else-if statement, 160–163
empty parentheses, 31
endless loops, 186
EOF (end of file), 170
EOR (&) bitwise operator, 344
equal sign (=)
  location, 314
  numeric variables and, 80
equal to (==) comparison operator, if statement, 151
error messages
  components of, 23
  GCC compiler, 24

line numbers, 24
linker and, 26
semicolons, 24
ERROR.C, 22–27
errors
bugs, 27
compiler errors, 27
critical errors, 25
fatal errors, 25
linker and, 26
linker errors, 27
null pointer assignment, 27
parse errors, 23
source code, 22–27
syntax errors, 23
escape clause, loops, 197
escape sequences, printf(), 44–45, 306–308
execute
definition, 160
do-while loops, 227
exit command, 351
exp() function, 319
exponents, math operations, 314–315
extended ASCII codes, 129

• F •

%f conversion character, printf() function, 311
\f, printf() escape sequence, 306
fatal errors, 25
fflush() function, 170–171
file size, 346
filenames, extensions, 13
files
folders, 361–362
header files, # include and, 294–297
source code, 12
text, size, 262
flexibility of C, 222–223
float keyword
format, 113
numeric data types, 109
float variable, declaring, 113
floating-point values
double keyword, 118
formatting, 119–120
JUPITER.C, 114–115
negative, 112
numeric data types and, 108
positive, 112
ranges, 114
variables, 99
folders, 361–364
for keyword
description, 188
parentheses, 189, 190
for loops
decrementing, 206–207
do_this statement, 189
introduction, 186
nested, 233
printf() statement, 188
variables, 191
while loop comparison, 219–220
while_true keyword, 189
for (; ;) loops
break keyword, 237
while loops and, 220–222
format strings, printf() function, 310
formats
char variable, 122
E notation, 117
floating-point values, 119–120
functions, 262–263, 289–291
if statement, 154–155
printf() and, 46, 310–311
scanf(), 49
strings, 46
text, 47–49
fpurge() function, 171
FreeBSD
compiler, 360
folders, 362
functions
{} (curly braces) and, 31
abs(), 319
acos(), 319
arguments, 46, 282
asin(), 319
atan(), 319
atio(), 81–82, 136
bonus(), 288–289
calling, 254
calling, variable names and, 279–280
case sensitivity, 264
conversion characters, 46
cos(), 319
creating, 254
declaring, 263
defining, 263
defining, returning values and, 282
delay(), 269
dropBomb(), 265–266
exp(), 319
fflush(), 170–171
formats, 262–263, 289–291

functions *(continued)*
  formatting strings, 46
  fpurge(), 171
  getchar(), 126
  gets(), 65–67
  getval(), 284
  header files and, 296
  input requirements, 275
  introduction, 30
  jerk(), 256–258
  library, 255
  log(), 319
  log10(), 319
  main(), 30
  math, 319–320
  mathematical operators, 134
  naming, 263–264
  necessity, 253
  output, 275–276
  parameters, 279
  parentheses, 254, 262
  pow(), 315
  printf(), 305–312
  procedures and, 253
  prototyping, 258–262
  putchar(), 127–128
  puts(), 67–71
  rand(), 326–328
  redundancy and, 256
  return keyword, 285–287
  scanf(), 40
  seedrnd(), 329–331
  sending values to, 276–277
  sin(), 319
  sleep(), 234
  sqrt(), 317–319
  srand(), 329
  strings and, 42
  tan(), 319
  time(), 332
  types, 275–276
  values, declaring as variables, 276
  values, passing, 279
  values, passing multiple, 280–282
  values, returning, 255, 282–289
  variable naming and, 96
further reading, 358

• G •

%g conversion character, printf() function, 311
gcc command, math library links, 317
GCC compiler
  error messages, 24
  introduction, 15
  Windows, 365–367
GENIE1.C, 148–150
GENIE2.C, 162–163
GENIE3.C, 163–164
getchar() function
  reading text from keyboard, 126
  returning values, 283
  returns, 168
  single character reading, 171
  standard input and, 168
gets() function
  INSULT1.C, 66
  introduction, 65–66
getval() function, 284
global variables
  declaring, 270–271
  description, 269
GOODBYE.C
  compiling, 15–16
  creating, 13–14
  recompiling, 21–22
  running program, 16
  typing tips, 14
goto keyword, loops, 186
greater than (>) comparison operator, if statement, 152
greater than or equal to (>=) comparison operator, if statement, 152
GREATER.C
  comparisons, 167–168
  standard input reading, 170
GRID.C, 234–235

• H •

.H file extension, 296
header files
  compiler and, 296
  functions and, 296
  #include construction and, 294–297
  library files and, 300
  programming code, 300
  STDIO.H, 297–298
  writing, 298–299
HEAD.H, 298–299
HEIGHT.C, 135–136
HEY.C, 216–217
high-level languages, 10
history, command line, 347
history of C, 9–11

• I •

%i conversion character, printf() function, 311
ICKYGU.C, 98–99
IDE (Integrated Development Environment), command prompt window, 350
if command. *See* if keyword
if keyword
  BLOWUP1.C, 173–174
  comparisons and, 148, 150–151
  introduction, 147–148
  logical operators, 180–182
  math and, 148
  operators, 151–152
  parentheses, 150
  selection statements, 148
  string comparison, 174
  TAXES.C, 155–157
  test, 150
  values and, 165
if statement
  block, 150–151
  format, 154–155
if-else structure
  definition, 158
  either-or decisions, 158–159
if-then statement, 154
imaginary number, 319
INCODD.C, 321
incrementation. *See also* decrementation
  ++ operator, 202–203
  a++, 320–321
  ASSESSED.C, 140–141
  assignment operators, 212
  five count, 211
  for loops and, 188
  introduction, 137
  LARDO.C, 138–140
  loops and, 201–202, 209
  operator location, 322–323
  operator shortcuts, 212
  post-incrementing, 322–323, 351
  pre-incrementing, 322–323, 351
  skipping values, 210
  values, 138–139
indents, source code, 14
infinite loops
  conditions, 196
  FOREVER.C, 195
  while loops, 217
input
  functions, 275
  getchar() and, 168
  GREATER.C, 170
  STDIO.H, 297–298
input bounds, do-while loop number checking, 229–230
INSULT1.C
  gets() function and, 66
  puts() function, 68–69
INSULT2.C, 69–70
int data types, 108
int integer, 110–111
int keyword
  main() function and, 79
  numeric data types, 108
  placement in program, 78
  range, 78
  unsigned int keyword, 109
int main, 31
integers
  binary numbers and, 112
  floating-point number format, 119–120
  versus floating-point numbers, 110
  int, 110–111
  introduction, 78–79
  long int, 110–111
  METHUS1.C, 79–80
  negative numbers, 111
  reasons to use, 110
  types, 110–111
  value conversion from string numbers, 81–82
  value range, 78
  variables, declaring, 110–111
IQ.C
  getval() function, 284–285
  type-casting and, 286

• J •

jerk() function, 256–258, 278–279
JUPITER.C, 114–115
justified text, 47–49
JUSTIFY.C, 47–49

• K •

keyboard
  numeric values, 81
  reading text from, 125–126
  reading text to, 127–128

keyboard overflow, 67
keywords
  break, 198–199
  break, nested loops and, 235–237
  case, 244
  case sensitivity, 33
  char, 50, 108
  const, 106
  continue, 235–236, 237–238
  do, 227
  double, 109
  float, 109, 113
  goto, 186
  if, 148
  int, 78, 108
  introduction, 32
  long, 109
  return, 285–287
  short, 108
  short int, 108
  struct, 341–342
  switch, 243–244
  unsigned char, 109
  unsigned int, 109
  unsigned long, 109
  unsigned short, 109
  variable naming and, 96
  while, 218
kitty variable, 76–77

• L •

languages, high-level, 10
LARDO.C
  ++ operator, 203–204
  incrementation, 138–140
leaping loops, 210
learn directory/folder, 363–364
less than (<) comparison operator, if statement, 151
less than or equal to (<=) comparison operator, if statement, 152
libm library, 319
library files
  header files and, 300
  libm, 319
  math library links, 317
library of functions, 255
LIGHTS1.C, 316–317
LIGHTS2.C, 318–319
line numbers
  commands, text editor, 349
  error messages, 24
linked lists, 343
linker
  errors and, 26, 27
  introduction, 15
linking
  compiling and, 17
  FreeBSD, 368–370
  Linux, 368–370
  Mac OS X, 368–370
  math library, 317
Linux
  compiler, 360
  folders, 362
lists, linked, 343
literal strings, 53
LOBBY1.C, 240–243
LOBBY2.C, 248–250
local variables, 270
log() function, 319
log10() function, 319
logic
  if command and, 180–182
  introduction, 175–176
logical operators
  &&, 180
  ||, 178, 180
  AND, 180
  if command, 180–182
  OR, 178
long int integer, 110–111
long keyword
  numeric data types, 109
  unsigned long keyword, 109
loops. *See also* for loops
  100.C, 192–193
  ;; in for loops, 220–222
  backward counting, 205
  break keyword, 198–199, 235–236, 352
  conditions, 196
  continue keyword, 235–236, 237–238
  delay loops, 233
  description, 185
  do-while, 186
  endless loops, 186
  escape clause, 197
  for loops, 186, 188–189
  goto keyword, 186
  incrementation, 201–202, 209
  infinite loops, 195–196
  leaping loops, 210
  looping statements, 185
  nested, 231–235
  OUCH.C, 187–188
  stopping, 193–195, 197–198
  switch-case, 239–247

variable initialization, 217
while, 186, 215–216
lowercase text, 13, 33
low-level programming languages, reasons to use, 10
ls command, 350
Lvalue errors, math, 314

• M •

Mac
compiler, 361
folders, 362
Mac OS X
compiler, 360
folders, 362
machine language, 10
macros, 303–304
MADLIB1.C
comment styles, 58–59
comments and, 56–57
magic pellets problem, order of precedence, 144–145
main() function
int keyword, 79
introduction, 30
returning values and, 287–288
math
exponents, 314–315
functions, 319–320
if command and, 148
imaginary number, 319
incrementation, 137–139
Lvalue errors, 314
order of precedence, 314
pow() function, 315
square root operations, 314, 317–319
math library, links, 317
mathematical operators, 86–88
+ (addition), 87, 134
/ (division), 87, 134
* (multiplication), 87, 134
order of precedence, 141–146
shortcuts, 212
- (subtraction), 87, 134
values, 134
variables, 134
MATH.H header, pow() function, 315
MDAS mnemonic, 142–143
METHUS1.C, 79–80
METHUS2.C, 83–85
METHUS3.C, 85–86
METHUS4.C, 88–90
METHUS5.C, 90–92
MiniGW compiler, 360
mnemonic for order of precedence, 142–143, 335
modulus (%)
introduction, 333
math operator, 314
MSVC (Microsoft Visual C++) compiler, 360
multiplication symbol (*), 87
My Dear Mother's Aunt Sally mnemonic, 142–143

• N •

\n (newline character)
printf() escape sequence, 306
RULES.C, 36–37
naming
functions, 263–264
variables, 95
variables, calling functions and, 279–280
variables, guidelines, 95–96
variables, tips for, 351
negative numbers
E notation, 117
floating-point, 112
integers, 111
numeric data types, 111–113
nested comments, problems with, 62–63
nested loops
break keyword, 235–237
continue keyword, 235–236, 237–238
definition, 231
for loops, 233
GRID.C, 234–235
while loops, 233
newline character, 31, 71
0*nn*, printf() escape sequence, 307
not equal to (!=) comparison operator, if statement, 152
NULL character, strings, 341
null pointer assignment error, 27
numbers
absolute value, 320
ASCII characters, 122
checking in do-while loops, 229–231
converting string to integer values, 81–82
floating-point *versus* integers, 110
precision, 118
random, 325–326
scientific notation, 115
strings and, 82
variable naming and, 96

numeric constants
description, 101
shortcuts, 102–104
numeric data types
character types, 108
double-precision types, 109
integer types, 108, 109
introduction, 107–108
negative numbers, 111–113
positive numbers, 111–113
ranges, 108–109
short integer types, 108
signed, 111–113
single-precision types, 109
unsigned, 111–113
unsigned character types, 109
unsigned integer types, 109
variables, 108–109
numeric variables
description, 93
integers, 78–79
introduction, 77–78
value assignment, 80–81, 97
nv command, 350

• O •

%o conversion character, printf() function, 311
object code files, OBJ extension, 15
OLLYOLLY.C, 204
operating system interaction, 345
operators
-- (decrement), 207–208, 322
++ (incrementation), 202–203
binary, 344
bitwise, 344
comparison operators, 151–152
comparison operators with if statement, 160
description, 34
if comparisons, 151–152
logical, 178
mathematical, + (addition), 134
mathematical, / (division), 134
mathematical, * (multiplication), 134
mathematical, - (subtraction), 134
shortcut for math, 212
optimizers, 357–358
OR (&) bitwise operator, 344
OR logical operator
examples, 181
if command and, 178
order of precedence
DENTIST.C, 141
introduction, 141
magic pellets problem, 144–145
mnemonic, 142–143, 337
parentheses, 144, 145–146
PELLETS.C, 144–145
OS (operating system), 27
OUCH.C, 187–188
output
functions, 275–276
STDIO.H, 297–298

• P •

PacMan example of variables, 76
parameters, functions, 279
parentheses
empty, 31
for keyword, 189, 190
functions, 254, 262
if command, 150
order of precedence and, 144, 145–146
source code, 13
statements, 34
strings, 31, 42
switch-case loops, 247
parse errors, 23
passing values, to functions, 279–282
PELLETS.C, 144–145
pipe character, 178–179
pointers, 343
positive numbers
floating-point, 112
numeric data types, 111–113
post-incrementing, 322–323, 351
pow() function
double variables, 316
introduction, 315
MATH.H header, 315
pre-incrementing, 322–323, 351
precedence. *See* order of precedence
precision, numbers, 118
preprocessor directives, 30
printf()
backslash, 305
conversion characters, 311
description, 31
escape sequences, 44–45, 306–308
flags, 312
for loops, 188
format, 42, 46, 310–311

format strings, 310
input-size specifiers, 312
newline character and, 71
precision specifiers, 312
puts() and, 71
review, 305
special characters, 306
text display, 306
variable contents, 71
variable display, 305
variables, 46
width specifiers, 312
PRINTFUN.C, 307–309
printing
text, 42–44
variables, 70
procedures, functions and, 253
program size, 346
programmer, 11
programming
breaking up code, 354
breakpoints, 356
talking through program, 355
programming code. *See* source code
programming languages
B, 10
BASIC, 10
low-level, 10
machine language, 10
programs
running, 17
saving to files, 361–362
troubleshooting, 353–358
prototyping functions
BIGJERK3.C, 261–262
delay() function, 269
introduction, 258–259
semicolons, 260
value returning and, 283
pseudorandom numbers, 328
putchar() function, reading text to keyboard, 127–128
puts() function
INSULT1.C, 68–69
INSULT2.C, 69–70
introduction, 67
printf() function and, 71
STOP.C, 68
string variables, 71
text, 67, 71
variable printing, 70
pwd command, 351

• Q •

quotes. *See also* double quotes
char variable, 123
formatting strings, 46
strings, 42–43

• R •

\r, printf() escape sequence, 306
rand() function
introduction, 326–328
seeds, 328–329
RAND_MAX, value, displaying, 330
random numbers
introduction, 325–326
pseudorandom numbers, 326
seeding, 326, 328–329
random-sampler variable program, 98–99
RANDOM1.C, 327–328
RANDOM2.C, 329–330
RANDOM3.C, 331–333
RANDOM4.C, 335–336
ranges
floating-point numbers, 114
int integer, 111
long int integer, 111
numeric data types, 108–109
reading text
from keyboard, 125–126
to keyboard, 127–128
recompiling source code, 21–22
ren command, 350
reserved words, 33. *See also* keywords
resources, 358
return command, 31
return keyword, 285–287
return statements, BONUS.C, 288–289
returning values
atoi() function, 283
functions, 255, 282–289
getchar() function, 283
main() function and, 287–288
Ritchie, Dennis, 11
rm command, 351
RULES.C, 36–37

• S •

%s conversion character, printf() function, 311
saving, source code, 16

scanf() function
  COLOR.C and, 51–52
  format, 49
  introduction, 40
  null pointer assignment errors and, 51
  reading text from keyboard, 125–128
  string variables, 49
scientific notation
  E notation, 116–117
  introduction, 115
seeding random numbers, 326, 328–329
seedrnd() function, 329–331
selection statements
  if keyword and, 148
  switch-case loops, 241
semicolons
  case statement, 247
  compilers and, 31
  constants, 269
  do-while loops, 227
  else keyword, 159
  errors and, 24
  gets(), 66
  if test, 150
  prototypes, 260
  variable declaration, 276
  while keyword, 219
shell command, 345
short int keyword, numeric data types, 108
short keyword
  numeric data types, 108
  unsigned short keyword, 109
shortcuts for math operations, 212
signed numeric data types, 111–113
sin() function, 319
single quotes, char variable, 123
single-character variables, 122–123
single-line comments, 59
single-precision data types, 109
slash (/)
  with asterisk (/*), 56
  double (//), 60
sleep() function, 234
source code
  blank lines, 14
  case sensitivity, 13
  coding programs, 12
  compiler and, 14–15
  editing, 19–21, 24–25
  errors, 22–27
  filename extensions, 13
  files, 12
  header files, 300
  indents, 14
  linker, 15
  parentheses, 13
  recompiling, 21–22
  saving, 16
  text editors, 12
  tweaking, 20
  twiddling, 20
  typing tips, 14
special characters, printf() function, 306
SPEED.C, 101–104
split lines, 37–38
sqrt() function, 317–319
square root math operations
  introduction, 314
  sqrt() function, 317–319
srand() function, 329
standard input, getchar() and, 168
statements
  case, 243
  case keyword, 244
  description, 34
  disabling with comments, 61
  do-while loops, 227
  else, 157–158
  else-if, 160–163
  if block, 150–151
  if-then, 154
  selection statements, 148
  while keyword, 218
STDIO.H, 31, 297–298
STDLIB.H, 83
STOP.C, 68
string constants
  #define directive and, 105
  description, 53, 101
string variables
  description, 94
  scanf() and, 49, 57
strings
  comparing with if keyword, 174
  description, 32, 340–341
  formatting strings, 46
  functions and, 42
  gets() function, 66–67
  literal strings, 53
  NULL character, 341
  number conversion to integer value, 81–82
  numbers and, 82
  parentheses, 31, 42
  printing, 42–44
struct keyword, 341–342

structures, 341–342
styles of comments, 58–60
subtraction symbol (-), 87
switch command, 243, 247
switch keyword, 243–244
switch-case loops
  break command, 244–245
  case keyword, 244
  case statements, 244
  default statements, 244
  introduction, 239
  LOBBY1.C, 241–243
  parentheses, 247
  selection statements, 241
  while loops and, 248–250
symbolic constants, 103
symbols, mathematical, 86–88
syntax, 24
syntax errors, 23

• T •

\t, printf() escape sequence, 307
talking through program, 355
tan() function, 319
TAXES.C, 155–157
text
  display, printf(), 306
  formatting, 47–49
  justified, 47–49
  lowercase, 13
  printing, 42–44
  puts() function, 67, 71
  reading from keyboard, 125–126
  reading to keyboard, 127–128
  strings, 32
text editors
  context-colored, 348–349
  line-number commands, 349
  running, 364–365
  source code, 12
  windows, 348
text files
  size, 262
  source code, 12
text strings, 31
time() function, 332
tweaking source code, 20
twiddling source code, 20
type command, 351
TYPER1.C, 197–198
TYPER2.C, 220–222
typing, source code, 14

• U •

%u conversion character, printf() function, 311
underline, variable naming and, 96
Unix, compiler, 361
unsigned char keyword, numeric data types, 109
unsigned character data types, 109
unsigned int keyword, numeric data types, 109
unsigned integer data types, 109
unsigned long keyword, numeric data types, 109
unsigned numeric data types, 111–113
unsigned short keyword, numeric data types, 109

• V •

\v, printf() escape sequence, 307
values
  absolute, 320
  arrays, 340
  constants, 91
  declaring as variables, 276
  floating point, 99
  functions, returning, 282–289
  functions, sending to, 276–277
  if keyword, 165
  incrementation, 138
  keyboard entry, 81
  mathematical operators, 134
  numbers and, 82
  numeric variables and, 80–81, 97
  parameters, 279
  passing multiple to functions, 280–282
  passing to functions, 279
  predefining in variables, 124
  return keyword, 285–287
  returning from functions, 255
  returning, main() function and, 287–288
  variables, 96–98
  variables, char, 124
variables
  ++ operator, 321
  arrays, 339–340
  BOMBER.C, 265–269
  char keyword and, 40, 123–124
  character, comparing, 166
  comments, 95
  constants and, 101
  contents, 76

variables *(continued)*
  dead_horse, 223
  declarations, 40
  declarations, multiple, 100–101
  declarations, reasons for, 94–95
  declaring values as, 276
  description, 75–76
  double, pow() function, 316
  dual, BOMBER.C, 267
  float variable, 113
  floating-point values, 99
  for loop, 191
  global, 269
  global, declaring, 270–271
  initializing, loops and, 217
  integer, declaring, 110–111
  kitty (string variable), 76–77
  local, 270
  mathematical operators, 134
  METHUS1.C, 79–80
  names, calling functions and, 279–280
  naming, 95
  naming guidelines, 95–96
  naming tips, 351
  numeric, 77–86, 93
  numeric data types, 109
  PacMan example, 76
  printf() function, 46, 71, 305
  printing, 70
  programming tips, 356
  puts() function and, 70
  random-sample program, 98–99
  scanf() and, 49
  single-character, 122–123
  storage location, 76
  string, 94
  string, scanf() and, 49
  value assignment, 80–81
  value assignment, char, 124
  value incrementation, 138
  value, predefining, 124
  values, 96–98
vertical bar (pipe character), 178
vim text editor
  context-colored, 348–349
  line-number commands, 349
viruses, keyboard overflow and, 67

• W •

WHICH.C, 129
while keyword, statements, 218
while loops
  break statement, 221
  controls, 216
  do-while loops, 225–231
  for loop comparison, 219–220
  for (;;) loops and, 220–222
  infinite loops, 217
  introduction, 186
  nested, 233
  overview, 215–216
  repeat rate, 216
  switch-case structure and, 248–250
while true condition, 218–219
while_true statement
  for loops, 189
  while loop, 218
WHORU.C
  compiling, 40–41
  I/O and, 39
Windows
  compiling, 367–368
  folders, 361–362
  GCC compiler, 365–367
  linking, 367–368
windows, editor view, 348
Windows Notepad, filename extensions, 13
worms, keyboard overflow and, 67
writing, header files, 298–299

• X •

%x conversion character, printf() function, 311
xnnn, printf() escape sequence, 307
XOR (&) bitwise operator, 344

• Z •

zeroes, floating-point number format, 119–120